T0287624

Soli Sorabjee

Soli Sorabjee

Life and Times
An Authorized Biography

Abhinav Chandrachud

PENGUIN
VIKING

An imprint of Penguin Random House

VIKING

USA | Canada | UK | Ireland | Australia
New Zealand | India | South Africa | China | Singapore

Viking is part of the Penguin Random House group of companies
whose addresses can be found at global.penguinrandomhouse.com

Published by Penguin Random House India Pvt. Ltd
4th Floor, Capital Tower 1, MG Road,
Gurugram 122 002, Haryana, India

Penguin
Random House
India

First published in Viking by Penguin Random House India 2022

Copyright © Abhinav Chandrachud 2022

All rights reserved

10 9 8 7 6 5 4 3

The views and opinions expressed in this book are the author's own and the
facts are as reported by him which have been verified to the extent possible,
and the publishers are not in any way liable for the same.

ISBN 9780670096411

Typeset in EB Garamond by Manipal Digital Systems, Manipal
Printed at Replika Press Pvt. Ltd, India

www.penguin.co.in

This is a legitimate digitally printed version of the book and therefore might not
have certain extra finishing on the cover.

To Radha,
For reminding me that 'love . . . is an ever-fixed mark
That looks on tempests and is never shaken'.

Contents

1

The Last Soliloquy

How does a Parsi lawyer, deeply influenced by the principles of Roman Catholicism, fall in love with a Bahai and go on to become the Attorney General of India for a Hindu nationalist Bharatiya Janata Party (BJP)-led coalition government? How does a boy with a broken leg, who studied in a Gujarati-medium school and lost his father at the age of 19, go on to mount a heroic defence of the Janata government's decision to dissolve Congress state legislatures in the Supreme Court in 1977? How does a newspaper columnist who admires Nehru,[1] who criticizes the BJP for being 'obsessed' with 'demolishing mosques' and advises them to replace 'Hindutva' with '*Bharatva*' or 'Indianness', get chosen by Prime Minister Vajpayee to represent the government in the Supreme Court in many cases, including the Ayodhya case? How does a lawyer with a humdrum customs and excise law practice, whose grandfather sold horse-drawn carriages in Bombay, become a UN human rights rapporteur and repeatedly defend the fundamental right to free speech and expression in the Supreme Court of India?

On a warm summer day in May 2018, I met Soli Sorabjee (1930–2021) at his residence at Neeti Bagh in New Delhi to ask him these and scores of other fascinating questions about his life. I was there to convince him to write his autobiography. Equipped with my cell phone, on which I recorded around 6–7 hours of my conversations with him (with his permission) over the next several days, I had hoped to put together a preliminary draft of an autobiography for Sorabjee which he could then build upon, edit and publish. In my mind, Sorabjee's autobiography would bear the title: 'The Last Soliloquy'. In the 2000s, Sorabjee used to write a wonderfully witty, humorous and informative column in the *Indian Express* called 'Soli Loquies'. It was a play on the word 'soliloquy'—a monologue by a character on stage who speaks only to the audience and not to any other character in a play. Sorabjee was especially fond of the 'To be or not to be' soliloquy in Shakespeare's *Hamlet*, in which the prince of Denmark (Sorabjee wanted to name his eldest son 'Hamlet'[2]) complains of the 'pangs of despised love' and 'the law's delay'.[3] In his column, Sorabjee spoke directly to us, the readers, and not only to the world of courts, judges and lawyers, of which he was a part. In his autobiography, I had hoped that he would speak to us, and to posterity, once again.

Unfortunately, I soon realized that this would not be possible. While Sorabjee had an excellent memory for the things that had happened to him in the early stages of his life—his Jesuit teachers at St Xavier's College, the lawyers and judges he encountered at the Bombay High Court in the 1960s, the poems of Wordsworth and Shakespeare that he had read as a child—his memory was not as sharp for the relatively recent past. When I asked him about the politician L.K. Advani, for instance, he told me about Hotchand Advani instead, a generous lawyer who had a chamber alongside his at the Bombay High Court in the early 1970s.

This book is, therefore, a modest replacement for the autobiography that never was. In it, we will see how Sorabjee's grandfather, Hormasjee, made a fortune selling imported horse-drawn carriages and cars in Bombay; how Sorabjee left his Gujarati-medium school at the age of 12 and developed a fondness for English literature and Roman Catholicism in Father Bonet's classes at St Xavier's College; and how he permanently damaged his leg in a motorcycle accident at the age of 18 and lost his father a year later. In the pages of this book, we will read about the awkward relationship Sorabjee had with his senior at the Bombay High Court, Kharshedji Bhabha; his first brief, in which he failed to get an adjournment; the first case that he ever argued (and lost) on his own in the Supreme Court for the notorious smuggler Mayer Hans George; how he won a Supreme Court case for the first time; got his own chamber; declined an offer to be a judge and became a senior advocate.

It was Indira Gandhi's 'phoney' Emergency of 1975 which brought Sorabjee into his element and catapulted him into the national arena. Until then, Sorabjee had primarily been a customs and excise lawyer. The Emergency transformed him into a defender of citizens' rights. He began appearing in many criminal cases for perhaps the first time in his career—preventive detention cases where he asked the courts to release Indira Gandhi's political prisoners. He mounted a heroic defence of free speech in the *Freedom First* case in the Bombay High Court and saved many pieces of journalism from the ruthless scissors of the censor. Realizing that copies of anti-government judgments were barred from being published during the Emergency, he subversively wrote a book with the only intention that his readers would get to read the pro-free-speech judgments that were set out in the book's appendix. He joined the board of directors of the *Statesman* and fought the government's secret instructions that no government company should advertise in that newspaper.

As the Additional Solicitor General (and later, Solicitor General) for India with the Janata government (1977–80), Sorabjee played an important part in the Janata government's policy of dismantling Indira Gandhi's Emergency-era excesses. He successfully defended the government's decision to impose President's Rule on nine Congress state governments. He helped defend the government's decision to impound the passport of Maneka Gandhi, Indira Gandhi's daughter-in-law, so that she could not avoid attending the various judicial commissions that had been set up to investigate her family's alleged misadventures. In the *Kissa Kursi Ka* case, he called Sanjay Gandhi the 'personification of untruths' to his face in open court. At the same time, Sorabjee started appearing in intellectual debates on a unique, new medium, television, and was called a 'scintillating media star' by the *Times of India*. He became an internationally known figure and was invited to attend events in New York and Geneva.

As the Attorney General of India with V.P. Singh's National Front government (1989–90), Sorabjee convinced the Supreme Court to partly modify its controversial decision to allow the government to settle the Bhopal gas tragedy case for $470 million by reviving the criminal cases against Union Carbide's management. He set a very high bar for himself, promising that he would never be the mere mouthpiece of the government. Sorabjee was never seen as a political partisan. Vajpayee's BJP decided to pick him as the Attorney General despite the fact that he had successfully argued cases which the BJP was ideologically opposed to (e.g., a free speech case concerning the famous television show *Tamas* that the BJP wanted to ban).

Though this book is a biography, it is not an obituary or eulogy for Sorabjee. In fact, Sorabjee was against falsely praising and lying about people after they are no more. 'Obituary references to the departed soul', he once wrote in the pages of the *Indian Express*, 'are the most common form of lying in public.'[4] 'It is unkind to speak ill of a person who is dead and gone', he added, '[b]ut is it necessary to discover hidden talents and imaginary virtues in the deceased?'[5] This book will not try to conceal Sorabjee's flaws or whitewash the contentious moments of his career. As the Attorney General of India with the BJP-led coalition government between 1998 and 2004, Sorabjee was harshly criticized by the outgoing law minister Ram Jethmalani for, among other things, altering his written opinion in order to allow the government to bail out telecom companies. During this time, Sorabjee had an awkward equation with one of his most famous juniors, Harish Salve. In his book on free speech,

Sorabjee (perhaps unwittingly for that era) picked up a passage from a book written by a foreign author without attributing the source. During his first stint as the Attorney General of India, his effigy was burned by critics who were unhappy with his arguments in the Mandal Commission case. Sorabjee had some eccentricities too. He once impersonated the Italian ambassador and tried to get the Tata group to halt the night-time construction of the Taj Mansingh hotel so that he could get some sleep in his nearby residence. He would ask a client or advocate to leave a meeting if he or she showed any signs of having a cold or cough.

Despite his shortcomings, Sorabjee's life teaches valuable lessons to the next generation of lawyers: always maintain your independence from your client and never be the mere mouthpiece of your client; take up cases which you can argue yourself rather than only assisting senior advocates; do not think winning or losing a case is important (Sorabjee's win–loss ratio as a private lawyer was, roughly speaking, fifty-fifty), what matters is the effort you put into preparing for a case; do not allow any single client or attorney to control your destiny (Sorabjee was briefed by a vast pool of lawyers and never relied on any one lawyer or client for his bread and butter); and it is important to socialize outside the court.

This book is not only a biography of Sorabjee but a history of the times that he lived in. Through the lens of Sorabjee's life, this book examines the changes that were occurring all around Sorabjee and the Sorabjee family between 1853 and 2004. For instance, a few decades before Sorabjee visited the Bombay racecourse to witness his father's horse, Doodal Dandy, win a race, we will see how the Turf Club in Bombay installed a new machine called the 'totalizator' (or 'tote') which revolutionized the method in which the odds of a horse race were calculated, far before the tote was introduced to horse racing in London. As Sorabjee entered the portals of the Gujarati-medium Bharda New High School at Waudby Road in Bombay, we will see the debates that were taking place on 'Anglo-Vernacular' education in colonial India. When Sorabjee was a private lawyer in the 1980s, we will see how the

INSAT-1B satellite, launched in 1983, was responsible for bringing about Sorabjee's first and most important free speech case at the Supreme Court concerning the sensational television serial *Tamas*, which had followed a string of newly successful soap operas on TV including *Hum Log* and *Buniyaad*. In 1975, we will see how Indira Gandhi tried to justify imposing the Emergency in India by citing, among other things, an attempt that had been made on the life of Chief Justice A.N. Ray. We will witness the kind of tactics that were used by her government to silence its critics like the *Indian Express*, by cutting off their electricity and directing nationalized banks not to offer them any credit. Through the *Bandit Queen* case which Sorabjee argued in the 1990s, we will see how India came to terms with depictions of nudity on the large screen.

In some places, this book may make us pause and reflect on the status of the legal profession. We may ask ourselves why Constitutional Court judges in India retire between the ages of 62 and 65, when arguably the most important phase of Sorabjee's career, as the Attorney General of India with the BJP-led coalition government, only began when he was already 68 years old. We may wonder why each time Sorabjee became a government lawyer, his win–loss ratio suddenly shot up. As a private lawyer, Sorabjee won around 50 per cent of his cases, but as a law officer with the Janata, National Front and National Democratic Alliance (NDA) governments, he won approximately 70 per cent of his cases. Surely Sorabjee's advocacy skills did not substantially improve each time he became a government lawyer. Perhaps the government was a more responsible client and only chose those cases to contest which were winnable. Perhaps as a law officer, Sorabjee had the discretion to settle cases that he thought the government would lose and fight those that he knew it could win. Or perhaps courts in India adopt an attitude of deference towards the government in many cases, regardless of which political dispensation is in power. After all, when a litigant challenges a law, the court begins by presuming that the law is constitutionally valid and it is for the petitioner to establish that the law is unconstitutional, regardless of how important the fundamental right which is at stake might be.

This book relies on interviews that were conducted by the author with Sorabjee, members of his close family, his juniors and well-wishers, in order to recreate Sorabjee's life and times. It relies on reports and articles that were published in the *Times of India* and the *Indian Express*, especially those written either about Sorabjee or by him.[6] It looks at 1,124 reported cases decided by the Supreme Court, High Courts and tribunals, in which Sorabjee appeared, that are available on the SCC Online and Manupatra databases.[7] Unfortunately, there is no culture of preserving private papers in India, and I did not have access to any of Sorabjee's letters and personal papers. Further, though more than 30 years have gone by since Sorabjee was the Additional Solicitor General for India with the Janata government and the Attorney General with the National Front government, his official records do not appear to have been declassified by the government and made available on the Abhilekh Patal database. This is despite the fact that Sorabjee believed that the opinions of Attorneys General, except on 'sensitive matters of security, confidential intelligence, and the like', ought to be published.[8] Therefore, we will not be able to see the confidential advice that Sorabjee gave the government during his tenure as a law officer.

2

Hormasjee Sorabjee & Sons

Soli Sorabjee was born to a prominent Parsi business family of substantial means. His grandfather, Hormasjee Sorabjee,[1] was born around 1853. At the age of 16,[2] Hormasjee joined the firm of a prominent Muslim Kutchee-Memon[3] businessman in Bombay, Haji Currim Mahomed Sulliman, who was known by his nickname 'Cummoo'.[4] Though Cummoo's brother, Hajee Jaffer Sulliman, had founded the firm known as Jaffer Sulliman & Co., after his death in 1869[5] Cummoo continued to use his brother's name while carrying on the business. At their showroom in Girgaum,[6] Jaffer Sulliman & Co. sold horses, horse-drawn carriages, furniture, chinaware and other miscellaneous items, many of which were imported from England.

For instance, in 1861, Jaffer Sulliman ran a classified advertisement in the *Times of India* informing his patrons that he was offering for sale various pieces like 'Air Beds and Pillows', 'Mackintosh Coats' for the monsoon and a 'Selection of Electroplated Goods and Chinaware', which had recently arrived from three ships known as the *Bengal*, *Cassipore* and *Art-Union*.[7] Also on offer were a '[First rate] second hand Rosewood Cottage Piano', and an eight-year-old 'grey Arab riding horse', which, for some reason Sulliman made it a point to add, had 'been constantly ridden by a Lady' (perhaps thereby implying that the horse had not been overburdened).[8] In another such advertisement carried in 1872, Jaffer Sulliman & Co. told their customers that they were selling new and second-hand English-built 'Barouches' and 'Mall Phaetons' (types of horse-drawn carriages), apart from 'a large assortment of unique patterns in Crockery and Glass-ware'.[9] Besides, in the 1870s, they built a special stand in which ticket-paying customers could watch the horse races in Bombay[10] and one such race was even called the 'Jaffer Sulliman Cup'.[11] They carried out other kinds of odd businesses. For instance, they offered to hire out a yacht to wealthy patrons and once had on sale a 'first class Jubbulpoor [Jabalpur] Swiss Cottage Tent'.[12] They described themselves as 'general agents and upholsterers', and their showrooms contained a 'general furnishing bazaar'.[13]

Business was booming and Cummoo became a wealthy merchant and philanthropist in Bombay. He regularly donated money to charities, built sanatoriums[14] and constructed a rest-house or *dharamsala* for weary travellers.[15] However, perhaps his greatest charitable contribution came in the form of donating a sum of Rs 20,000 in 1883 for setting up the 'Jaffer Sulliman Dispensary' for treating women and children under the charge of female doctors in Bombay.[16] One of the first female doctors in India, Dr Edith Pechey, arrived in Bombay in December 1883,[17] and treated patients there. Until then, many women were not permitted to even see a male doctor because they were forced to live their lives in complete seclusion.[18] On rare occasions, male doctors were permitted to examine female patients through a thick curtain.[19] The Jaffer Sulliman Dispensary was declared open in March 1886 by the wife of the Governor of Bombay, Lady Reay, who was felicitated with a huge garland of flowers by Cummoo on the occasion.[20] Attached to Cama Hospital,[21] which was built for women with a charitable donation by a wealthy Parsi merchant,[22] the dispensary still exists in Mumbai today.

The 'portly'[23] big-boned Cummoo was a prominent and highly regarded resident of Bombay. When Queen Victoria was declared the Empress of India in 1877, Cummoo was selected to be on a committee to organize celebrations to mark the occasion.[24] He was a Justice of the Peace.[25] Afflicted with numerous ailments including rheumatism and dropsy, Cummoo died in 1886 at the age of 57, leaving behind a widow and a minor daughter.[26]

Hormasjee had joined Cummoo's firm around 1869, initially earning a salary of Rs 15 per month.[27] After Cummoo died, Hormasjee, at the approximate age of 36, managed the business of Jaffer Sulliman & Co. for several years.[28] In 1889, for instance, a classified advertisement was published in the *Times of India* announcing the sale of the property of a British member of the armed forces, Major Gerald Martin, including his horses, horse-carriages and harnesses and offering to lease out Martin's Malabar Hill bungalow. Interested patrons were asked to contact 'Mr Hormusjee of Cummoo Jaffer Sulleman & Co.'[29] He soon branched out on his own and obtained 'abkari contracts' (probably for the manufacture or sale of liquor) in Nasik and Poona.[30] However, he continued to sell the possessions (usually horses and horse-carriages) of British officials in Bombay who were going back home. For instance, in 1900, Hormasjee offered to his customers the horses and 'tonga' of R.B. Stewart, a member of the Indian Civil Service who was departing for England.[31]

Much of Hormasjee's business therefore depended on his good relations with British officials stationed in Bombay. He went about collecting testimonials from many satisfied Britons to whom he had offered his services. For example, in 1894, before departing for England, the Chief Justice of the Bombay High Court, Charles Sargent, wrote a letter to Hormasjee in which he expressed his 'high opinion' of Hormasjee as being 'a straight-forward honest man of business' for the 12–15 years that he had known him. Sargent initially met Hormasjee at Jaffer Sulliman & Co., but even after Hormasjee set up his own business,

Sargent had always found him to be 'a most reliable and satisfactory person to have dealings with'.[32] Another such testimonial was written by Charles Ollivant in 1892, who had only recently stepped down as the Municipal Commissioner of Bombay. Ollivant, who later became a member of the Governor's executive council in Bombay, wrote that he had a 'high opinion' of Hormasjee's 'intelligence and respectability' and that he thought that he would 'execute any honest commission with zeal and tact.'[33]

The name 'Hormasjee Sorabjee' was quite a common Parsi name in Bombay at the time and there were other merchants who went by that name as well. A prominent bookseller at Medows Street, for example, carried on business under the name 'Hormusjee Sorabjee & Co.' Sorabjee's grandfather, however, often used the last name 'Lelinvala'. For instance, his passbook with the National Bank of India carried the name 'Hormusjee Sorabjee Lelinvala Esq.'[34] When he was sued in the Bombay High Court by a plaintiff who claimed he had not been paid for the tents he had supplied Hormasjee and others (a case which Hormasjee eventually won), Hormasjee was sued using this last name.[35]

Hormasjee contributed to charitable causes, offering a sum of Rs 10 to the Ichhapur Relief Fund[36] after a massive fire broke out in Ichhapur, Bengal, in 1888, leaving around 100 people homeless.[37] Between 1896 and 1897, when the bubonic plague arrived in Bombay and eventually grew into becoming a worldwide pandemic,[38] Hormasjee rendered 'meritorious services' to the government.[39] In 1902, Hormasjee was in charge of making arrangements for the stay of Indian princes in England at the coronation of King Edward VII.[40] In 1903, he was present at the Victoria Terminus railway station to receive the Nizam of Hyderabad in Bombay.[41] All this suggests wealth and position for Hormasjee at the turn of the 19th century.

. . .

In 1902, a classified advertisement appeared in the *Times of India* under the name of 'Hormasjee Sorabjee & Sons'.[42] By now, Sorabjee's father Jehangir, who was born in 1878, was in his early twenties. Jehangir Sorabjee was, thus, one of the 'Sons' in Hormasjee's business.[43] Hormasjee Sorabjee & Sons were in the business of selling, hiring out and repairing imported horse-carriages and cars. This was not too far off from the business of Jaffer Sulliman & Co. In 1902, in their showrooms at Queen's Road in Bombay, they offered for sale one 'Rubber-tyred Victoria with a handsome and fast grey Arab Horse', and a Cabriolette (a kind of horse-carriage) 'with Bicycle Wheels'.[44] Queen's Road was in a posh locality frequented by Europeans.[45]

In 1908, the Continental Motor Tyres company purchased a full-page advertisement in the *Times of India* in which they informed patrons that Hormasjee Sorabjee & Sons was one of the Bombay firms that would supply their 'excellent' and 'reliable' tyres at the 'latest reduced prices'.[46] The following year, Hormasjee's firm offered for sale two horse-drawn carriages belonging to the Commissioner of Police in Bombay, H.G. Gell. One of these carriages was an 'English-built canoe-shaped Victoria' (an open-air carriage), while the other was a 'single seat Office Brougham' (an enclosed carriage). Also available for sale that year were a pair of 'well matched' and 'absolutely quiet' Bay Waler Cobs (horses) belonging to Commissioner Gell.[47] The firm continued to make charitable donations. In 1908, it contributed a large sum of money, Rs 100, to a fund meant for looking after destitute peons.[48]

As the years rolled on, Hormasjee Sorabjee & Sons sold French, American and English cars like De Dion,[49] Hotchkiss,[50] Overland,[51] Oldsmobile[52] and Swift,[53] and the tyres of companies like Dunlop,[54] Good Year[55] and Continental Motor Tyres to wealthy patrons. In 1929, the firm advertised an American car, a 'Chandler', for sale. This car, they assured their patrons, was '[g]uaranteed to do over 85 miles an hour', and had been '[s]pecially tuned by the famous [American] Race Driver, Ralph Mulford',[56] who participated in the first ever Indianapolis-500 or Indy-500 car race.[57] Hormasjee travelled to England 16 times in his lifetime.[58] In the 1920s, he was said to have spent several months abroad at a time and to have maintained an apartment in London and Paris. He would come back to Bombay only in the winters. He ran petrol pumps. His firm also entered the business of real estate broking. Towards the end of the 1920s, Hormasjee Sorabjee's firm advertised three bungalows in Mahabaleshwar, 'Parvati Villa', 'Maneck Villa' and 'Valley View', to be given out on rent.[59]

Sorabjee was born on 9 March 1930. Hormasjee passed away in 1931.[60] His wife, Soonabai, had died sometime before then. Sorabjee, therefore, never knew his paternal grandparents. Thereafter, Hormasjee's sons started businesses in their own names. In 1936, Jehangir Sorabjee used his own name to inform patrons that the 6-bedroom Mahabaleshwar bungalow 'Valley View', which had earlier been advertised under his father's firm's name, was available to be rented out.[61] Similarly, in 1938, Maneckji Hormasji Sorabji (who also sometimes used the last name 'Lelinvala'[62]), Jehangir's brother,[63] used his own name to inform customers that the Mahabaleshwar bungalows 'Maneck Villa' and 'Parvati Villa', previously let out by Hormasjee Sorabjee & Sons, were available for renting.[64]

Jehangir Sorabjee cut a handsome figure. He was not a lawyer and had never attended university. Even so, as a wealthy merchant in Bombay the colonial government made him an Honorary Presidency Magistrate, akin to a Justice of the Peace in England. In this capacity, it was his duty to decide minor traffic cases at the Honorary Magistrates' court in Girgaum (now Girgaon) in Bombay.[65] Ironically, therefore, a merchant who imported and sold foreign cars in India presided over cases of rash and negligent driving in the city. In 1928, he attended a farewell banquet hosted by the Society of Honorary Presidency Magistrates for Leslie Wilson, Governor of Bombay.[66]

Sorabjee's mother, Khorshed, a soft-spoken and gentle soul, was born in 1896. She married Jehangir in 1922, when she was around twenty-six years old, which was quite late by the standards of the time. Jehangir himself was forty-four when he married—there was a gap of nearly twenty years between Khorshed and Jehangir. Sorabjee was born eight years into the marriage when Jehangir was around fifty-two years old. He was the only child, and Jehangir's blue-eyed boy. As Sorabjee's son later jokingly put it, Sorabjee was thoroughly spoiled by his father and Sorabjee's own children had to bear the consequences of this for several decades! Though Sorabjee had no siblings, he had two dogs he was very fond of, who would keep him company whenever he was lonely.

One of Sorabjee's earliest memories was of accompanying his father to the Honorary Magistrate's court at Girgaum. A Parsi defendant had parked his car in a no-parking zone. His excuse was that the car had broken down. The case came up before Jehangir who took a practical, lenient view of the matter and let the man off with a warning. Though Jehangir did not have a university education, he was quite bright. He pushed Sorabjee into excelling in scholastics. Sorabjee was quite devoted to his father and believed that he got his intellectual bent of mind from him.

A man of leisure, Jehangir owned around 15–20 horses and a few stables. In 1935, his horse named 'Saint Fortunat' won a 1-mile long race in Kolhapur.[67] That year, another horse, 'Grey Beauty', fared quite well in a race of 6 furlongs in Colombo, Ceylon (now Sri Lanka).[68] However, with the outbreak of the Second World War in 1939, Jehangir's business fell on difficult times. Cars could no longer be imported for sale in India and the petrol pump business came to a grinding halt because of war-time rationing. Slowly but surely, Hormasjee's sprawling business started to crumble in Jehangir's hands and the family lived off its property. Compared to Hormasjee, Jehangir had to endure a relatively frugal life. However, the family was certainly not poor.

Sorabjee's maternal grandfather, Ardeshir Bomanjee Dubash, was a wealthy merchant who had business interests in fields as diverse as shipping, banking and cotton textiles. He served as a director of the Central Bank of India[69] and of the Bombay Cotton Manufacturing Company.[70] Between 1913 and 1914, Dubash was involved in a heavily contested law suit at the Bombay High Court against a firm called Andrew Yule and Company.[71] Andrew Yule and Company were agents who supplied coal from Bengal collieries to industries in Bombay. They hired a ship called the 'Gymeric' to make twelve trips from Bengal to Bombay for the purpose. However, after only four such trips were completed some legal complications arose[72] and Ardeshir Dubash purchased the vessel from the owner, paying him a whopping advance of Rs 2,20,000 for it. Dubash then refused to allow the ship to complete the remaining eight trips to Bengal. Andrew Yule and Company sued Dubash in the Bombay High Court. The case eventually went up in appeal before a division bench headed by Chief Justice Basil Scott, who held that Dubash would have to honour the agreement in favour of Andrew Yule and Company.

The case was extensively reported in the press,[73] and Dubash engaged Chimanlal Setalvad to appear for him. Setalvad eventually served as an additional judge of the Bombay High Court, member of the Governor's executive council, and acting president of the Central Legislative Assembly.[74] Setalvad's son was the first Attorney General of independent India. Among the other lawyers who appeared in the Dubash case were M.A. Jinnah (the founder of Pakistan) and Bhulabhai Desai (a legendary advocate who represented three leaders of the Indian National Army at the Red Fort after the Second World War[75]).

Ardeshir and his wife, Maneckbai, owned properties all over the presidency. They belonged to the notable Parsi Dubash family, which had made its fortune in the business of stevedoring. Maneckbai, who suffered from diabetes for much of her life, insisted that not only the sons in the Dubash family but also the daughters would inherit their family property and wealth. It was for this reason that their daughter, Khorshed, received one such property, a spacious bungalow on Nepean

Sea Road called Hill Side Villa in a quiet neighbourhood, a part of the West Hill Compound. Until 1935, Sorabjee lived at Queen's Road—the very road on which his grandfather and father had sold cars and horse-carriages to wealthy patrons at the turn of the century. Thereafter, the family moved into his mother's bungalow, Hill Side Villa, where Sorabjee continued to reside until he left for Delhi as a law officer.

As a child, Sorabjee enjoyed memorizing railway tables and could recite the arrival and departure timings of trains from memory. His cousins, for instance, would ask him to recite the departure time of the Frontier Mail, a train which was inaugurated in 1928 and carried mail and passengers between Bombay and Delhi in 23 hours and 35 minutes.[76] He would respond in a heartbeat. Trains always fascinated him. At the age of seven when Sorabjee had his thread ceremony (Navjot), he requested his maternal grandmother Maneckbai for a 'full railway set with engine, carriages, signals, etc.' as a present. He wished to be 'an engine driver in charge of the then mighty Punjab Mail roaring down from Bombay to Nasik, Mammad, Itarsi, Jhansi and then to Delhi.'[77] He was only nine years old when the Second World War broke out in 1939, and there was little that a child of his age could do to occupy himself besides things like reading railway timetables and horse-racing books. He read these from cover to cover, over and over again.

. . .

Horse racing in colonial Bombay was a big deal. The Governor of Bombay had his own private box in the Grand Stand at the racecourse.[78] While visiting Bombay, the Viceroy of India sometimes attended the races.[79] It was quite common to see royalty like the Maharaja of Kashmir or the Amir of Afghanistan (whose stay arrangements in Bombay had been made by Hormasjee himself[80]) in attendance.[81] Built on land leased by the government,[82] the racecourse at Mahalakshmi had an impressive appearance: a central entrance for carriages and cars on arrival, separate 'enclosures' or seating areas for members of the Western India Turf Club and the ordinary public, the 'totalizator' betting machine which was installed in 1911–12, the 'paddock' where the winning horses would line up, a string of stables with 36 stalls, and the Grand Stand with its reserved boxes for dignitaries.[83] In 1949, the Mahalakshmi racecourse in Bombay was the first Indian racecourse to install the new 'photo-finish camera' to help judges ascertain the winner of each race.[84]

Patrons turned out for the races in their finest attire and the *Times of India* frequently reported on the prevalent fashion available on display.[85] It also reported the results of the races, setting out the names of not merely the horses that had won the race but those who 'also ran' the race[86] (the phrase 'also ran' is now often used to describe those whose performance in any endeavour is forgettable). Horse racing most frequently occurred in Bombay and Poona, though races also took place in other parts of the presidency like Kolhapur,[87] Ahmednagar[88] and Mahabaleshwar.[89] A special fast train belonging to the Great Indian Peninsula Railway ferried patrons from Poona to Bombay and back on race days.[90] Once at the venue, horse racing enthusiasts would have to watch out for pickpockets,[91] thieves[92] and illegal bookmakers (bookies).[93]

In the decades leading up to Sorabjee's birth in 1930, heated debates had taken place concerning the betting and gambling elements of horse racing. Between 1911 and 1912, the Bombay government decided to abolish the system of licenced bookmakers or bookies who offered odds to racing patrons in the 'ring' located within the premises of the racecourse.[94] Though the Turf Club's Stewards (i.e., officials in charge of the rules of horse racing, often members of the military[95]) disagreed with the proposal, there were several reasons for the government to do so. As they were so easily accessible on the premises, bookmakers encouraged betting. They engaged with stable owners, trainers and jockeys in what we would now call match-fixing. Since bets were taken on credit as opposed to an up-front cash payment, they encouraged patrons to financially ruin themselves by betting beyond their means.

They also offered arbitrary odds to customers which were not rooted in any scientific calculations.

It was with all this in mind that in 1911–12 the Bombay government abolished bookmakers and installed a revolutionary betting machine called a 'totalizator' (or 'tote'[96]) in the premises of the Mahalakshmi racecourse, where bets could only be offered upon making an upfront cash payment.[97] The totalizator was essentially a machine that calculated the amount that would be paid to those who had bet on the winning horse on the basis of an old French formula called the 'pari mutuel', which took into account the total amount of bets placed in the race.[98] It was only after looking at the successful operation of the tote in India, among other colonies, that the tote was introduced in the Jockey Club in London in 1927.[99] In America, the totalizator machine in horse racing was used for the first time in 1933.[100] In 1911–12, the government decided to reduce the number of days on which betting could be carried on at the Mahalakshmi racecourse premises.[101] They were also asked to consider clamping down on 'bucket shop' owners or bookies outside the premises of the racecourse who offered odds on horse racing.[102]

In the 1920s and 1930s, government regulation of horse racing sought to prevent poor people from attending the races. Government officials felt that since the tickets for the second and third enclosures at the racecourse were very affordable, poor people were attending the races, placing bets and ruining themselves financially.[103] In 1946, Gandhi wrote that while gambling on horse races was a lesser evil as compared to consuming alcohol, the government ought to 'put an end to the evil' nonetheless.[104]

Sorabjee developed an interest in horse racing during his school and college days. He would wake up at 5.30 a.m. and visit the Mahalakshmi racecourse where he would time the horses in order to figure out which of them were in form and likely to do well in the race. He would also keenly read and memorize the horse racing books which would contain statistics on each horse. Consequently, as a child, Sorabjee knew crucial details about the performance of horses—weight, timing, pedigree, present form and condition, handicap, ability of the jockey[105] and so on. At the Sorabjee family's sunday lunches, Jehangir would ask Sorabjee, a little boy of eight, which horse to bet on because of the amount Sorabjee knew about the horses. Attending the races was also a way for the father and son to bond. Sorabjee spent a great deal of time at the races with his father.

His father would worry that he would miss school or college if he went to the races in the mornings, but Sorabjee assured him that he would not miss class, and it was on this assurance that Jehangir permitted Sorabjee to indulge in this hobby. Though he enjoyed horse racing, he was never really interested in betting or gambling. Of course, as an adult Sorabjee might have placed the odd bet on a horse once in a while but that was more to keep things interesting than out of any compulsive need to gamble. He also never rode horses in the races himself, though he rode them for leisure at places like Mahabaleshwar and Matheran.

Perhaps the highlight of his adolescent life was in 1945 when he was just 15 years old. His father's horse, Doodal Dandy,[106] had won a race.[107] Sorabjee was allowed to 'lead in' Doodal Dandy by taking it to the paddock. One of the most thrilling moments in a horse race is when the winning horse is brought into the paddock, usually by the jockey and the owner. It is accompanied by a great deal of cheering from the onlookers lining the paddock. That day, Sorabjee was permitted to lead in Doodal Dandy. It was an unforgettable moment for him. Someone even objected to this, saying that he was too young to do so. However, nobody seemed to have paid much notice to the person who objected.

Later on in life, Sorabjee had a good memory as a lawyer. He was able to recall citations and paragraphs of judgments in the law reports with relative ease. If memory is like a muscle, then one wonders whether the time Sorabjee spent memorizing horse racing statistics and railway timetables as a child helped contribute to that essential skill. Sorabjee's cousins disliked his prodigious memory as a child. They would have to recite the prayers that the Zoroastrian priest had taught them, and Sorabjee was the only one among them who could recite the prayers very well, much to their own embarrassment. One of his cousins would sometimes exclaim, 'Soli will either be a complete lunatic or a brilliant person'. In his own self-deprecating way, Sorabjee would perhaps ask the reader today to wonder which of these he really became.

Having benefitted substantially from British rule in India, neither the Sorabjee nor the Dubash family played any part in India's freedom movement. They were wealthy elites who had been in Bombay for generations. However, they had not taken to university education or the learned professions.

3

Sorabjee, 'SJ'

Until the age of 12, Sorabjee attended the Bharda New High School at Waudby Road in Fort, Bombay, his father's alma mater. Founded in January 1891, the 'New High School', as it was originally called, was a private school which received no aid from the government[1] and had Gujarati as its medium of instruction.[2]

The school was founded by two Parsi graduates of Bombay University, Jalbhai Dorabji Bharda and Kaikobad Behramji Marzban, both of whom were the school's original headmasters.[3] When Bharda died thirty years later,[4] the school was renamed 'Bharda New High School' in his honour.[5] Like Bharda, Marzban had obtained a BA from Bombay University and he replaced Bharda as a Fellow at the university after the latter's death in 1921.[6] However, Marzban was perhaps the more accomplished of the two. He wrote a book on William Shakespeare,[7] delivered a lecture on Dadabhai Naoroji,[8] and served on a jury in a murder trial.[9] He was a Justice of the Peace;[10] a member of the Film Censor Board;[11] and a part of the Parsi Central Association,[12] a body formed to lobby the government to protect the interests of the Parsi community.[13] His grandfather had founded the first Gujarati newspaper and his brother owned the *Jamé Jamshed*, a leading Anglo-Gujarati daily.[14] However, he too passed away in 1933[15] before Sorabjee entered the school.

The Bharda New High School was a boys' school with a large number of Parsi students. Between 1916 and 1941, roughly 41 per cent of the school's pupils were Parsis, 38 per cent were Hindus and 20 per cent were Muslims.[16] This was despite the fact that Parsis constituted less than 5 per cent of the population of Bombay and 0.03 per cent of the population of India.[17] However, the vast majority of Parsis living in India were located in Bombay presidency. There were roughly 110,000 Parsis living in India in 1933, of whom 89,199 were in Bombay presidency and 57,765 in Bombay city.[18] Of course, these numbers paled in comparison with the general population of India which numbered 353 million at the time.[19]

Parsis were immigrants who arrived in India fleeing religious persecution in Persia sometime between the 8th and 10th centuries.[20] As a community, they had done well for themselves. They were highly literate. In the city of Bombay in 1931, 74.2 per cent of the Zoroastrian community was literate as opposed to 18.8 per cent of the Hindus, 19.3 per cent of the Muslims and 51 per cent of the Christians. Similarly, at that time, 53 per cent Zoroastrians in Bombay city were literate in English, as against 7.1 per cent Hindus, 4.9 per cent Muslims and 42.5 per cent Christians.[21] Between the 17th and 19th centuries, many Parsis made their fortunes as ship-builders, general merchants and by entering fields as diverse as trade with China, textile milling and railroad building.[22] However, though many Parsis like Sorabjee's grandfather and father had done well for themselves, the vast majority were not wealthy. Most of them were clerks, storekeepers, shopkeepers, domestic servants, etc.[23]

School attendance in British India was not compulsory.[24] There was no universal free primary education.[25] A typical Parsi school child attended school at least a year after an average English child and often studied in the dual-medium of Gujarati and English.[26] Even so, around 7 out of 10 Parsi children between the ages of 5 and 15 attended school in Bombay city.[27] There were more Parsi students at the Bharda New High School than in other prominent private schools at that time. In 1933, while there were 544 Parsi boys studying at Bharda, there were 400 Parsis studying at the Jesuit St Xavier's School and only 90 Parsis at the Anglo-Scottish Cathedral and John Connon School.[28]

In 1937, Sorabjee must have been one among the 1,800 boys who were enrolled to study under the 80 teachers at the Bharda New High School. The school often boasted that it was the largest private high school in the British Empire,[29] though this claim was not verified.[30] It was no stranger to lawyers. D.F. Mulla, a Parsi lawyer, who eventually became a judge of the Privy Council in London, taught in the school when it was originally founded.[31] One of its most famous alumni was Bhulabhai Desai,[32] who was, incidentally, engaged by Sorabjee's maternal grandfather in the Gymeric case that we have encountered in the previous chapter. Many of its alumni went on to become members of the legislative councils, joined the Indian Civil Service, and became lawyers, doctors and engineers.[33] However, the school did not have its own building and operated out of rented premises.[34]

The Bharda New High School seemed to emphasize excellence in sports, and Sorabjee was probably not too content in this environment.[35] By 1937, the school had won the popular Harris Shield inter-school cricket tournament 18 times.[36] It had a cricket club, a hockey club, a boxing class and a gymnasium.[37] Physical exercise was compulsory for every student unless excused by a doctor's note.[38] Students' height, weight and chest measurements were routinely recorded and preserved by school officials.[39] In 1933, a few years before Sorabjee entered the school, an observer used the school's data to conclude that 5.3 per cent of the Parsi boys at Bharda were 'fat', 31.2 per cent were 'well nourished', 38.1 per cent had received 'average nutrition', while 25.4 per cent were undernourished. Similarly, 62 per cent of the Parsi boys there that year, noted this observer, had decayed teeth while 23.9 per cent had poor vision.[40] The school boasted of having a music class, a debating union and an elocution competition, where Sorabjee might have felt more at home.[41]

Nearly all the pupils enrolled in the school were native Gujarati speakers.[42] The medium of instruction in the school was Gujarati. As the Bharda New High School had divisions going up all the way until matriculation (i.e., the school-leaving exam conducted by Bombay University),[43] this probably meant that the school was an 'Anglo-Vernacular School'. Such schools followed a pattern of education which was divided into three levels. At the primary school level, the medium of instruction was in the local language and English was not taught to the students at all. At the secondary school level, English was introduced as a subject to the students, but the medium of instruction continued to be in the local language. Finally, at the high school level, the medium of instruction entirely changed to English and was no longer in the local language. This is because the matriculation exam conducted by the University was to be written in English. The matriculation exam was meant to prepare students for education at the university level, which was also entirely in English.[44] Of course, not all schools in colonial Bombay were Anglo-Vernacular schools. There were some schools, typically run by the government or by Europeans, in which the medium of instruction was in English even at the primary level.

In fact, in 1912, several decades before Sorabjee was admitted into the Bharda New High School, a furious debate had taken place in the Bombay Teachers' Association as to whether English ought to be introduced as the medium of instruction at the primary level.[45] Introducing English to Indian students at the secondary and high schools levels, some argued, meant that Indian pupils were not entirely comfortable with the language.[46] Principal Bharda intervened in the debate and argued that teaching Parsi students in the medium of English at the primary level would be 'dangerous and unadvisable'. 'It would be impossible for a child which had formed its ideas and expressions in Gujarati,' he added, 'suddenly to recast them and take to another language.'[47]

. . .

In 1942, at the age of 12, when Sorabjee decided to leave Bharda New High School, he was probably at the stage where English had been introduced as a subject, but Gujarati remained the medium of instruction. The school he decided to move to was St Xavier's High School.

St Xavier's High School was an educational institution of greater vintage and of substantial official patronage as compared to Bharda. It received land from the government[48] and was founded with a large grant of over Rs 61,000 from the government of Bombay which matched contributions from private Bombay residents like Cowasjee Jehangeer Readymoney, a wealthy Parsi merchant.[49] The school building was constructed in a Western architectural style on the Esplanade or 'maidan' (open ground),[50] the area surrounding the old Fort of Bombay, where much of the new city developed in this period.[51] The school began its operations in 1870 and from 1877 onwards, it was visited by dignitaries like the Chief Justice of the Bombay High Court,[52] the Governor of Bombay[53] and the Viceroy of British India.[54] For instance, in 1903, Governor Northcote visited St Xavier's High School and advised its students not to engage in rote-learning but to learn how to apply the lessons contained in their textbooks.[55] The school and college remained in the same building until the year 1900, when the college got its own building.[56]

Parsi students were admitted into St Xavier's High School in substantial numbers, though they were outnumbered by Christian students. In 1903, for example, out of the 1,415 students in the high school, there were 830 (58 per cent) Christians, 270 (19 per cent) Parsis, 212 (14 per cent) Hindus, 90 (6 per cent) Muslims, and 13 (0.9 per cent)

Jews.[57] It was this mix of students from various communities that made one observer refer to St Xavier's as a 'cosmopolitan' institution.[58]

The number of students enrolled at the institution grew substantially over the years. The high school started with 300 pupils but it had over 1,400 students by 1908.[59] As opposed to Bharda New High School, it seemed to lay a greater emphasis on scholastic achievements over sports. A high proportion of its students successfully passed the matriculation examination of Bombay University. In 1886, for example, 77.1 per cent of its students passed the matriculation exam, though the general pass percentage that year was 36.7 per cent.[60] Similarly, 61 out of 61 boys matriculated in 1924, 56 out of 64 in 1925, 44 out of 53 in 1926 and 50 out of 53 in 1927.[61] Unlike at Bharda, participating in sports was not compulsory for students at Xavier's.[62] However, Sorabjee had 'some idea' of the game of cricket and he enjoyed watching the occasional contest between St Xavier's and Elphinstone College, particularly because the 'hard-hitting' Polly Umrigar, later the captain of the Indian cricket team, played for St Xavier's.[63]

The institution was set up by Roman Catholic priests of the Jesuit order. Chief among them was Father Joseph Anthony Willy, who belonged to the German province of Switzerland. Born in Switzerland in 1821, he became a member of the Society of Jesus in 1844 and arrived in Bombay in 1858. He was the first Superior or principal of St Xavier's School and College.[64] By 1905, the school had a teaching staff of 13 members of the Society of Jesus, 24 'secular' male teachers (i.e., teachers who were not priests), and 4 female teachers who taught the lower sections.[65] Though it was referred to as St Xavier's 'High School', it accepted students in the lower divisions as well, but it restricted the numbers of these students so as to promote parish schools in Bombay's Catholic districts.[66]

Except for a brief period during World War I when the German Jesuit priests of St Xavier's were interned,[67] the Jesuit priests who taught at St Xavier's were very highly regarded by the official administration. They were considered to be exceptionally devoted to their duty as teachers and to have provided a very high level of education. Of course, Xavier's was not the only educational institution set up by the Jesuit order in the colony, presidency or even in the city. Other Jesuit schools included St Mary's High School in Bombay, St Vincent's High School in Poona, St Patrick's School in Karachi, St Stanislaus's Institute in Bandra, and so on.[68] However, Protestant Britons residing in Bombay did not wish to send their children to a Roman Catholic school. It was with this in mind that a committee consisting of Protestant Britons was formed in 1878 to collect funds in order to set up the Cathedral High School in Bombay which would 'promote the education of the Christian youth of this Presidency according to the principles of the Church of England'.[69]

Sorabjee moved to St Xavier's High School because it had better prospects. It was a school of older vintage, it enjoyed greater patronage from the government and it had a stronger academic record. Despite having transferred from a Gujarati-medium background, Sorabjee excelled in subjects like English and French. He liked the atmosphere there. Charles Correa, later a famous architect, was one of his classmates. He revered the Jesuit priests at St Xavier's and developed a deep sense of fondness for them. Towards the end of his life, when his memory was no longer what it once was, he gleefully remembered the Jesuit priests who taught him at St Xavier's even though he might not have been able to recall the names of some of the more prominent politicians that he had encountered as the Attorney General of India.

Father Morant was the Principal at St Xavier's, and Sorabjee's teachers included Father Solagran, Father Tena (a particularly compassionate figure), Father Esteller and Father Jorda. If the students made too much of a ruckus, Father Jorda would get upset with them and stop teaching. Sorabjee admired his teachers' lessons in school. On 14 April 1944, Sorabjee was in his classroom at St Xavier's when the students heard loud explosions. Those were the days of World War II. All the students rushed out of their classrooms in order to figure out what had happened. They later learned that a British freighter called SS Fort Stikine, which had arrived from Karachi and was carrying explosives and ammunition, had exploded, causing serious casualties.[70] Father Bonet, another Jesuit instructor at school, had provided relief to the injured during that tragedy.

Sorabjee had a friend in school by the name of Nani Wadia. Wadia was not a very good student and used to believe that he would be promoted to the next level if he participated in the Boy Scouts programme. Father Bonet would firmly tell Wadia that this was not true. 'Wadio', he would say in his characteristic way, 'if you think you will get a form (to advance into the next standard) merely because you are in the Boy Scouts, you are mistaken. If you work, you will get a form.' Father Bonet frowned upon pupils who swore, even those who uttered the words 'Damn it'.[71] In a society fixated by race, caste and complexion, Wadia, a dark-skinned Parsi boy, was teased by his classmates about the colour of his skin. In turn, Wadia never lost his sense of humour. He and his classmates had once played a prank on someone. When the victim of the prank asked Wadia and others to apologize, Wadia asked him: 'Should we say sorry one by one, or together?' Wadia, Sorabjee and another classmate, Jimmy Umrigar, were called 'the gang of three' by their friends. They were sometimes ordered out of the classroom by the instructor.[72]

The Jesuit teachers at St Xavier's got Sorabjee interested in the principles of Roman Catholicism and he was deeply influenced by them. His classmates used to often tease him and say that the first two letters of his initials 'SJ' stood not for Soli Jehangir but for 'Society of Jesus'. Priests of the Jesuit order would write the letters 'SJ' after their names. The basic principles of Catholicism appealed to Sorabjee. Roman Catholicism struck him as a very gentle religion. He enjoyed reading the Sermon on the Mount in the New Testament, and felt that its lessons had to be practised in order to really bring about a true Catholic spirit in keeping with the requirements of the times.

His parents, on the other hand, were a bit concerned about his interest in Catholicism. They took steps to ensure that he would not convert to it. They tried to persuade him and instil in him the notion that Parsis believe in a particular faith because of the values that it represents. At that time, there was a Parsi woman called Dhalla who had converted to Catholicism and become a nun. The phenomenon of Parsis converting to Christianity and causing an upheaval in the community was not unique to that time. In 1839, for instance, two senior Parsi pupils at Wilson School converted to Christianity, creating an uproar in the community.[73] Predictably, there was quite a commotion in the Parsi community when Dhalla converted in Sorabjee's time. In fact, Sorabjee's family knew Dhalla's father distantly. Interestingly, many years before, as a student at Queen Mary School in Bombay, when Sorabjee's own mother won a prize in Biblical scripture, her father promptly pulled her out of the school and put an end to her education for fear that she might convert to Christianity.

Despite such fears, however, the Parsi community took to English education in the Jesuit St Xavier's High School and College in large numbers. In retrospect, Sorabjee believed that he never came close to converting to Catholicism, though he was certainly influenced by it. He did not, for instance, make it a habit of regularly going to Church, though on some occasions like Christmas Mass he may have attended Church. The Jesuit instructors at St Xavier's made absolutely no attempt to convert Sorabjee. As he later confessed to an alumni audience, though he was not converted at St Xavier's, he was transformed by the education he received there.[74] Many years later, as a lawyer in the 1960s, he made sure to visit the Vatican. Sorabjee later enrolled his sons, Jehangir and Hormazd, in a Jesuit educational institution as well. He was also quite pleased when he learned that his grandson, Raian, would be enrolled in a Jesuit institution.

St Xavier's High School encouraged its students to learn Latin.[75] Its students regularly performed plays written by William Shakespeare.[76] At a prize distribution ceremony in 1895, students performed scenes from the play *The Merchant of Venice*. The chief guest at the function, Justice

Badruddin Tyabji of the Bombay High Court, reminded the school's pupils that like the character Shylock in the play, 'they all had the same feelings and sentiments, and to whatever creed they belonged they must never regard themselves above the law or above other nationalities [i.e., races], and must treat others as they would themselves wish to be treated by them.'[77]

It was in Father Bonet's classes that Sorabjee developed his abiding love for English literature.[78] He won first prize in an elocution competition for his reading of John Keats's *Ode to a Nightingale*.[79] In the Bombay University matriculation exam held in 1946, Sorabjee stood first in English in the entire province.[80] Many years later, in his witty columns in the *Times of India* and the *Indian Express*, he quoted poets like Wilfred Owen, Emily Dickinson and Alexander Smith with ease.[81] It was perhaps here that Sorabjee developed his lifelong fondness for Shakespeare's sonnets, especially Sonnet No. 116, which he remembered to the end of his days: 'Love is not love/Which alters when it alteration finds/Or bends with the remover to remove./O no! it is an ever-fixed mark/That looks on tempests and is never shaken.' Borrowing the words of this sonnet, in newspaper columns and speeches he wrote and delivered in later years, Sorabjee repeatedly referred to India's judiciary as the 'ever-fixed mark' in an 'otherwise dark and depressing firmament'.[82]

It was also here that Sorabjee accidentally developed a lifelong love for jazz music.[83] The salesman at Bombay's record shop, Rhythm House, gave him a jazz record ('Tiger Rag' by the Benny Goodman trio with 'Sweet Sue' on the flip side) instead of Brahm's Hungarian Dance No. 5. When he heard the music, his anger at having received the wrong record instantly evaporated.[84]

After matriculating, Sorabjee initially enrolled as a science student at St Xavier's College though he quickly switched streams and pursued the two-year Bachelor of Arts programme in economics. He later regretted having picked economics, as he would have been 'more comfortable with literature or philosophy as [his] subject', even though his 'worldly-wise' advisors warned him that 'these subjects had no utilitarian value to get on in life'.[85] He was the first member of his immediate family to attend college, though an elder cousin had become a solicitor. He was an unremarkable college student[86] finishing the Intermediate Arts programme in 1948 with a second class[87] and getting his BA degree with just a pass grade,[88] though his academic performance might have been affected by the death of his father, as we shall see in the next chapter.

As a college student sitting in the canteen, Sorabjee discussed horse racing with some of his friends, many of whom were Anglo-Indians and Christians. A Christian friend by the name of Antao would speculate about which horses would win the races. Parsi students like Sorabjee were admitted into St Xavier's College in large numbers, such that they outnumbered even the Christians. In 1895, for example, among 286 students enrolled in the college, 149 (52 per cent) were Parsis, 87 (30 per cent) were Hindus, 35 (12 per cent) were Christians, 11 (3 per cent) were Muslims and 4 (1 per cent) were Jews.[89] In 1900, the Rector of the college expressed regret over the fact that 'the Christian community did not seem to appreciate sufficiently the benefits to be derived from a higher education'.[90]

Sorabjee's interest in Catholicism deepened as a college student. He continued to be fond of his Jesuit instructors in college. One such teacher was the legendary Father Duhr, who used to heavily criticize the philosophy of the Nazis in his classes on history. Sorabjee enjoyed attending his lectures and listening to him particularly because Father Duhr did not care whether Sorabjee got the right answers in class or not. He had a great personality and Sorabjee later wrote about him in his column in the *Indian Express*.[91] Another instructor, Father Raphael, used to play the piano in his free time and Sorabjee loved listening to his rendition of Beethoven's Emperor Concerto. Theophilis Aguiar, his professor of English at St Xavier's college, was another favourite. Sorabjee was quite upset with him when he did not visit Sorabjee in the hospital when he broke his leg in a motorcycle accident later on. In his college days, Sorabjee could not write very well because he had writer's cramp. Even his examination had to be written by somebody else under his dictation.

Of course, not every lecturer at St Xavier's College was universally admired. There was a professor called Father Fell, the sports director who taught poetry in the first year.[92] In their youthful way, students would say behind his back, 'Father Fell, Go to Hell'. Sorabjee developed an aversion towards poetry in Father Fell's classes only to fall in love with poetry all over again in 1961 during a case at the Bombay High Court.[93] Father Noguera, a well-built instructor, would point to his large forearm and threaten students by saying, 'Do you see this?', when a student got on his wrong side during a lesson.

4

Chamber No. 1

Two incidents in Sorabjee's early life had a profound impact on the years to come. The first occurred on 30 January 1948, coincidentally the date on which Mahatma Gandhi was assassinated. Sorabjee had borrowed the motorcycle of a friend, Shiavax Dadabhoy, who lived across the road from him. While riding the bike on Marine Drive along Kennedy Sea-Face, with his friend Cedric Santos[1] riding pillion, Sorabjee got into an accident in which he fractured his leg. On his way to the hospital, Sorabjee heard that Mahatma Gandhi had been assassinated. He hoped to himself that the assassin was not a Muslim, as he feared that there would otherwise be substantial rioting and communal violence across the country.

His father, Jehangir, was distraught when he heard about the accident. Sorabjee had to lie in bed and wear a plaster on his leg for the longest time thereafter. However, something had gone wrong. The doctor did not set his leg correctly (or perhaps the doctors back then lacked the facilities to ensure that the alignment of bones in the leg was correct). After the accident, Sorabjee's leg was forever crooked. In the years that followed, his leg always gave him trouble. He could never again run or sprint like other young boys. He felt that he was not fully normal after that. He could not even wear a pair of shorts again, since his leg was noticeably crooked. Later, he prohibited his children from riding a motorcycle.

The second defining episode of Sorabjee's early life was the death of his father in 1949, when he was only 19 years old. As an only child, Sorabjee had to grow up overnight, getting involved in the process of liquidating his father's estate in order to pay off his debts. It was his father's death which set him on the path of pursuing a career in the legal profession. After his father's death, Sorabjee had to visit the office of his uncle who was appointed executor of his father's will. Sorabjee was treated quite poorly in that office and it was then that Sorabjee decided that he would pursue a profession in which he would be his own master, where he would not have to kowtow to any boss. He wanted to be on his own, to have his own mind, without having to carry out the dictates of any board of directors. Sorabjee's mother wanted him to become an accountant. However, Sorabjee preferred a career in law. It was there that he would be able to argue cases the way he would like to argue them, with independence, and to try and make his own name in the profession.

. . .

It was against this backdrop that in 1950, just as a new Constitution came into force in independent India, Sorabjee entered the portals of the Government Law College at Churchgate in Bombay. In two important respects, the Government Law College was different from the educational institutions that Sorabjee had attended in the past. Firstly, this was a government college as opposed to Bharda and Xavier's which were private institutions. Though there were educational institutions run by the government which had excellent reputations (e.g., Elphinstone College), Government Law College in Bombay had a historically poor reputation, albeit one which was on the mend. Secondly, this was the first educational institution attended by Sorabjee where Hindus were in the majority. At both Bharda and Xavier's College, Parsis outnumbered every other community. At Xavier's High School the significant population of Parsi pupils was second only to its Christian counterpart. At Government Law College, on the other hand, Hindus had always been in a large majority, while Parsis occupied a sizeable minority of seats. Broadly speaking, between 1871 and 1903, for instance, Parsi students held around 20 per cent of the seats at Government Law College.[2]

In the colonial period, students who attended Government Law College (which was, until 1925, called 'Government Law School'[3]) had a long list of grievances against the institution. For quite some time, the college had no full-time faculty members.[4] It had no building where students could imbibe their lessons (classes were held at Elphinstone College).[5] For long, Government Law College was the only law school in the entire presidency and yet, there was no hostel or dormitory where students who came to Bombay from the mofussil (i.e., the interiors of the presidency) could reside. This made studying at Government Law College prohibitively expensive for those who came from outside Bombay, many of whom had to work in order to sustain themselves in the city.[6] The study of law was a part-time endeavour. In the colonial period, classes were typically held in the evenings.[7] Professors, who were juniors at the Bombay Bar, would sometimes rush through lessons, omitting important topics altogether.[8] Students received no practical training.[9] Obtaining a law degree from Government Law College was not even absolutely necessary in order to practise law. For example, those who had passed the pleader's exam[10] or become barristers in England did not need a law degree in order to practise at the Bombay High Court. At times, students would show up at lectures only for a few minutes so that they could mark their attendance[11] and those who stayed on raised a ruckus if the professor exceeded the class duration by even a few minutes.[12]

By the time Sorabjee joined Government Law College in 1950, however, many of these problems had been resolved. Professors started being appointed to the college who were required to have some standing at the Bombay Bar,[13] many of whom went on to become judges of the Bombay High Court.[14] A principal was appointed as the head of the college towards the end of the 19th century,[15] whose appointment was designed to ensure that professors would not cut corners while delivering lectures.[16] The number of professors at the college steadily increased. By 1923, it had 14 professors who delivered around 84 lectures in a year.[17] From 1938 onwards, some faculty members in the college were appointed as full-time professors.[18] The college got its own building at 'A' Road in Churchgate in 1941.[19] A hostel was available to outstation students when Sorabjee entered the college's portals in 1950.[20]

In June 1950, when Sorabjee was interviewed by Principal S.G. Chitale[21] for admission into the first year of the two-year LLB programme,[22] Government Law College had nearly doubled[23] its students with around 900 seats, and the college had decided to become a little more selective in its admissions process.[24] The study of law was a popular fallback option for students who could not do what they really wanted to. As the editor of Government Law College's magazine wrote in November 1950, '[s]tudents of science, commerce and arts, if they cannot do medicine, engineering or business, study law'.[25]

Sorabjee's years at law school were quite eventful. He won a 'hat speech' debating competition in his first year, where students picked debating topics out of a hat and were expected to speak extempore. Among the twenty competitors in the contest, Sorabjee spoke with 'an air of easy confidence'.[26] The hat-speech debating competition was won by Ashok Desai, another future Attorney General, the following year.[27] In the law college magazine, Sorabjee wrote a review of a book on the art of cross-examination in which he quoted from one of his favourite books, Charles Dickens's *The Pickwick Papers*, and lamented how some people condemned 'all lawyers as scoundrels'.[28] He was a member of the magazine committee in which he helped edit the pages of the law college magazine.[29] He also participated in an inter-collegiate Gujarati dramatics competition.[30]

In November 1951, when Sorabjee was in his second year at college, the Chief Justice of the Supreme Court of India, Harilal Kania, passed away. Prior to his elevation to the bench, Kania had been the junior of a legendary Parsi advocate at the Bombay Bar, Jamshedji Kanga. Under the presidentship of Kanga, a fund was raised to perpetuate the memory of Kania and in September 1953, after Sorabjee had finished his final year, a reading room called the 'Sir Harilal Jekisondas Kania Reading Room' was inaugurated at the Government Law College where students could read law reports and periodicals.[31]

At that time, the LLB degree was a two-year programme after BA,[32] but it was possible to study law straight after high school, though it then took three years to complete. For instance, Jehangir Gagrat, whom everyone knew by the nickname 'Jangoo', did not pursue a BA programme and instead, he studied law at Government Law College over three years immediately after high school.[33] Though Sorabjee had an arts degree, he too went through three years at Government Law College—the third year was spent as a fellow at the college.[34] He was enrolled as a lawyer on 16 October 1952,[35] but was a member of the magazine committee at Government Law College in the academic year 1952–53.[36]

Owing to its location in Bombay and its physical proximity to the Bombay High Court, over the years, a number of leading lawyers and judges visited Government Law College and offered advice to students on how they could fashion a successful career at the Bombay Bar. For instance, students were told that the practice of law required patience and perseverance; that after graduating from law school, it would take some time before they would start getting briefs to appear in cases.[37] They were told not to make earning money their sole aim in life.[38] They were informed that the law was a jealous mistress, and that the practice of law required many hours of hard work.[39] They were advised to go to the law courts and observe lawyers arguing cases in order to truly understand how the profession functioned.[40] They were told not to make copious notes as lawyers and to rely on their memory instead.[41] They were counselled that winning or losing a case did not matter as long as a lawyer poured his 'heart and soul' into the case.[42] They were informed that a sound knowledge of English was essential to a successful career at the Bar.[43] They were introduced to several witty and irreverent anecdotes involving courtroom humour.[44] There is no doubt that Sorabjee must also have received some such lessons during his three-year stint as a student at Government Law College.

There were many reasons why Sorabjee chose to remain in India rather than going to England to get called to the Bar at one of the Inns of Court, as some prominent colonial era Bombay lawyers had done. 'I want to make my mark here; why go abroad?' he thought to himself. To do well in India, he would have to know Indian law. It was around five years since the end of the Second World War and England was in a bad shape. Sorabjee's father had died, and Sorabjee still had a lot of businesses and family affairs to clear up after him. Debts had to be settled, properties had to be sold off. Sorabjee had no brother or sister and he had to do all this himself. There was nobody to guide him in his career. At the age of 20, a career in law seemed like quite a gamble. Who knew if his practice would work out? Was it really worth investing such a large sum of money and taking such a huge risk to move to England to get called to the Bar? Interestingly, most of the top-level Bombay lawyers in that generation studied in India and did not go to England. Nani Palkhivala, H.M. Seervai, Fali Nariman and many others back then studied law in India alone.

At Government Law College, Sorabjee had two excellent part-time professors. The first of them was Nani Palkhivala, who taught the law of evidence. That was the only class Sorabjee did not bunk.[45] Palkhivala was so precise, so clear in his lectures, that it was difficult not to listen in rapt attention. He gave a completely different complexion to the subject. The other was Y.V. Chandrachud, who later became the Chief Justice of the Supreme Court of India. Chandrachud taught Sorabjee torts and expounded the subject very well. Palkhivala and Chandrachud were friends. They both ceased to be professors at Government Law College in 1953.[46]

Government Law College had a remarkable group of students at that time—Fali Nariman, Ashok Desai, Anil Divan, Jangoo Gagrat[47] and Jehangir Khambata (also known by his nickname 'Jangoo') who later became the Managing Director of Glaxo in India—were all students there. Fali Nariman, a brilliant student who won many academic accolades,[48] was older and senior to Sorabjee by two years. Jangoo Khambata, assistant editor of the law college magazine,[49] was a very good natured and sweet man. There was a constant friendly rivalry between Sorabjee and Khambata during their law college days about who would get better marks. Eventually, Khambata felt that going to court and arguing cases every day was not for him, and he joined Glaxo. Sorabjee and Khambata remained good friends even thereafter. Towards the end of his life, Sorabjee recalled the days when Jangoo and his wife Eva were courting. Sorabjee and his wife Zena would catch them in the theatre and tease them. Eva was very beautiful and was an excellent debater.

Sorabjee frequently took part in the student parliament which was held at Government Law College. He was sometimes the prime minister or the leader of the house,[50] sometimes in the opposition, and was once elected as the speaker of the house.[51] Ashok Desai, Anil Divan (another brilliant student[52]), and Jangoo Gagrat used to participate in it as well. It was in the student parliament that Sorabjee sharpened his debating skills, which helped him as a lawyer. He was not a very studious pupil and thought that he would fail in the first year of the LLB exam. However, he was surprised when someone told him that he had been awarded the Kinloch Forbes Gold Medal in Roman Law and Jurisprudence in the first year LLB examination in June 1951,[53] a prize which had been won by his future senior Kharshedji Bhabha in 1936.[54] He enjoyed his young days and did not take college too seriously. He was part of a small band in which he played the clarinet. He only stopped playing the instrument once his law practice became heavy, as he could not find the time for rehearsing and practising at home.

While Sorabjee was still a student at Government Law College, he used to go back to St Xavier's College in order to help out with their dramatics. It was there, in 1952, that he met his future wife, Zena, who subscribed to the Bahai faith. At the time, she was an Inter-Science (12th standard) student at the college. Both of them were fond of dramatics. Zena used to take part as an actor while Sorabjee, given his fondness for western classical music and jazz, used to help out behind the scenes with the music. Zena acted in Gujarati plays like *Shirin Bai Nu Shantiniketan* by Adi Marzban (a famous director of Gujarati and English plays), and in English plays like *In a Glass Darkly*. These plays were performed in the hall at St Xavier's College. Sorabjee and Zena dated for around a year or so and then he proposed to Zena on 18 December 1952. He was still a law student then, about 22 years old, while Zena was 17. They were married in October 1953. Zena's sister, Mona Fozdar (later Mona Chinubhai) also studied at Government Law College.

. . .

After Sorabjee graduated from Government Law College, he wanted to join the chambers of Kharshedji Bhabha, a Parsi advocate who was a junior in the chambers of Jamshedji Kanga. Kharshedji was married to Sorabjee's first cousin, Naju, and it was through this connection that Sorabjee hoped to secure a place in the chamber. Kharshedji first refused to admit Sorabjee into the chamber, citing a lack of physical space. The High Court annexe building had not yet been constructed and Kanga had a crowded chamber on the ground floor of the High Court at that time.[55] It measured about twenty by twenty feet.[56] It was due to the lack of space that Nani Palkhivala, a junior himself in Kanga's chamber, used to have conferences with clients in his car parked outside the premises. Sorabjee then went back to Kharshedji and promised him that he would not occupy any physical space in the chamber and he would sit in the High Court library instead. On that assurance, Kharshedji admitted him into the chamber. Sorabjee's mother might also have pressurized Kharshedji into taking him on as a junior.

Around 38 years old at the time,[57] Kharshedji himself had only recently started doing phenomenally well at the Bombay Bar.[58] In the seven years between 1942 and 1949, Kharshedji only had around eight reported cases to his credit (i.e., cases that were reported in the law reports or even in the *Times of India*). However, in the next three years alone, while Sorabjee was still in law school, Kharshedji added another 30 reported cases to his name. In other words, his career at the Bombay High Court took off while Sorabjee was studying law.

The mustachioed Kharshedji cut quite a dashing figure. He was a first-generation lawyer whose family, like the Sorabjees, was quite well off. His wife, Naju, of whom he was said to be quite afraid, was a part of the wealthy Dubash family. His cousin Homi J. Bhabha was a famous nuclear physicist. His juniors called him 'Kharshedji', not 'Sir'. He had some eccentricities. He wore an old gown which had holes in it, and once kicked a junior under the table, in court, because he was displeased with him. He had a colourful vocabulary replete with unmentionable Gujarati epithets which he would not hesitate to use when he was annoyed.

Between 1942 and 1968, including the years that Sorabjee spent with him, Kharshedji appeared on the Original Side of the Bombay High Court. In other words, the cases he took up originated in the city of Bombay and did not come to the High Court from the districts. He appeared mostly in the Bombay High Court though, on occasion, he travelled to the Supreme Court or to other High Courts like the Gujarat High Court. He regularly appeared before both the 'single judge' (i.e., the judge who heard cases at the first instance in the High Court) and before the 'division bench' (i.e., a bench of two judges, hearing intra-court appeals from the single judge).[59] The judges he most frequently appeared before were Chief Justice M.C. Chagla (the first Indian Chief Justice of the Bombay High Court) and Justice N.H.C. Coyajee, a Parsi judge, whose father, H.C. Coyajee, had also been an acting judge of the Bombay High Court in the colonial period.[60]

One such case in 1952 in which Kharshedji appeared was a suit filed by one Mr Tyebbhai M. Koicha against the Mullaji Saheb, the head of the Dawoodi Bohra community. In 1934 and 1948, the Mullaji Saheb had issued an edict excommunicating Koicha from the Dawoodi Bohra community. In 1949, the Bombay government enacted a statute called the Bombay Prevention of Excommunication Act, which prohibited excommunication altogether. Appearing for Koicha in the Bombay High Court, a team of lawyers, including Kharshedji, argued that the Bombay statute did not violate Article 26 of India's new Constitution, which gave a religious denomination like the Dawoodi Bohra community the right to 'manage its own affairs in matters of religion'. Accepting this argument, the Bombay High Court held that a law which barred the Mullaji Saheb from excommunicating any of the members of the community did not prohibit the community from managing its own affairs in matters of religion and therefore did not interfere with Article 26.[61] The decision was eventually overruled by the Supreme Court in a famous decision around ten years later, in 1962.[62]

Another such case in which Kharshedji appeared in 1952 was a suit filed by one Parsram Parumal Dabrai against Air India. The plaintiff, Dabrai, had given Air India a parcel of gold worth Rs 1.80 lakhs in Karachi and had asked them to deliver it to Bombay. Air India did as they were told and transported the gold, keeping it in an iron cage in their Bombay office on arrival. However, the gold was then suddenly stolen from the iron cage, and Dabrai asked Air India to compensate him. The contract between Dabrai and Air India absolved Air India of any liability if the gold was lost or stolen, even if Air India had been negligent in looking after it. Interestingly, Dabrai had already recovered the value of the stolen goods from his insurance provider. Further, Air India had prosecuted one of its sweepers for the theft, and the police had recovered some part of the gold from him. Air India engaged Kharshedji to present their case in court. Relying on the contract between the parties, the Bombay High Court dismissed Dabrai's suit, but directed the police to return the recovered gold to him.[63]

Kanga's chamber, of which Kharshedji and his juniors were a part, buzzed with activity. It had lawyers like Nani Palkhivala, H.M. Seervai, Fali Nariman, Rustom Kolah, R.J. Joshi, Behram Palkhivala, Marzban Mistry, and others. When the new High Court annexe building was constructed in the mid-1950s, Kanga's chamber was relocated to Chamber No. 1 in the annexe building. Since then, Kanga's chamber has always been referred to as 'Chamber No. 1'.

Kharshedji himself appeared in a wide variety of commercial cases. Between 1942 and 1968, he most frequently appeared in property disputes, for e.g., cases where private property had been requisitioned by the Bombay government for public use, or cases concerning land left behind by 'evacuees' who had migrated from Bombay to Pakistan. However, he appeared in a broad array of general commercial cases, touching on subject areas as diverse as customs, excise, labour, suits for money, intellectual property disputes involving Bollywood films, company cases against cotton textile mills and so on.

The Original Side of the Bombay High Court, in which Kharshedji practised, followed the 'dual system', a kind of division of labour between two branches of the profession—'advocates' and 'attorneys', akin to barristers and solicitors in England. Attorneys were the ones who directly interfaced with clients, briefed advocates, filed cases and looked after the paperwork and logistics of the case. Advocates, like Kharshedji, on the other hand, addressed the court, argued cases, and made submissions to judges. Kharshedji was briefed by a very diverse group of law firms and solicitors. The ones who briefed him most frequently— Little & Company, Payne & Company and Ambubhai & Diwanji— accounted for only around 27 per cent of his work. In other words, he was doing so well in his career at that time that even if any single firm or client decided to stop briefing him, it would not have made much of a difference to his career.

Between 1942 and 1968, Kharshedji appeared most often for private clients. In only about 23 per cent of the cases that he appeared in, during that period, did he represent the government. He had a formidable win–loss record in those years, winning around 54 per cent of the cases he contested and losing around 28 per cent, with the rest ending in a draw. Statistically speaking, Sorabjee quickly became Kharshedji's most preferred junior. Kharshedji appeared with Sorabjee more often between 1953 and 1968 than with any other junior. Kharshedji was assisted by Sorabjee in 10 per cent of his cases, followed by Fali Nariman (5 per cent) and D.P. Madon (3 per cent) (who later became a judge of the Supreme Court of India).

Perhaps the earliest case that Sorabjee appeared in along with Kharshedji was a petition filed by a bank called Gadodia Bank against the government of Bombay. Gadodia Bank owned premises on the fourth floor of a building on Meadows Street in Bombay. After the bank's tenant vacated the premises, the government of Bombay issued an order by which it requisitioned the premises, taking them over for the residence of a government employee. The case came up in December 1953, perhaps around six months after Sorabjee's fellowship at Government Law College had come to an end. Appearing for the bank before the Bombay High Court, Kharshedji and Sorabjee argued that the requisition order was void because it was issued after the prescribed time-limit within which it could have been legally issued. Justice Tendolkar rejected this submission and held that the requisition order was valid.[64]

In many respects, however, Kharshedji's practice between 1953 and 1968 was different from what Sorabjee's would eventually become. Kharshedji appeared in only a few cases of constitutional significance, the Mullaji Saheb case being one of them. Kharshedji was primarily a commercial lawyer. Further, he was not a public figure. He did not write any books or columns in newspapers. He did not make speeches that were prominently reported in the press. Like Nani Palkhivala, but unlike Sorabjee,[65] he also ventured outside the legal profession when, in the 1960s, he became a director on the board of directors of companies like the Bank of India[66] and Warner-Hindustan Ltd.[67]

Even towards the end of his life, Sorabjee acknowledged the huge debt that he owed Kharshedji. However, the two of them did not have a perfect relationship. Kharshedji, who had a feisty personality, at times tended to be rough with his juniors.[68] Sorabjee was no exception. In his early days in the chamber, Sorabjee often came back with tears in his eyes, having been scolded by Kharshedji in court. If Kharshedji lost a case in which Sorabjee appeared with him, he would blame the defeat on Sorabjee. In later years, Sorabjee's own meteoric rise in the profession, at a time when Kharshedji's practice was on the decline, also made things awkward between them.[69]

5

'Judges Must be Expensive'

A lawyer's first brief is always considered to be very memorable. Sorabjee's first brief was given to him by a Parsi attorney, Naval Vakil, a partner at Little & Company, a firm which used to heavily brief his senior, Kharshedji Bhabha. It was not a very serious brief. Sorabjee just had to ask Justice S.T. Desai for an adjournment in the case. Vakil sent Sorabjee the brief along with a thoughtful note. It said: 'I hope it leads to more success.' However, in this, his very first case at the Bombay High Court, Sorabjee failed. The judge refused Sorabjee his adjournment. Even so, Sorabjee marked a fee of two 'gold mohurs' for his appearance in the case, equivalent to thirty rupees. Since the colonial period, Bombay advocates marked their fees in gold mohurs, where one gold mohur was worth fifteen rupees. Even today, it is common to see fees being marked in gold mohurs or 'gms' on the Original Side of the Bombay High Court.

Sorabjee's practice started slowly. Between 1953 and 1955, in the first ten important cases that he appeared in (i.e., cases that were either reported in the law reports or written about in the *Times of India*), Sorabjee was led by a senior and did not offer any independent arguments in court. Naturally, the senior advocate he was 'led by' most often in his cases in the early days was his own senior, Kharshedji. By 1957, however, around 4 years into his practice, Sorabjee started arguing cases on his own in the Bombay High Court. Between 1953 and 1970, before Sorabjee became a senior, he argued 63 per cent of the important cases that he appeared in himself. In other words, even as a junior, the majority of the briefs that Sorabjee received were those in which he had to stand up in a packed courtroom, face the judge, make his arguments, and try to obtain a favourable outcome for his client. This number rose substantially after he became a senior advocate. Between 1971 and 1975, after Sorabjee became a senior and up to the eve of Indira Gandhi's Emergency, Sorabjee argued 81 per cent of the important cases that he appeared in himself. Like Kharshedji, Sorabjee appeared mostly on the Original Side of the Bombay High Court. Like him, Sorabjee appeared both before a single judge and division bench in equal proportions.[1]

There is no doubt that Parsi connections helped Sorabjee. He grew up in a wealthy, well-connected Parsi family. He was privileged. He did not have to worry about earning money in the early days of his law practice, to pay rent or to support a family. He studied in schools that had a high proportion of Parsi pupils. He got into the chamber of a prominent Parsi advocate, Kharshedji, his cousin's husband. He got his first brief from a Parsi attorney. However, that is as far as Parsi connections could take him. In order to succeed at the Bombay Bar, Sorabjee had to perform well as a lawyer, in the absence of which his benefactors would soon have abandoned him. Most of the judges and clients were non-Parsis. Between 1953 and 1975, for instance, in the 132 reported cases in which Sorabjee appeared, only 22 (16 per cent) had a Parsi judge on the bench.

Sorabjee started getting noticed by the judges of the Bombay High Court a few years into his practice. In 1957, Chief Justice M.C. Chagla, a non-Parsi judge, appointed Sorabjee as an 'amicus curiae' or 'friend of the court' to assist the court in a divorce case under the Hindu Marriage Act, 1955. Chagla must have seen a spark in Sorabjee and tried to encourage him by appointing him as an amicus. Chagla concluded his short judgment in the case with the following line: 'We are thankful to Mr Sorabjee who assisted this Court as amicus curiae.'[2] In many cases, Sorabjee did things that might have helped him gain the trust of the court. He cited judgments against himself—informing the court about cases that were decided against the point that he was making.[3] Judges therefore knew that Sorabjee was not the kind of lawyer who would obtain favourable orders by hiding things from them. He made concessions in court, giving up legal points that he felt were not worth arguing. In a case in 1969, for instance, the additional judicial commissioner in Goa noted in his judgment: 'Shri Sorabjee, appearing for the petitioner, candidly conceded, and I think very appropriately, that the petitioner had not been able to substantiate the allegation of mala fides.'[4] In important cases, he went to the court prepared to argue a series of well-articulated propositions.[5] All this earned him praise from the bench. In one case in 1965, which he argued against the rising star of the Kharshedji chamber, Fali Nariman, Justice V.D. Tulzapurkar remarked: '[B]oth Mr Nariman and Mr Sorabjee submitted arguments with great ability'.[6] Nariman and Sorabjee appeared against each other often, each one getting the better of the other in nearly equal proportions.[7]

Between 1953 and 1975 Sorabjee had a large customs and excise practice (an 'excise' tax was a tax on goods produced or manufactured in India[8]—it was replaced by the 'goods and services tax' or GST in 2017[9]). About 26 per cent of his work at this time was in that branch of law. However, his other large practice areas included labour cases, company cases, landlord–tenant disputes, tax cases, commercial suits, cases involving evacuee property or land requisition and cases concerning foreigners or passports. He was primarily a 'writ court lawyer'—a High Court lawyer who appears in the court that hears 'writ petitions' as opposed to 'suits'. A 'writ petition' is typically a case filed against a government body under the Constitution and does not involve any evidence or cross-examination. In this phase of his career,

Sorabjee overwhelmingly had private clients. Between 1953 and 1975, he represented the government in only 13 per cent of his cases. In other words, he was mostly on the petitioner's side in the writ court. In a memorable case, which required him to travel abroad with B.N. Kirpal, a future Chief Justice of the Supreme Court, he was appointed to represent Japan Airlines in a court of inquiry set up to investigate the crash of a DC-8 aircraft in June 1972.[10] He also had an impressive win–loss record during that period, winning 59 per cent of the important cases that he appeared in between 1953 and 1975.

Sorabjee learned early on that as an advocate, he was not the hired mouthpiece of his client. Of course, he listened to his clients' instructions, but he did not consider himself to be bound by them. While arguing cases at the Bombay High Court, he paid close attention to the judge's questions and comments. After listening to how the judge was responding to his arguments in court, he could tell which points were appealing to the judge and which were not. He would then pursue those points which seemed to find favour with the court.

He also learned the important skill of throwing his opponent off course, without interrupting him or causing a disturbance in court. In one case, for instance, Sorabjee felt that his opponent was making his submissions quite well. Sorabjee then whispered something to his own junior, loud enough that his opponent could hear what he was saying. This annoyed his opponent, who flew into a rage. Sorabjee then stood up and said to the court, innocently, 'My lord, I am only whispering.' 'Whispering?' his opponent thundered, 'Your whispers can be heard all across the courtroom!' The interruption had its desired effect. His opponent lost his composure and rhythm, which was hard for him to regain thereafter.

Up to 1966, around 13 years into his practice, Sorabjee appeared overwhelmingly in the Bombay High Court, travelling to other courts very rarely. During that time, he appeared in the Bombay High Court 93 per cent of the time, appearing occasionally in the Supreme Court and Gujarat High Court. However, from 1967 onwards, his Supreme Court appearances increased substantially, such that he started spending nearly half of his time in the Supreme Court or in High Courts outside Bombay. From 1967 onwards, he appeared in the Bombay High Court in around 52 per cent of his cases. In other words, only 14 years into his practice, at the age of 37, even before being designated a senior advocate, Sorabjee had one foot in the Bombay High Court and the other in the Supreme Court.

In his junior days, Sorabjee had all his meetings with clients and solicitors in the library on the second floor of the Bombay High Court. There was just no space in Chamber No. 1 for Sorabjee to have his conferences there. However, Sorabjee's fortunes turned when he got his own chamber in the Bombay High Court around 1968 after Manek Jhaveri, a very senior and astute lawyer, passed away. Jhaveri used to sit in Chamber No. 8 in the annexe building. In the ordinary scheme of things, the chamber would have gone to a lawyer more senior to Sorabjee, a lawyer by the name of Mukund Mody, who had been a judge of the Gujarat High Court. Despite being a Parsi like Sorabjee, Chief Justice S.P. Kotval of the Bombay High Court was not willing to overlook Mody and give the newly vacant chamber to Sorabjee. However, Mody graciously agreed that Sorabjee should be the one to get Chamber No. 8, and so in 1968, from having only a cubicle in Kharshedji's chamber (Fali Nariman had a table), Sorabjee got his own chamber in the High Court premises. He asked two of Kharshedji's juniors, Avinash Rana and Obed Chinoy, to join him as juniors. They readily agreed as they too would get their own independent tables and a desk to keep their books and briefs in Sorabjee's new chamber. Interestingly, Rana was actually older than Sorabjee. Coincidentally, Mody's son, Jaydev, and Sorabjee's daughter, Zia, eventually got married.

Sorabjee's practice improved dramatically once he got his new chamber. In 1969, about a year after he got the keys, he appeared in fourteen reported cases, including five cases in the Supreme Court, two in Goa and one in Gujarat—the highest volume of work that he had done in a single year, until then. In that same year, Kharshedji had hardly any reported cases to his credit. Getting a chamber meant that Sorabjee's clients could now come and brief him more comfortably in a private environment as against being in the bustling, public High Court library. Sorabjee was happier when he got his chamber than he was on the day when he was designated a senior. Sorabjee threw a party to celebrate his new chamber. He did no such thing when he became a senior advocate in 1971.

After spending around 6 years at the Bar, Sorabjee started occasionally appearing in cases against his own senior, Kharshedji. In 1959, for example, Sorabjee appeared in a land requisition matter against Kharshedji and lost the case.[11] However, after getting his own chamber, Sorabjee started getting the better of Kharshedji in their contests in court. In a case decided in 1969, for instance, 75 bars of silver belonging to one of Sorabjee's clients had been confiscated by the customs department on the grounds that they were going to be illegally exported out of India. Kharshedji appeared for the customs department in the Bombay High Court. Sorabjee won the case and the High Court directed the department to return the silver to his client.[12] Perhaps the most significant of these encounters between master and apprentice occurred in 1970 in Nirlon's case. Sorabjee's client, Nirlon Synthetic Fibres and Chemicals Ltd., was unhappy over the fact that the excise department wanted to charge excise duty on the polymer chips that they used for manufacturing nylon yarn. Sorabjee successfully argued that since the polymer chips never left Nirlon's factory premises, no excise duty could be charged on them. Bhabha, who appeared for the central excise department, lost the case.[13] This case in particular marked a turning point in Sorabjee's career. It was Sorabjee's moment of liberation, when he felt, for the first time, that he had perhaps proved to be a worthy match for his senior.

The senior advocate along with whom Sorabjee would most often be briefed, apart from Kharshedji, was Nani Palkhivala. Between 1953 and 1975, Sorabjee appeared with Palkhivala, who occupied Chamber No. 3 in the annexe building of the High Court, in a number of cases, especially in the Supreme Court. It was therefore no surprise when, in 1973, even as a senior advocate, Sorabjee was briefed to assist Nani Palkhivala in perhaps the most important case of his life until that point in time, Kesavananda Bharati v. State of Kerala.[14] In that case, a bench of 13 judges of the Supreme Court—a bench strength of unprecedented size—held that the Constitution of India has certain basic or essential features which cannot be altered, amended or destroyed by Parliament. In other words, it was in that case that the Supreme Court held that the High Courts and Supreme Court have the power to strike down a constitutional amendment—to say that a constitutional amendment itself is unconstitutional.

Palkhivala, Sorabjee's former evidence law professor at Government Law College, was around 10 years older than Sorabjee, having been born in 1920. During the case, Sorabjee stationed himself in Delhi and did not get much of a chance to come back to Bombay even over the weekends. His son, named Jehangir after his own father—visited Sorabjee in Delhi. Palkhivala had a big suite at the Oberoi. The waiting and living rooms of the suite were stacked with the case papers. All the top lawyers and solicitors on Palkhivala's side used to meet there to prepare for the case, including the famous solicitor of that time, J.B. Dadachanji, who regularly briefed Sorabjee in cases at the Supreme Court. Conferences were 'brief and concentrated'.[15] Though Palkhivala was unfailingly courteous to juniors who were well-prepared,[16] the atmosphere in those meetings used to be tense, which suggests that perhaps some juniors were not prepared to meet Palkhivala's expectations. Palkhivala famously never wanted to waste even a moment's time during that case. When he arrived for dinner, for instance, the food had to be there waiting for him. In other words, he did not have enough time to order food and wait around at the dinner table. He was always in a rush.

On Fridays, Palkhivala would travel out of Delhi in connection with his work for the Tata group. Before leaving, Palkhivala would give Sorabjee the key to his suite, and Sorabjee and Jehangir would then move in, since all the papers and books were there. Palkhivala relied on Sorabjee in that case. There is no doubt that at least some part of the credit for developing the basic structure theory (i.e., the argument that the Constitution has an unamendable basic structure) must go to Sorabjee. Sorabjee got an opportunity to address the court himself only towards the end of the case.

Palkhivala and Sorabjee grew to be close friends. Palkhivala would send Sorabjee's children birthday presents. He never had time to visit bookshops. He would visit Sorabjee's home, go through Sorabjee's library, pick out the books he wanted, and ask Sorabjee to order new copies of those books for him. Palkhivala often spent New Year's Eve with the Sorabjees at Valley View in Mahabaleshwar. Sorabjee's closest friends, however, were three non-lawyers: Minoo Davar, Yusuf Curmally, and Suresh Mirajkar.

. . .

It was a customs case which first brought Sorabjee to the lectern at the Supreme Court. In November 1962, a German national by the name of Mayer Hans George boarded a Swiss Air plane at Zurich to fly to Manila in the Philippines. The flight had a short layover in Bombay. When the plane landed in Bombay, two customs officers, acting on a tip, boarded the flight and asked George whether he was carrying any gold. George shrugged his shoulders and said, 'No'. Unsatisfied with his answer, the customs officials took George to the baggage hall, where they found that he was wearing a specially prepared jacket with 28 compartments, containing 34 slabs of gold, weighing 1 kg each. They arrested him and charged him with smuggling.

George, however, had an interesting response. He said that in August 1948, the Reserve Bank of India had issued a notification which allowed a person to carry gold, in transit, through India. Though this general notification had been withdrawn by the Reserve Bank in November 1962, George said that as a German national, he was unaware of the 1962 notification. He was therefore not guilty of any crime, he pleaded. Rejecting this argument, the presidency magistrate had held that even if George had not actually received a copy of the 1962 notification, he was deemed to have known about it the moment it was published in India's official gazette. In other words, ignorance of the law was not an excuse, even for a foreign national like George. George was sentenced to a year in prison.

Sorabjee was retained to argue the case in the High Court. The case was decided in December 1963 by a bench headed by Justice Y.V. Chandrachud, Sorabjee's former torts professor at Government Law College. Among the various propositions that Sorabjee meticulously formulated for the court in the case, one argument was particularly interesting. Sorabjee submitted that since his client, a German national, was not aware of the existence of the 1962 Reserve Bank notification, his client lacked the *mens rea* or criminal intent necessary for committing any crime. In fact, Sorabjee and his future junior, Avinash Rana, had looked high and low for the 1962 Reserve Bank notification and had been unable to trace it. If they could not find it even in the Bombay High Court library, Sorabjee argued, then how could George be expected to have located it in Zurich?[17]

The High Court agreed with this submission. It found that the mere fact that the 1962 Reserve Bank notification was published in the official gazette did not mean that George was actually or even constructively aware of it. Of course, if an act of Parliament is published in the official gazette, then everyone, including foreign nationals like George, is deemed to be aware of its contents. However, the 1962 notification was not an act of Parliament but only a Reserve Bank notification. How could someone be aware of it merely because it is published in the official gazette? Since no Central statute prescribed how Reserve Bank notifications of this kind were required to be published, merely printing the notification in the official gazette was not enough.[18] George was directed to be released immediately.

The case was carried in appeal to the Supreme Court by the government of Maharashtra. In the Supreme Court in 1964, the Solicitor General of India, H.N. Sanyal, appeared against Sorabjee, who was at that time a junior lawyer of just over ten years' standing. The case came up before a bench of three judges: K. Subba Rao (a famous dissenter, who later became the Chief Justice of the Supreme Court and resigned in order to contest elections for the President of India), N. Rajagopala Ayyangar and J.R. Mudholkar.[19] Though Sorabjee had appeared in the Supreme Court before,[20] he had never argued a reported case there himself.

Two judges, Ayyangar and Mudholkar, disagreed with Sorabjee and reversed the Bombay High Court's decision. They held that the Foreign Exchange Regulation Act, 1947, under which the Reserve Bank notifications had been issued, did not make *mens rea* a necessary ingredient for constituting the offence of smuggling. In other words, since George had voluntarily brought the gold to India (i.e., he had not been tricked into doing so, and the plane had not been forced to land in Bombay due to a technical difficulty), he was guilty of the offence of smuggling. It did not matter that he may not have known that bringing gold to India was a crime.[21] The court especially took this view because the statute they were interpreting was designed to conserve India's foreign exchange—'essential to the economic life of a developing country'.[22] The court also found that publication of the notification in the 'usual form', i.e., in the official gazette, was enough to presume that even a foreign national like George was aware of it.[23]

However, disagreeing with the majority, Justice Subba Rao, in one of his characteristic dissents, held that though George appeared to be an 'experienced smuggler of gold' and though the customs authorities had acted 'bona fide and with diligence', Sorabjee's arguments were convincing and George did not have the necessary *mens rea* in order to be considered guilty of the offence of smuggling.[24]

Since a majority of the judges of the court had found George to be guilty, the question which then arose was what sentence George should be made to undergo. The court noticed, however, that George had already spent a year in prison, which was the sentence that had been issued by the presidency magistrate. The Supreme Court therefore directed George to be released immediately. Sorabjee's first important case at the Supreme Court had ended in failure. His client was no better off than if he had simply served out his sentence in jail. However, the judgment delivered by the Supreme Court in Meyer Hans George's case remains, to this day, an authority for the proposition that a notification becomes effective as soon as it is published in the official gazette.[25]

. . .

A few years after the George case, in 1967, Sorabjee argued three back-to-back cases in the Supreme Court.[26] One of these was Satwant Singh Sawhney v. D. Ramarathnam.[27] Sorabjee's client, Satwant Singh Sawhney, was an importer of automobile parts. Like Hormasjee Sorabjee in the 1920s, Sawhney had to travel abroad in connection with his import business. In 1966, the assistant passport officer in the ministry of external affairs wrote to Sawhney and asked him to surrender his passport. The government believed that Sawhney had violated the terms of his import licence and that he was going to flee the country, making it difficult to prosecute him. Sawhney challenged the order of the passport officer. The case came up before a bench of five judges of the Supreme Court, a 'Constitution Bench'.

This was not the first time that Sorabjee had encountered a case of this kind. A few years previously, in a case at the Bombay High Court, Sorabjee had successfully argued that the right to go abroad was a part of the right to life under Article 21 of the Constitution, and that a person could not be arbitrarily deprived of his passport by the government. Sorabjee had succeeded in that case not merely before the single judge[28] but also the division bench in appeal.[29] In fact, his success in the Bombay High Court in that case probably made him the ideal choice for arguing Sawhney's case before the Supreme Court. Though the Kerala and Mysore High Courts had taken a view similar to the Bombay High Court, i.e., that the right to 'personal liberty' under Article 21 of the Constitution includes the right to go abroad, the Delhi High Court had taken a contrary view.[30]

In his characteristic style, Sorabjee formulated five clear propositions in the Supreme Court. These were: (1) The right to travel abroad is a part of every person's fundamental right to 'personal liberty' under Article 21 of the Constitution. (2) It is impossible to travel abroad without a passport. (3) The government can only deprive a person of his or her right to 'personal liberty' under Article 21 of the Constitution by following a 'procedure established by law', but there was no law to deprive Sawhney of his passport. (4) The passport officer cannot have arbitrary and unfettered discretion to grant or deny a passport, as this would violate Article 14 of the Constitution (the right to equality) and the rule of law. (5) The passport officer has violated the principle of fair-play. On the other hand, the Additional Solicitor General of India, Niren De, argued that no person has a right to a passport, as it is merely a 'facility' offered by the government to its people, and the right to travel abroad is not a part of 'personal liberty' under Article 21 of the Constitution. Given the importance of the questions involved, the judges allowed Sorabjee's junior, Avinash Rana, to carry out research in the judges' library.[31] Sorabjee cited American and English law in support of his arguments.

This time around, Justice Subba Rao, the only judge who had agreed with Sorabjee in the George case, was now the Chief Justice of the Supreme Court. Subba Rao wrote the majority judgment for the court and agreed with Sorabjee once again. He held that the right to go abroad was a fundamental right, covered by the right of 'personal liberty' under Article 21.[32] He said that it was impossible to exercise that right without a passport.[33] He also added that since there was no law enacted by Parliament which prescribed the circumstances in which the government could revoke a person's passport, the government could not exercise its own discretion in revoking a person's passport. 'A person may like to go abroad for many reasons', said Justice Subba Rao, for e.g., to 'see the world', 'study abroad', 'undergo medical treatment', develop one's 'mental horizon' etc. The passport office could not hold on to an 'unchannelled arbitrary discretion' in the absence of any law enacted by Parliament in deciding when it would revoke a person's passport. 'Such a discretion patently violates the doctrine of equality,' said Justice Subba Rao, 'for the difference in the treatment of persons rests solely on the arbitrary selection of the executive.'[34]

After Satwant Singh Sawhney's case, India's Parliament enacted the Passports Act, 1967, which prescribed the conditions on the basis of which passports could be revoked. The judgment in Satwant Singh Sawhney's case remains a classic authority for the proposition that the government cannot deprive a person of his or her right to 'personal liberty' under Article 21 of the Constitution in the absence of a law, and that the government cannot arbitrarily exercise its discretion in the absence of some guiding principles.

. . .

It was around the time that he got his own chamber that Sorabjee was offered a judgeship at the Bombay High Court by Chief Justice S.P. Kotval. Sorabjee declined the offer because his third child, Jamshed, had special needs and Sorabjee would not have been able to afford his education in Bristol, England, on a judge's salary. A few years later, around 1971,[35] Sorabjee was designated a senior advocate. Unlike the procedure to become a senior today, Sorabjee did not have to apply to become a senior. He met Chief Justice Kotval in his chambers and told him that he wanted to be considered for seniority. Kotval said, 'yes, very good', and Sorabjee was designated a senior shortly thereafter. It is doubtful if, like today, the decision to designate senior advocates back then was taken in a full-court meeting consisting of all the judges of the High Court. Designating advocates as 'senior advocates' at the Bombay High Court was relatively new—it began after the Advocates Act was enacted in 1961.[36]

After becoming a senior, Sorabjee started writing opinion articles in the *Illustrated Weekly of India*, a weekly magazine published by Bennett, Coleman and Company Ltd., the owners of the *Times of India*. In one of his first articles, entitled 'Judges Must be Expensive',[37] published in August 1971, Sorabjee lamented the poor salary and working conditions of judges in India. The salary of a High Court judge at that time was Rs 3,500 per month. The net amount that a judge got in his hands after deducting taxes, provident fund contribution, and rent, came to around Rs 1,900 per month. Judges' pensions, after retirement, ranged between Rs 800 and Rs 1,300 per month.[38] Sorabjee noted, with alarm, that after being elevated to the bench, some judges had to 'dispense with the services of a chauffeur'.[39] Many of them were forced to form a carpool 'in order to save on the consumption of petrol'.[40] While Sorabjee himself was able to spend his holidays at his ancestral bungalows in Mahabaleshwar or Matheran, few judges were 'able to enjoy their long vacation by going out to distant hill-stations' because they simply had no money to do so.[41] Sorabjee wrote his article in response to the government's recent decision not to increase the salary of judges despite the fact that salaries of officers in the executive government had been increased. The chief secretary in Maharashtra, for instance, earned Rs 4,000 per month.[42] Likewise, in England, judicial salaries had doubled between 1956 and 1966.[43]

The salary of a High Court judge in India had not changed since 1950. 'I cannot conceive of a single instance', Sorabjee wrote in his article, 'where wages and salaries have remained exactly the same, be he a sweeper or a chauffeur, a clerk or a secretary, a mill-hand or a white-collar worker.'[44] Judges were being paid the same salary for the past two decades, he wrote, despite the fact that the 'fall in the value of the rupee' had been 'precipitous'.[45] Judges, he said, were not 'disembodied spirits whom inflation dare not touch', adding, 'rising prices do not freeze in their tracks in the face of the stern majesty of law.'[46]

Quoting from his favourite Shakespearean sonnet on love, which we saw in a previous chapter, Sorabjee referred to the judiciary as the 'ever-fixed mark' in 'an otherwise dark and depressing firmament',[47] a phrase he used on more than one occasion.[48] He also noted that the work of judges had substantially increased. In the past, weekends were 'days of leisure and recreation for the judges and there was not a single working Saturday'.[49] However, by the time Sorabjee wrote his article, weekends were spent by judges 'in reading the growing number of matters, both civil and criminal, coming up for admission, dictating judgments and doing several other judicial chores at home in order to save the time of the Court', including hearing urgent applications 'at any time of day or night'.[50]

In the colonial period, judges were paid very handsomely and a lawyer who was offered a High Court judgeship rarely refused it. In 1935, the Chief Justice of the Bombay High Court drew a higher salary than the Chief Justice of the US Supreme Court.[51] However, by the time Sorabjee wrote his article, prominent lawyers like Sorabjee were, for perhaps the first time in the court's history, refusing to accept judgeships of the High Court. In June 1966,[52] a sitting judge of the Bombay High Court, H.R. Gokhale, resigned from the court on account of the poor salary. His move was described by the Advocate General of Maharashtra,

H.M. Seervai, as 'revolutionary'.[53] Given the poor salaries of judges, '[i]s it surprising', Sorabjee asked, 'that in the last few years many able members of the Bar have had regretfully to refuse judgeships?'[54]

Retired judges had to work as lawyers or serve on tribunals in order to earn a living. A retired High Court judge could practise law in a different High Court or in the Supreme Court. Sorabjee considered this to be beneath the dignity of a High Court judgeship. 'I have always felt', he wrote, 'that it detracts from the high stature of judicial office that its former incumbents should be flitting from Court to Court or should preside over Tribunals whose orders and proceedings they have quashed and set aside in the recent past.'[55] He recommended that judges should at least get rent-free accommodation, a motor-car allowance, free electricity, gas and water, which would reduce the expenses required to be borne by them.[56]

Sorabjee concluded his article by launching an attack on the prevalent ideology of Nehruvian socialism. Some believed, he wrote, that a judge 'discharges public service and must not be impelled by materialistic consideration in our socialistic society, but should act in a spirit of service and sacrifice'. Others, he added, felt that 'a member of the Bar must accept judgeship as a call to duty'. These arguments, he said, were 'plainly meretricious'—they were facially attractive, but lacking in substance. '[A]ll this talk of sacrifice and small incomes in a socialistic society', he wrote, 'has a sanctimonious ring.'[57] 'Let us never forget', he concluded, borrowing the words of A.P. Herbert (though without giving him any credit),[58] an English writer and politician,[59] 'that if justice must be cheap, judges must be expensive.'[60]

Sorabjee's article, perhaps his first in a newspaper, was illustrated by the now famous cartoonist R.K. Laxman, who sketched several comical drawings to enhance the point Sorabjee was making. In one such cartoon, Laxman drew a judge in a wig and gown holding up a placard which said 'We Too Want Justice'. In another cartoon, the same judge, holding books in both hands, was waiting at a bus stop, while one onlooker at the bus stop whispered to another, 'I understand they can't afford a car.'

In one of its following issues, the *Illustrated Weekly of India* published a letter written by an irate reader in response to Sorabjee's article, one of many such readers who would write angrily to the editor disagreeing with Sorabjee's articles in the press. The reader wrote, sarcastically:

'Tears rolled down my cheeks as I read of the plight of the poor judges . . . How can a person possibly live on a meager Rs. 42,000 for 365 long days? I offer to donate a portion of my salary towards the uplift of this community as an interim measure. By the way, I happen to be an overpaid engineer (of considerable experience) and have the rare distinction of getting full Rs. 526 plus some paise per month, and that too subject to a mild grinding by the Income Tax Department.'[61]

6

'This is Nothing to Panic About'

At 8 a.m. on 26 June 1975,[1] Prime Minister Indira Gandhi addressed the nation in an unscheduled radio broadcast. Speaking first in Hindi and then in English,[2] she said: 'The President has proclaimed an Emergency. This is nothing to panic about.'[3] In the coming days, the government offered five reasons why the Emergency had to be declared in India: a students' movement in Gujarat, George Fernandes's plans for a nationwide railway strike, Jayprakash Narayan's call for a 'total revolution' in Bihar, the assassination of the union railways minister and the attempt on the life of Chief Justice A.N. Ray. However, to many observers, a judgment delivered by the Allahabad High Court earlier that month was the sole reason why the Emergency had been declared.

In July 1973, when Chimanbhai Patel was sworn in as the Chief Minister of Gujarat,[4] India was in the midst of a crisis of inflation, food scarcity and mass unemployment.[5] In the ordinary scheme of things, Patel's Congress government would have enjoyed a five-year term in office. However, in January 1974, barely six months into Patel's tenure, rising prices and food shortages prompted students in Gujarat to protest against the government.[6] The movement, though peaceful in parts, descended into violence. Fair price shops were looted,[7] milk booths[8] and bus stands[9] were set on fire, while schools were forced to close down.[10] Rioting occurred in places like Ahmedabad, Baroda,[11] Dahod and Jhalod.[12] The police opened fire on rioting students at a number of places.[13] The army and the Border Security Force were called in to maintain law and order,[14] and a 'shoot at sight' order was given to them in some places.[15]

On 9 February 1974, Patel and his ministers resigned, and President's Rule was imposed in Gujarat.[16] However, the aim of the student movement, in which opposition leaders soon got involved, was for the entire democratically elected legislative assembly in Gujarat to be dissolved and for fresh elections to be held. Members of the legislative assembly were threatened in order to get them to resign.[17] Morarji Desai undertook a fast unto death and vowed to eat again only once the Gujarat legislative assembly was dissolved.[18] In the Lok Sabha, Prime Minister Indira Gandhi alleged that a conspiracy was afoot to remove her from power. The incidents against the Congress government in Gujarat, she said, were really a rehearsal for what lay ahead in India.[19] On 15 March 1974, the democratically elected legislative assembly in Gujarat was dissolved by the Governor. By that time, out of around 168 members, only some 73 legislators remained in office, while the rest had resigned.[20] The dissolution of the assembly was celebrated with sporadic incidents of looting.[21] According to the government, the Gujarat students' agitation left 95 dead and 933 injured. There were 896 cases of looting and arson, with property worth over Rs 2.50 crores being damaged.[22] More importantly, a government which had democratically won a mandate for a full five-year term in office was forced to abdicate. A non-Congress government came to power in Gujarat in the elections which were held thereafter.[23]

In May 1974, George Fernandes, a trade union leader,[24] planned a nationwide railway workers' strike[25] which, the government feared, would paralyse India's economy, resulting in the closure of thermal and steel plants,[26] and halting the supply of essential goods like coal,[27] foodgrains, and petroleum products.[28] The strike, which lasted between 8 May and 28 May 1974,[29] was less harmful than expected,[30] especially because the government arrested Fernandes and around a thousand other railway employees, including prominent union leaders.[31]

Later that year, Jayprakash Narayan, a Sarvodaya leader,[32] called for 'total revolution' in Bihar.[33] Modelled on the Gujarat agitation, the movement called on elected leaders in Bihar to resign. It was a movement aimed at eradicating corruption, unemployment, price-rise,[34] black marketeers, profiteers, hoarders[35] and the excesses of capitalism.[36] Narayan, fondly called 'JP', asked people to stop paying their taxes[37] and argued that the people had the power to recall state legislators and parliamentarians if they failed to honour their electoral promises.[38] He advocated the establishment of 'janata sarkars' or parallel governments in every village.[39] Though JP urged protestors to be peaceful, according to the government, there were 544 incidents of violence in Bihar during the JP agitation.[40] The police opened fire on 54 occasions.[41] Once again, democratically elected legislators in the state were surrounded (gheraoed) by protestors and forced to resign.[42] However, what the Indira Gandhi government seemed to be most concerned about was that JP had allegedly made a speech in which he asked members of the army and police force and government servants to disobey orders they considered illegal.[43] The government also had recorded instances where JP had asked police officers to refuse to open fire on peaceful demonstrations and not to obey the illegal orders of their superior officers.[44]

All these movements were taking place in India against the backdrop of the 'cultural revolution' in China, in which Chairman Mao Tse-tung was purging the leadership of the Chinese Communist Party.[45] The Indira Gandhi government believed that both JP and Fernandes were admirers of Mao Tse-tung.[46]

In January 1975, union railways minister, L.N. Mishra, was injured in a bomb explosion which occurred at the Samastipur Railway

Station in Patna where he had gone to inaugurate a new 53-km railway line.[47] He succumbed to his injuries the following day.[48] A few months later, an attempt was made on the life of the Chief Justice of India, A.N. Ray. In 1973, Prime Minister Indira Gandhi had superseded three senior judges[49] who were in line for the post of Chief Justice of India, as they had held against her in cases that were important to her administration. Ray had been appointed to the post of Chief Justice in their place. The three superseded judges had resigned. On 20 March 1975, while Ray was in his car waiting at a signal on his way back home from court, he felt something hit his left shoulder and fall at his feet.[50] A similar object fell at the feet of his son, who was on his right.[51] The objects were two standard 35-mm grenades weighing 2.5 pounds each.[52] Thankfully, they failed to explode as they were old and had weak springs.[53]

However, perhaps the single most important factor which contributed to the declaration of Emergency on that fateful day in June 1975 was a judgment delivered by the Allahabad High Court. In the 1971 general elections, Raj Narain, a member of the Samyukta Socialist Party, contested the election against Indira Gandhi in the Rae Bareli constituency in Uttar Pradesh. Gandhi defeated him with over 100,000 votes.[54] Narain then filed an election petition in the Allahabad High Court alleging that she had won by corrupt means. In particular, he argued that she had used government officials to help her during the election, she had exceeded the permissible expenditure on her campaign, she had used the image of a cow and calf as her electoral symbol (thereby exploiting popular religious sentiments) and used Indian air force planes to fly around during election tours.[55]

The courtroom on the first floor of the 60-year-old[56] building of the Allahabad High Court, where the trial was to take place, had to be given a face-lift. A wooden platform was erected just beneath the judge's dais for Indira Gandhi to depose as her own witness.[57] In March 1975, amidst tight security arrangements, she was cross-examined by Shanti Bhushan,

Narain's counsel, for close to four hours.[58] She was given a chair to sit on.[59] None rose for her when she entered the courtroom, as Justice Jagmohan Lal Sinha, the presiding judge, had reminded everyone that the convention in courts was that one only rose for the judge. However, some forgot this rule and rose for Indira Gandhi anyway when she got up to leave the courtroom at the end of her evidence.[60]

On 12 June 1975, Justice Sinha delivered his judgment. Finding the Prime Minister guilty of electoral malpractices, he debarred her from holding elective office for the next six years. After reading out the operative portion of the order, Justice Sinha went back to his chamber amidst 'deafening cheers and clapping'.[61] However, Indira Gandhi's counsel, S.C. Khare, requested him to stay his own judgment so that an appeal could be filed in the Supreme Court. Justice Sinha granted a stay for twenty days.[62] In other words, Indira Gandhi could continue to be the Prime Minister of India for a period of twenty days, or until she filed an appeal in the Supreme Court, whichever came earlier. In the meantime, opposition parties asked Indira Gandhi to resign.[63]

At the time, the Supreme Court was in the midst of its summer vacation. Sorabjee was away in London with his family on holiday. Indira Gandhi engaged J.B. Dadachanji, an advocate who used to frequently brief Sorabjee, to represent her in the Supreme Court.[64] In turn, Dadachanji retained the services of Nani Palkhivala, whom Sorabjee was briefed with regularly in the Supreme Court. Dadachanji's choice of counsels was interesting. Palkhivala had appeared against Indira Gandhi's government in several cases, including the basic structure case,[65] the bank nationalization case[66] and the privy purses case.[67] Indira Gandhi's draft appeal in the Supreme Court had been settled by the Additional Solicitor General for India, Sorabjee's chamber colleague, Fali Nariman.[68] Indira Gandhi's case came up before a single vacation judge, Justice V.R. Krishna Iyer. A judge with known communist leanings,[69] his appointment to the Supreme Court in 1973 had been opposed by a group of 150 lawyers, led by none other than Sorabjee.[70]

Sorabjee had later publicly withdrawn his opposition to Iyer on the eve of the latter's retirement in 1980.[71]

In the Supreme Court, Indira Gandhi's case was heard for a full five and a half hours.[72] Palkhivala asked Justice Krishna Iyer for an unconditional stay of the Allahabad High Court judgment, so that the Prime Minister could continue to hold her office. If this was not done, he argued, her political career would be ruined.[73] The arguments on whether a stay should be granted or not were so intense that Justice Krishna Iyer observed that the two counsels, Palkhivala and Shanti Bhushan, appeared to be 'shadow-boxing'.[74]

On the same day, i.e., 24 June 1975, Justice Krishna Iyer pronounced the judgment in his chamber in the Supreme Court. He had decided to grant a 'conditional stay' against the Allahabad High Court order. Indira Gandhi could remain in office as the Prime Minister and participate in the proceedings in Parliament. However, she could not vote in Parliament or draw any remuneration as a member of Parliament.[75] In Bombay, people scrambled to buy newspapers that came out in the evening in order to learn what had happened.[76] A special All India Radio Hindi bulletin at 4.02 p.m. broke the news.[77] M.C. Chagla, the former Chief Justice of the Bombay High Court, opined that Indira Gandhi ought to resign as she had lost the moral authority to retain her office.[78] Opposition leaders got ready to stage a nationwide protest until she stepped down.[79]

Indira Gandhi, on the other hand, offered journalists no comment on Justice Krishna Iyer's judgment.[80] Instead, the following day, 25 June 1975, she visited the President of India, Fakhruddin Ali Ahmed.[81] The next morning, on 26 June, she delivered her All India Radio broadcast, informing India that it was in a state of Emergency. In it, she said that there was a 'deep and widespread conspiracy' which began ever since she undertook measures to benefit the 'common man and woman of India'. 'In the name of democracy', she added, 'it has been sought to negate the very functioning of democracy.' 'Duly elected governments have not been allowed to function', she said, referring to Gujarat and Bihar, 'and in some cases force has been used to compel members to resign in order to dissolve lawfully elected assemblies.' 'Agitations have surcharged the atmosphere', she said, 'leading to violent incidents'. She referred to the 'brutal murder' of L.N. Mishra and the 'dastardly attack' on Chief Justice Ray. 'Certain persons', she said, without specifying who, 'have gone to the length of inciting our armed forces to mutiny and our police to rebel.' 'This is not a personal matter', she insisted, suggesting that the Allahabad High Court case had nothing to do with her decision, '[i]t is not important whether I remain Prime Minister or not'.[82]

However, Indira Gandhi had not consulted her cabinet before declaring the Emergency. None of the government reports suggested that the law and order situation was grave enough to justify declaring an Emergency.[83] Though she offered many justifications in support of the Emergency, and may even have believed them to be true,[84] to many observers, the Prime Minister's instinct for self-preservation seemed to be the only reason why the Emergency was declared.[85] Later, a one-man commission, headed by a retired Chief Justice of India, Justice J.C. Shah, found that there were no reasons justifying the imposition of the Emergency, that Indira Gandhi took the step only to save her own skin.[86] Both Fali Nariman, who resigned as Additional Solicitor General the day after the Emergency was imposed,[87] and Sorabjee, later called the Emergency 'phoney',[88] because 'there was no real cause for it'.[89]

The Indira Gandhi government cracked down on its opponents during the Emergency with an iron fist. Opposition leaders were arrested under the Maintenance of Internal Security Act (MISA).[90] It was the *New York Times* which reported that dozens of India's opposition leaders, including JP and Morarji Desai, had been arrested.[91] This information was withheld from India's people by its press, under the government's gag orders. In London, Sorabjee's eldest son, Jehangir, noticed that something was wrong when he saw an article in a newspaper which said that an Emergency had been imposed in India. Sorabjee refused to believe it. He rushed to the Air India office in London, and got his hands on a reliable newspaper. It was true. The Prime Minister of India, it said, had declared an Emergency. Sorabjee cut his trip short and returned to India immediately.

. . .

People in India were accustomed to living in Emergencies.[92] A 'considerable part of the life of free India', until then, was spent in a state of Emergency. However, this Emergency was different in at least two ways—the draconian arrest and detention of opposition leaders, and the extensive censorship of the press. Press censorship had not been imposed in any of the three prior Emergencies when India was in a state of war against Pakistan or China.[93] Sorabjee was aghast at what he saw and decided to catalogue instances of press censorship in two books that he planned on writing. At the time, newspapers that wished to publish stories about the Emergency (e.g., the President's order suspending habeas corpus, the condition of detenues under MISA, etc.) had to seek the censor's prior approval.[94] The censor issued directions, often bordering on the inane, to the editors of newspapers from time to time. Even 'sober and moderate' criticism of the government was prohibited. Quotations of Gandhi, Tagore and Nehru had to be blacked out. Court decisions that went against the government could not be reported by the press,[95] nor could the press report about how the government was interfering with the independence of the judiciary by transferring judges.[96] The government barred the press from reporting the story of the Bollywood actress, Nargis, being arrested in London for allegedly getting involved in shoplifting.[97] An article written by Sorabjee himself was censored by the government during the Emergency.[98]

After a few days of token resistance, the press, Sorabjee wrote in one of his books on press censorship, responded with 'meek submission',[99] either because they were afraid of what the government could do (an internationally acclaimed journalist, Kuldip Nayar, was arrested by the government)[100], or because they wanted to earn the rewards that the government put on offer. For instance, newspapers that supported the government received an adequate supply of newsprint, plenty of government advertisements and were included in 'official delegations visiting foreign countries'.[101] In one of his books on press censorship, Sorabjee was particularly peeved with the *Hindustan Times* which, he wrote, became 'an unabashed supporter of the government'.[102] It was in this manner that the 'first and most crucial round of the battle for freedom of the press and civil liberties was lost without a struggle in the first week after the Emergency'.[103] To those who knew how vibrant the Indian press was before the Emergency, wrote Sorabjee, its 'virtual self-emasculation' during the Emergency was 'a Himalayan tragedy'.[104]

Newspapers which offered any resistance were viciously harassed. Two prime examples were the *Indian Express* and the *Statesman*. When the *Indian Express* published stories that were critical of the administration, the government subjected it to harsh pre-censorship. It cut off its electricity supply and sealed its premises on the purported grounds that its electricity dues and property taxes had not been paid. It even issued an instruction to the nationalized banks to refuse credit to the *Indian Express*.[105] The *Statesman*—Sorabjee was on its board of directors during the Emergency[106]—met with a similar fate. The government attempted to appoint its own nominees on its board of directors. It prosecuted its Managing Director, C.R. Irani, on trumped up charges, and impounded his passport. It threatened to forfeit its printing press, attempted to buy a majority shareholding in the company and even issued secret instructions to government companies not to advertise in the *Statesman*.[107] These and other horror stories of press censorship during the Emergency were documented by Sorabjee in one of his books on press censorship.

Sorabjee's law practice was busier than ever during the Emergency. Between June 1975 and March 1977, he spent around 42 per cent of his time in the Bombay High Court, and the rest in the Supreme

Court and other High Courts like those of Delhi, Madhya Pradesh and Karnataka.[108] The cases he was engaged in at the Supreme Court came not merely from Maharashtra, his home state, but also from other states like Gujarat, Bihar, Madhya Pradesh and Orissa. He remained primarily a customs and excise lawyer, with 42 per cent of his practice devoted to this branch of law. His involvement in cases concerning plane crashes continued. For instance, he was engaged by Indian Airlines to represent them before a panel which was set up to investigate a crash which had occurred in October 1976.[109] However, during this time, he appeared in a number of cases concerning the Emergency—cases of press censorship, preventive detention and freedom of assembly.

Prior to the Emergency, in 1974, Sorabjee had appeared in a few preventive detention cases on behalf of the Central government, justifying the detention of suspected smugglers under MISA.[110] However, he now appeared on behalf of the government's political opponents, challenging their illegal orders of detention under MISA.[111] He also appeared in cases concerning important questions of constitutional law, e.g., in Reverend Stainislaus's case in January 1977, where he unsuccessfully tried to convince Chief Justice A.N. Ray that the freedom to profess, practise and propagate religion under Article 25 of the Constitution included the right to convert to a different religion.[112] He remained a writ court lawyer, arguing most of his cases himself, appearing mostly for private clients. His win–loss record remained roughly the same—out of sixteen reported cases in which he appeared where there was a clear winner and loser, Sorabjee won nine cases and lost seven.

Nobody really knew how long the Emergency was going to last and there was a great deal of uncertainty and fear. When Sorabjee wrote a letter to someone, he would have his eldest son, Jehangir, type it out in code, so that even if it were to be intercepted, the government would not be able to understand what its contents were. When he wrote a letter to his junior, Avinash Rana, he would not disclose his identity in it. However, he would write the letter in such a manner that when Rana read it he knew that the letter had come from Sorabjee.[113] Sorabjee was socially isolated and ostracized by some of his fun-loving friends who thought that the Emergency was a good thing, that it brought much-needed discipline to the country. Khushwant Singh, editor of the *Illustrated Weekly of India* and Sorabjee's good friend, was one such supporter of the Emergency.[114]

. . .

One of the most significant cases that Sorabjee appeared in during the Emergency was the *Freedom First* case, involving press censorship. Minocher ('Minoo') Masani, a member of the Constituent Assembly, former Indian ambassador to Brazil and Mayor of Bombay,[115] edited an English journal called *Freedom First*. In July 1975, Masani submitted to the state censor the entire journal that he wished to carry in the first August issue. The censor prohibited him from printing eleven articles while permitting the rest. The eleven censored articles dealt with a whole range of issues—press reports containing domestic and international news, letters to the editor, opinion articles, quotations of famous personalities, and so on. Sorabjee appeared for Masani, a regular client and good friend of his, without charging any fees. In fact, Masani knew JP quite well and he had even asked Sorabjee to help JP write his will while JP was being treated at Jaslok Hospital in Bombay.

In the *Freedom First* case, Sorabjee succeeded in having the censorship order set aside before the single judge. The government went up in appeal before the division bench of the Bombay High Court. The case was heard by Justice D.P. Madon (later a Supreme Court judge) and Justice M.H. Kania (later the Chief Justice of the Supreme Court).[116] The court held that despite the imposition of the Emergency, though the fundamental right to free speech had been suspended by the government, Masani was still entitled to challenge the censorship of his newspaper on the grounds that none of the articles were prejudicial to the internal security situation in India. Though India was in a state of Emergency, said Justice Madon in his judgment, the rule of law continues to prevail.[117] The censor has to apply his mind and cannot abuse his powers.[118] 'True democracy', wrote the court, 'can only thrive in a free clearing-house of competing ideologies and philosophies.'[119] 'The day this clearing house closes down would toll the death knell of democracy.'[120]

The censor had clearly gone above and beyond the call of duty in censoring some of Masani's articles. For instance, in one article, Masani had quoted the words of J.L. Nain, the chairman of the Monopolies and Restrictive Trade Practices Commission and a retired judge of the Bombay High Court.[121] Nain had said that '[p]ublic-sector commercial corporations are resorting to unfair trade practices without any hindrance'.[122] The court rejected the government's fantastic argument that publishing this quotation would undermine public confidence in national credit and government loans.[123] In another article, *Freedom First* had merely informed its readers that a weekly newspaper called *Swarajya* had challenged a government censorship order issued against it, that the case had been admitted by the Madras High Court and an interim order had been passed in its favour.[124] Justice Madon strongly deprecated the censor's attempt to ban such articles that it found 'unpalatable'. A third article was a letter to the editor. In it, a *Freedom First* reader asked the American Ambassador to India to halt America's financial aid to India. The government argued that this article would harm India's friendly relations with the US and cause foreign aid from the US to dry up. 'This is crediting the writer of the said letter', wrote the court, 'with too much importance which even he in his wildest dreams must not have attributed to himself.'[125] 'Surely, American aid is not given or reduced or withdrawn', the court added, 'in proportion to what is written in letters to newspapers and journals.'[126] The court permitted *Freedom First* to carry an article which said that Amnesty International had urged police officers to disobey orders to torture people in their custody.[127] However, it allowed two of the eleven articles to be censored.[128]

Incidentally, Sorabjee's opponent in the *Freedom First* case was H.G. Advani, a generous man, who occupied the chamber next to his in the Bombay High Court.[129] Sorabjee once needed to use the telephone in Advani's chamber. Advani insisted that Sorabjee make not one phone call but two. Sorabjee, a talented mimic who spared no one in his impersonations, often imitated Advani's mannerisms. Sorabjee was particularly known for his mimicry of H.M. Seervai, the long-standing advocate general of Maharashtra and constitutional law scholar, who had a reputation for perhaps taking himself a little too seriously at times. He also imitated judges like Justice V.D. Tulzapurkar and Justice Y.V. Chandrachud. Legend has it that on one occasion he inadvertently imitated Justice Tulzapurkar while arguing a case in Justice Tulzapurkar's own court. Another story goes that when H.M. Seervai once called someone, the recipient of the call hung up the phone thinking that it was Sorabjee on the line imitating Seervai.

In its correspondence, the censor would often speak of 'killing' news articles instead of banning them. In a case Sorabjee was once appearing in, Justice D.M. Rege of the Bombay High Court was alarmed when he read the word 'kill' in the case papers, wondering if the censor had more nefarious designs in mind. 'Kill?', he kept repeating in court.

Between February 1976 and April 1976,[130] Sorabjee wrote one of his books on press censorship. His real objective in writing it was to publish, in the book's appendices, landmark censorship judgments delivered by the Bombay and Gujarat High Courts which Indian newspapers were afraid of writing about for fear of incurring the wrath of the censor.[131] However, Sorabjee was worried that the government might raid his home and confiscate the manuscript. He hid his papers next door in an aunt's home. He would visit his aunt or his High Court chamber in order to work on the book. Once it was ready, several publishers, including the Tata Press,[132] refused to print it, fearing reprisal by the government. It was published by N.M. Tripathi in April 1976.[133] One thousand copies were printed, of which 100 were kept aside for clandestine circulation should the book be banned.[134] The censor wanted to ban the book but given the book's 'legal garb' it did not want to suffer an adverse order of a court.[135]

Courageously written, Sorabjee's book would have served as a handbook for journalists who had been subjected to the censor's indiscriminate scissors. It was a scholarly book which ripped apart Emergency-era pre-censorship laws in its meticulous analysis. However, in the introductory chapter of the book, Sorabjee reproduced a paragraph written by an American author, Corliss Lamont, in a book published in 1956, without citing the source or giving Lamont any credit or attribution.[136]

Two days before the *Freedom First* judgment was delivered by the High Court,[137] Sorabjee wrote an article in the *Illustrated Weekly of India* in which he highlighted how important courts were during the Emergency. 'Doctors capriciously refused passports, petty traders illegally deprived of licences, Government servants wrongfully removed, innocent persons illegally detained and the countless victims of discrimination'—all of them, he wrote, were 'beholden to fearless judges'. It was the 'independent court of law' which prevented the 'Rule of Law being supplanted by the rule of the lathi'.[138]

In April 1976, however, Sorabjee appeared in a case in which the Supreme Court failed to live up to the lofty ideals he had espoused in his article. In Additional District Magistrate, Jabalpur v. Shivakant Shukla,[139] a bench of five judges of the Supreme Court considered the question of whether a petition for habeas corpus could be filed (challenging the government's orders of detention) despite the fact that an Emergency had been imposed and the right to life had been suspended under the Constitution. Nine High Courts[140] had taken the view that the government's illegal or arbitrary orders of detention could still be challenged, especially if they were mala fide or not in accordance with the provisions of MISA. In the Supreme Court, the bench was presided over by Chief Justice A.N. Ray. The attempt on his life the previous year had been cited by Prime Minister Indira Gandhi as one of the justifications for imposing the Emergency. Also included in the bench were Justice Y.V. Chandrachud (Sorabjee's former torts professor) and Justice P.N. Bhagwati (previously a Bombay lawyer who had appeared against Kharshedji in many cases). Apart from Sorabjee, one of the advocates who argued the case against the government was Shanti Bhushan, who had famously cross-examined Indira Gandhi for several hours in the Raj Narain case.

Adopting his line of arguments in the *Freedom First* case, in the Supreme Court, Sorabjee argued that even though the government had declared an Emergency and suspended the fundamental right to life, the rule of law continued to prevail in India. The 'fundamental principle of the rule of law', he added, was that 'the executive could not interfere with the liberty of a person unless it could support the legality of its action before a court of law.' In arguments reminiscent of his submissions in the Satwant Singh Sawhney case, Sorabjee said that the rule of law obliged the government not to take any prejudicial action against a person without having the sanction of a valid law and without the action being in accordance with law. The rule of law ensured that an arbitrary exercise of power would be eliminated.[141]

After two months of hearing comprehensive arguments,[142] with '14 ceiling fans whirr[ing] overhead',[143] the court held, by a majority of 4–1, that illegal orders of detention could not be challenged in the courts during the Emergency since the right to life had been suspended and the very existence of the state was at stake. Justice H.R. Khanna was the only judge who wrote a dissenting judgment. Newspapers were prohibited, by the censor, from reporting the dissent.[144] 'This disastrous judgment', wrote Sorabjee in a footnote in one of his books on press censorship, 'provided a carte blanche for uncontrolled arbitrariness on the part of Mrs Gandhi's officials.' 'The faith of the common man in the independence of the judiciary', he added, 'was badly shaken.'[145]

7

'Court to Keep Maneka's Passport'

Nobody quite understood why Indira Gandhi impulsively decided to dissolve the lower house of Parliament in January 1977 and hold a general election,[1] even though her government had an extra year remaining in office because of an amendment that she had introduced into the Constitution in 1976.[2] 'To be candid,' wrote Sorabjee, 'even the most optimistic among us would not have believed that we could have got rid of the yoke [of the Emergency] within 20 months—so soon, so smoothly, so painlessly.'[3] In the elections which were held in March 1977, the Congress was resoundingly defeated by the Janata party—the first time in India's history that a non-Congress government came to power at the Centre. Sorabjee learned of the election result late at night. He drove his son Jehangir to Fort in south Bombay, next to the High Court, where the electoral outcome was displayed on a chalk board. It was clear that the Congress had been decimated. Indira Gandhi herself lost her election in Rae Bareilli to her nemesis Raj Narain,[4] by over 55,000 votes.[5]

On 24 March 1977, the 81-year old Morarji Desai, dressed in a spotless white kurta and a Gandhi cap, took his oath of office in Hindi at Rashtrapati

Bhavan in Delhi.[6] Janata MPs (Members of Parliament) took their pledge at Raj Ghat, paying their respects to Mahatma Gandhi.[7] A motley crew of 18 parliamentarians were inducted into Desai's cabinet, including Shanti Bhushan, the advocate who had grilled Indira Gandhi for four hours in Allahabad and who had argued the habeas corpus case alongside Sorabjee in the Supreme Court.[8] Bhushan was made law minister.

After the swearing-in ceremony, a press correspondent asked Prime Minister Desai an interesting question. Though Janata had come to power at the Centre, the Congress was still in office in many states in India—the very states which had unequivocally voted against the Congress in the general election. Despite the elections, the Congress remained in power in many states and consequently, it held the reins of power even in the upper house of India's Parliament, the Rajya Sabha, whose composition is controlled by the states. Would Morarji Desai, asked the correspondent, dissolve the state legislatures in which the Congress party was in power and hold fresh elections? Desai answered by saying that the Janata government would not resort to tactics that had been adopted by the last government. We will not 'topple' state governments, he said.[9]

A few weeks later, Sorabjee heard the telephone ringing in his bedroom. When he answered it, he recognized the voice of Shanti Bhushan at the other end of the receiver. 'Would you like to come to Delhi as the Additional Solicitor General for India?', Bhushan asked him. Sorabjee sat up in his bed. The question did not come as a surprise to him. He had expected that he would be made a law officer if the Janata government came to power. His arguments in preventive detention and press censorship cases during the Emergency had not gone unnoticed. However, the 47-year-old Sorabjee thought that he might have been offered a higher post. He told Bhushan that he would think about it, though he was inclined to say yes. Sorabjee then asked his wife, Zena, what he should do. It was clear to them that their son, Jamshed, who had special needs and who was now in a school in Bombay, could not be relocated to Delhi. There were no great schools or facilities there at that time for children with special needs. The principal of Jamshed's school also felt that he was beginning to do well and that his routine should not be disturbed. After some thought, Sorabjee and his wife decided that Zena would stay back in Bombay with the children, though she might spend a few days a month with him in Delhi.

Sorabjee's appointment as Additional Solicitor General for India was reported in the *Times of India* on 12 April 1977.[10] Zena went to Delhi to look for a good house for him. The government gave them a few choices in Lutyens' Delhi. Zena liked the house which was available on Aurangzeb Road, but Sorabjee picked the bungalow at Motilal Nehru Marg, which is now the official residence of the Attorney General of India. Along with Sorabjee, S.V. Gupte and S.N. Kacker were appointed Attorney General and Solicitor General, respectively. S.V. Gupte was a prominent Bombay lawyer[11] who had appeared against Sorabjee's senior, Kharshedji, in a number of cases. Kacker, a former Advocate General of Uttar Pradesh,[12] later became the law minister under the Janata government[13] and was replaced by Sorabjee as Solicitor General.

Sorabjee's home, on Motilal Nehru Marg, shared a wall with a new 11-storey 350-bed hotel which was being built[14] by the Taj group at 1, Man Singh Road, now the famous Taj Man Singh Hotel—a favourite for lawyers travelling to Delhi. Rumour had it that the Tata-owned company, Indian Hotel Co. Ltd., was only permitted to construct the hotel on the site by Sanjay Gandhi once Nani Palkhivala resigned from the company's board of directors.[15] While the hotel was being built, the noise was unbearable. Sorabjee would constantly call up the Taj group and complain about the loud racket, especially at night. The Italian ambassador to India used to live across the road. One night, in his desperation to get some sleep, Sorabjee called up the Taj group, pretended to be the Italian ambassador and asked them to stop the construction. Eventually, the hotel construction crew soundproofed

Sorabjee's bedroom so that he would not be bothered by the incessant construction-related commotion.

Sorabjee and his wife were social animals. They frequently threw parties at their residence in Delhi which even sitting judges of the Supreme Court attended.[16] It was not frowned upon, in that era, for judges to socialize with the very lawyers who would be appearing before them the next day. Sorabjee and Zena also had dinners in honour of retiring judges.

A few days after his appointment, certain events occurred which set the stage for Sorabjee's first big appearance at the Supreme Court as a law officer. On 18 April, the new Janata Home Minister, Charan Singh, wrote a letter to the Chief Ministers of nine Congress-run states.[17] In it, he requested the Chief Ministers to ask their respective state governors to dissolve their legislative assemblies and hold elections. This was because, he wrote, '[e]minent constitutional experts' were of the view that state legislatures ought to be dissolved when they no longer reflected the will of the people. Charan Singh wrote this letter despite the assurance given by Morarji Desai, on the day he was sworn in as Prime Minister, that he would not 'topple' Congress-run state governments. Two of these Congress governments, in Uttar Pradesh and Orissa, had only recently come to power in 1974.[18]

Charan Singh's letter did not come as a big surprise to anyone. A few weeks before, in a 30-minute press conference at Jaslok hospital, an ailing JP had said that the state legislatures ought to be dissolved in view of the election results.[19] A few days after Charan Singh's letter, Law Minister Shanti Bhushan hinted, in an interview on the radio, that Charan Singh's politely worded letter was not really a request—the government would ask the President to dissolve Congress-run state legislatures if Charan Singh's letter was not complied with.[20] The case soon travelled to the Supreme Court when six[21] of the nine states to whom Charan Singh had written his letter filed suits against the Central government under Article 131 of the Constitution, which gives the Supreme Court the power to hear disputes between the 'Government of India and one or more States'.[22] A bench of seven judges, headed by Chief Justice M.H. Beg, was constituted to hear the case.

The five-day hearing of this case in the Supreme Court was explosive. On the first day of arguments, R.K. Garg, who was appearing for three Punjab MLAs, requested the court to prevent the Central government from dissolving the state legislatures while the case was being heard by the Supreme Court. '[T]he court should not be faced with a fait accompli tomorrow', he said. If the Central government dissolved the state legislatures while the case was going on, there would be nothing left for the Supreme Court to decide. Justice Y.V. Chandrachud then looked at Sorabjee and said, '[t]his court must be treated with respect'. In other words, the Janata government should not, while the Supreme Court hearings were on, dissolve the Congress state legislatures. Sorabjee told Chandrachud that he would convey this to the government. 'We do not pass any midnight order', he said.[23]

That same day, a heated exchange occurred between the court and the former Attorney General of India, Niren De. Justice Y.V. Chandrachud told De that the case presented a 'plain political problem, and all these years we have scrupulously kept away from political issues.' Whether the President should dissolve the state legislatures or not appeared to be a political matter. After some back and forth between De and the court on this question, De seems to have told the court that the judges were being paid to hear him argue (i.e., that they were being paid their salaries to do their jobs and hear advocates like him argue).[24] The court took a serious view of these remarks and Justice Bhagwati informed De: 'It was not right on your part to have said that we are being paid to hear you.'[25] Chief Justice Beg dropped a hint to De that the Congress had dissolved state legislatures in the past. How could they now object to the Janata government dissolving Congress state legislatures? 'What is sauce for the goose is not sauce for the gander', he remarked, to which Justice Gupta added, 'Sauce is the same but the difference is between the goose and the gander'.[26]

Sorabjee addressed the court on the third day of arguments. He made three brief submissions to the court.[27] Firstly, he argued that the suits filed by the state governments were not maintainable. Article 131 of the Constitution gives the Supreme Court the jurisdiction or power to decide disputes between the Government of India and one or more states. This case, however, was a dispute relating merely to the composition of state legislatures, which did not affect the states themselves. Governments may come and go but the state will continue to exist and survive. Secondly, he submitted that the President's decision to dissolve the state legislatures under Article 356 of the Constitution was 'non justiciable' (i.e., it could not be reviewed by the court), except on very limited grounds. Of course, if the President's decision was 'demonstrably absurd or perverse or self-evidently mala fide', if there was no nexus at all between the President's reasons for dissolving the state legislatures and the purpose for which the President may dissolve state assemblies under Article 356 of the Constitution, then the court could intervene, but not otherwise.[28] Thirdly, he argued that in this case, there were justifiable grounds for dissolving the state legislatures. Two days later, Sorabjee submitted written propositions to the court encapsulating his arguments.[29]

Arguments were concluded on the fifth day of the case, on 29 April. The court took a short recess. When it returned, it informed a packed courtroom that the bench of seven judges had unanimously decided to dismiss the case.[30] The judgments containing their reasons were delivered a few days later.[31] By a narrow majority of 4–3, the court rejected Sorabjee's first argument and held that a suit under Article 131 of the Constitution was maintainable when the President sought to dissolve a state legislative assembly.[32] However, it agreed with Sorabjee's second and third propositions. The grounds on which a court could interfere with the President's decision to dissolve state legislative assemblies were very narrow. If the President decided to dissolve the state legislature for wholly extraneous, grossly perverse or mala fide reasons, then the court could interfere, but not otherwise.[33] For instance, if the President dissolved the state legislature because the Chief Minister belonged to a particular caste[34] or because the Chief Minister was below five feet in height,[35] then the court could interfere.[36] The court agreed with Sorabjee's third proposition and held that there were sufficient reasons, in this case, for the President to dissolve the state legislatures, in view of the large electoral verdict against the Congress government in the general elections.[37]

The judgments delivered by the court ended this case with even greater controversy. One of the judges, Justice Goswami, concluded his judgment with what he called a 'cold shudder', referring to how the acting President of India, B.D. Jatti, had met Chief Justice Beg sometime between 29 April and 6 May, and spoken about the case. After giving this matter 'the most anxious thought', Justice Goswami expressed the hope that the 'majesty of the High Office of the President, who should be beyond the high-watermark of any controversy, suffers not in future.'[38] Chief Justice Beg was livid when he read this paragraph in Justice Goswami's judgment and issued a press release clarifying that President Jatti had only met him to invite him for his son's wedding.[39] There were figurative fireworks on display in the Supreme Court's judgment.

After the court's decision, the Janata government advised the President of India to dissolve the state legislatures in the nine Congress-run states.[40] In the elections which followed, the Janata party was elected to power in most of the states.[41] Sorabjee had succeeded in his first important case as a law officer.

. . .

In the coming months, the Janata government instituted a number of probes to investigate accusations of wrongdoing against Congress leaders. The Shah Commission, headed by the retired Chief Justice of India, Justice J.C. Shah, was appointed to inquire into excesses committed by the government during the Emergency.[42] The Shah Commission eventually found that Indira Gandhi had imposed the Emergency only to hold on to her own office.[43] The Gupta Commission, manned by a sitting judge of the Supreme Court, Justice A.C. Gupta, found that Sanjay Gandhi promoted his Maruti car business by using his political clout.[44] Two commissions were headed by another retired judge of the Supreme Court, Justice Jaganmohan Reddy. One was constituted to investigate allegations of corruption against Bansi Lal, the former Congress defence minister.[45] The commission soon found that as the Chief Minister of Haryana, Bansi Lal had allotted contracts to Sanjay Gandhi's company, Maruti Ltd., in order to please him.[46] The other Reddy Commission inquired into allegations that a sum of Rs 60 lakhs was fraudulently withdrawn from the vault of the State Bank of India by a former army officer called R.S. Nagarwala, with a view to enriching Sanjay Gandhi.[47] These commissions were open to the public. As the Additional Solicitor General for India, Sorabjee appeared before the Jaganmohan Reddy Commission concerning Bansi Lal.[48]

After setting up these bodies, the government took steps to ensure that Indira Gandhi and members of her family, who would be required to appear before these probes, did not flee the country. The pilot licences of Sanjay and Maneka Gandhi, Indira Gandhi's younger son and daughter-in-law, respectively, were suspended.[49] Their passports were also impounded[50] under the Passports Act, 1967, a law which had been enacted after Satwant Singh Sawhney's case—Sorabjee's first reported victory arguing on his own at the Supreme Court. When Indira Gandhi applied for a passport, her application was refused.[51] Maneka Gandhi alleged that her phone line was being tapped and that intelligence officers were following her husband around.[52]

Maneka Gandhi filed a petition in the Supreme Court challenging the order of the regional passport officer impounding her passport. Her advocate argued that she had not been given a hearing by the passport officer and no copy of the passport officer's order had been provided to her, which were violations of the principles of 'natural justice'. The Supreme Court admitted her petition, and as an interim measure, issued a direction that her passport would be kept with the registrar of the Supreme Court until the court decided the case.[53]

The case came up for hearing before a bench of seven judges of the Supreme Court. Sorabjee did not make any arguments in this case but only assisted the Attorney General of India, S.V. Gupte. In Satwant Singh Sawhney's case, the Supreme Court had already held that the right to go abroad was a part of the fundamental right to 'personal liberty' under Article 21 of the Constitution. Under Article 21, the 'personal liberty' of a person cannot be deprived by the government without following a 'procedure established by law'. In Satwant Singh Sawhney's case, Sorabjee had argued that his client's passport had been impounded by the government without any procedure being established by law. There was no Passports Act, 1967, at that time. In other words, the government had deprived Sorabjee's client of his right to 'personal liberty' (i.e., his right to go abroad) without there being any 'procedure established by law', in violation of Article 21 of the Constitution. This argument had been accepted by Chief Justice Subba Rao in Satwant Singh Sawhney's case.

However, there was now an obstacle facing Maneka Gandhi in her case. After Satwant Singh Sawhney's decision, the government had enacted the Passports Act, 1967. This law now allowed the government to impound a person's passport in certain situations. In other words, there was now a 'procedure established by law' for depriving Maneka Gandhi of her right to personal liberty (i.e., her right to go abroad). Could her passport, therefore, be impounded without a hearing being given to her since there was now a 'procedure established by law'? Answering this question in the negative, Attorney General S.V. Gupte conceded and the Supreme Court accepted the proposition that the procedure which is established by law for depriving a person of his or her personal liberty under Article 21 of the Constitution cannot be 'arbitrary, unfair or unreasonable'.[54] The court held that a government officer who acts in an arbitrary manner violates the right to equality under Article 14 of the Constitution.[55] The court decided that it was incumbent upon the passport officer to give Maneka Gandhi a hearing— even a 'post-decisional hearing' (i.e., a hearing given after the decision to impound her passport had been taken) would suffice in urgent cases.[56] A copy of the order containing reasons had to be furnished to her as well.[57] The duration of the order impounding Maneka Gandhi's passport had to be limited in nature and could not extend over an indefinite period of time.[58]

In the ultimate result, Attorney General Gupte conceded that the government would give Maneka Gandhi a hearing, and if an adverse order was passed against her, impounding her passport again, the order would be limited to six months in duration. Given these concessions by the Attorney General, the court decided not to pass any formal order. Maneka Gandhi's passport was to remain in the custody of the registrar of the Supreme Court until further orders.[59] The following day, on 26 January 1978, which was Republic Day, a small article appeared on the front page of the *Times of India* under the title: 'Court to keep Maneka's passport'. The judgment of the Supreme Court in Maneka Gandhi's case remains, to this day, one of the leading judgments on Articles 14 and 21 of the Constitution.

. . .

During his tenure as Additional Solicitor General for India and, later, Solicitor General for India under the Janata government, between April 1977 and January 1980,[60] Sorabjee's law practice substantially changed. Previously, he would appear in the Supreme Court around half the time, spending his remaining moments in the High Courts. Now, he was almost exclusively a Supreme Court lawyer, appearing in the Supreme Court in 87 per cent of his reported cases during this time. Around 29 per cent of those cases were decided by benches consisting of five judges or more—referred to in legal parlance as 'Constitution Benches'. The cases he appeared in came to the Supreme Court from all over the country, and not merely from Bombay, where he was from.

The volume of Sorabjee's practice also picked up substantially in his years as a law officer in the Janata government. Until he became the Additional Solicitor General for India, the highest number of reported judgments that he had in any single year was in 1969. That year, immediately following the year in which he got his new chamber, he had 14 reported judgments to his credit. In other words, he appeared, that year, in 14 cases that were considered important enough by the judge hearing the case for the judgment to be published in the law reports. The average number of reported judgments per year that Sorabjee had in the 1960s was 6. Between 1970 and 1976, the average number of reported judgments that Sorabjee had to his name each year was 9. When Sorabjee became a law officer, however, this number began to substantially increase. In 1978, he had 17 reported judgments to his credit. In 1979, this figure increased to 23.

It was during this time that Sorabjee started appearing in television debates and talk shows with increasing regularity.[61] In fact, one commentator in the *Times of India* felt that he was over-exposing himself on television and radio. In a single week in April 1977, for instance, Sorabjee was on two different television discussions and on one radio show. As the *Times of India* admiringly wrote of him in May 1977, though Sorabjee was 'a real find on the mass media scene' and a 'scintillating media star', seeing him so often was 'like having caviar every day'.[62] In December 1977, Sorabjee was on television speaking about the rule of law (a favourite topic of his) at 9.15 p.m. when, at precisely the same moment, his chamber colleague and rival, Fali Nariman, was speaking about the Shah Commission in an All India Radio broadcast.[63]

Viewers could not decide which programme to tune-in to and 'veered from one to the other'.[64] In a television programme in December 1978, Sorabjee, in his 'usual assured and relaxed self' debated Professor Upendra Baxi, 'who seemed rather stiff-starched and laboured in contrast'.[65]

Sorabjee started becoming a figure known beyond legal circles and outside India. He was invited to London to attend the centenary celebrations of the British Liberal party.[66] One of his books on press censorship during the Emergency was originally commissioned by the Writers and Scholars Educational Trust in the UK, and its introductory chapter was written by Professor W.H. Morris-Jones at the University of London.[67] In 1978, he chaired a UN seminar on human rights in Geneva.[68] In May 1979, on the 25th anniversary of the historic decision of Brown v. Board of Education,[69] where the US Supreme Court had held that schools in America should not be segregated on the basis of race, Sorabjee spoke at an NAACP[70] event at Columbia University, New York.[71] In other words, as a law officer with the Janata government, Sorabjee reached a wider audience.

In his days of private practice, he was primarily a customs and excise lawyer. This now changed. While he continued to appear in a fair number of customs and excise cases, he now appeared in diverse fields of law, wherever his services were required by the government. He appeared in more criminal cases as a law officer under the Janata government than in customs and excise cases combined. As a private lawyer, he had hardly any criminal law practice at all. Many of these criminal cases are now classics. A prime example is Gurbaksh Singh Sibbia's case,[72] where the court rejected Sorabjee's argument that anticipatory bail (or pre-arrest bail) should only be granted to a person who shows the court that the police might arrest him or her for mala fide or oblique reasons.[73] A series of directions were issued by the court in that case on the factors that criminal courts must bear in mind while deciding cases of anticipatory bail. In Bachan Singh v. State of Punjab,[74] the Supreme Court held that the death penalty should only be imposed in the 'rarest of rare cases'.[75]

In the Sunil Batra cases,[76] the Supreme Court decided that convicts in prisons have fundamental rights,[77] that they cannot be held in solitary confinement,[78] saddled with bar fetters for an unusually long period of time,[79] or subjected to torture in custody.[80]

Of course, many of the civil law cases that Sorabjee appeared in during this period are considered classics as well. Apart from the state assembly dissolution and Maneka Gandhi cases, an instant hit which immediately comes to mind was the case of Mohinder Singh Gill v. Chief Election Commissioner,[81] where the court held that if a statutory authority passes an order, the order can only be justified by the government on the strength of the reasons contained in the order itself and not on the basis of reasons subsequently provided by the government on affidavit.

Sorabjee's win–loss record as a government lawyer changed dramatically. In his private practice days, Sorabjee, like Kharshedji, won around half the cases he appeared in, perhaps more. Now, he won approximately 70 per cent of the cases that he appeared in.[82] This, of course, does not mean that Sorabjee's advocacy skills had drastically improved in his years as a law officer. His win–loss record as a government advocate probably tells us something about the nature of our legal system. Among various possible explanations, it perhaps suggests that courts usually show a great deal of deference to the government in cases that come before it. Sorabjee won more cases as a government lawyer than he did as a private lawyer not because his advocacy skills had improved but because those cases were, in all likelihood, harder to lose. Further, Sorabjee now almost exclusively represented the government, or corporations like the State Bank of India and Municipal Corporation of Delhi. He appeared with three juniors in the vast majority of his cases—Girish Chandra, R.N. Sachtey and E.C. Agarwala.

In a number of cases, the court complimented Sorabjee for the high quality of his arguments,[83] the brevity of his submissions[84] and his 'characteristic fairness'.[85] Justice Krishna Iyer, to his credit, perhaps complimented Sorabjee the most during this period, despite the fact that

Sorabjee had initially opposed Iyer's elevation to the Supreme Court on the grounds that he was a Marxist.[86] In one of the Sunil Batra cases, for instance, Justice Krishna Iyer praised Sorabjee for arguing his case with 'commendable candour', 'benign detachment' and 'zealous concern'.[87] Never his client's mouthpiece, Sorabjee was able to take an independent view in the cases he argued and to admit that his client was wrong when he thought so. In one such case, C.B. Muthamma v. Union of India,[88] the first female[89] member of the Indian Foreign Service complained that she was being discriminated against and denied a promotion on the grounds that she was a woman. She was promoted before her case came up for final disposal, but was nonetheless concerned that she had, in the meantime, lost her seniority to junior male officers who had been promoted ahead of her while her case was pending. As the Solicitor General of India, Sorabjee persuaded the government to review her seniority,[90] so as to ensure that she regained seniority over her junior officers.

. . .

Between 1977 and 1980, Sorabjee was involved in one of the most sensational cases to have come to the Supreme Court, the *Kissa Kursi Ka* case. The case concerned a satirical film, *Kissa Kursi Ka*, which was critical of the Congress government. It told the story of how India's politicians used unscrupulous means to hold on to power. The film itself may have been quite crude, exaggerated and in bad taste. The producer, Amrit Nahata, submitted the film to the censor board in April 1975, a few months prior to the Emergency. As the censor certificate was not issued for some time, Nahata went to the Supreme Court which decided to see the film for itself in order to determine whether a censor certificate ought to be granted to it or not. The film was supposed to be specially screened for the Supreme Court on 17 November 1975, during the Emergency. Eleven days before that date, the film's negatives, which had been seized by the government, were hastily destroyed.[91]

After the Janata party came to power, the Central Bureau of Investigation (CBI) looked into the matter. In July 1977, the CBI filed a chargesheet in which they alleged that Prime Minister Indira Gandhi's younger son, Sanjay Gandhi, and the union minister for information and broadcasting, V.C. Shukla, were responsible for destroying the negatives of the film. Thirteen steel trunks containing 150 spools of the film were taken to the premises of Maruti Ltd. in Gurgaon, Haryana, and burned down.[92] Shukla himself, it was alleged, carried one print of the film in his own car to the residence of Prime Minister Indira Gandhi at 1, Safdarjang Road,[93] in order to enable its destruction. Nahata's case in the Supreme Court for a censor certificate came to an abrupt end when the government told the court that the negatives of the film were lost.[94] The CBI learned of all of this when they raided the Maruti premises.[95]

Named as an accused in the case, Sanjay Gandhi was summoned to appear in the court of the chief metropolitan magistrate in Delhi in August 1977.[96] '[F]renzied slogans' started being raised when Sanjay arrived in court on 27 August.[97] His supporters shouted slogans of 'Charan Singh hai-hai'. His detractors responded with their own slogan: '*Nasbandi Ke Teen Dalal* (the three brokers of forced sterilization)—Indira, Sanjay, Bansi Lal', referring to the forced sterilization programme during the Emergency. Sanjay's supporters formed a protective cordon around him and helped him inch towards the Tis Hazari building, up the crowded staircase and into the courtroom.[98] Members of the crowd attempted to manhandle Sanjay Gandhi. Many of the sloganeers had come to the court as organized groups in hired buses.[99] Sanjay was released on bail on a personal bond and surety of Rs 5,000.[100]

As the trial of the case commenced, witness after witness began to turn hostile.[101] In other words, prosecution witnesses who had, during the investigation, pointed a figure at Sanjay, started saying in court that they had been forced by the CBI to falsely implicate Sanjay Gandhi in the case. The government applied to the Delhi High Court for cancelling Sanjay's bail on the grounds that he was influencing witnesses. Sanjay Gandhi did himself no favours by the way in which he conducted himself in court. In April 1978, in the midst of the case, he called the special public prosecutor, S.B. Jaisinghani, a 'scoundrel', though the latter might have provoked him.[102] The government's application for cancelling Sanjay's bail was taken up by the Supreme Court.[103] In a 40-minute hearing before a bench presided over by Chief Justice Y.V. Chandrachud, Sanjay represented himself, though the Chief Justice told him that it would be better if he engaged an advocate on the next occasion. Ram Jethmalani was engaged by the Delhi government. The Chief Justice took note of the newspaper reports which had suggested unruly scenes in the sessions court during Sanjay's trial and the court remarked: 'Come what may, this court will not tolerate any violation of dignity or prestige of any court in the country. We cannot sit with folded hands.'[104]

On the next date, the court cancelled Sanjay's bail. It held that the fact that witnesses had turned hostile did not, by itself, mean that Sanjay had won them over.[105] However, the court found that there was evidence which suggested that Sanjay had, in fact, attempted to influence witnesses.[106] The prosecution feared that Sanjay would try and suborn Maruti witnesses. Since the government was going to take one month to examine these witnesses, Sanjay's bail was cancelled by the Supreme Court for one month.[107]

As Chief Justice Chandrachud delivered the court's verdict, Sanjay, dressed in a white kurta, walked up the aisle and spoke to the court directly, telling the judges that he feared bodily harm if he were arrested. Sorabjee, appearing in the case as the Additional Solicitor General, objected to these remarks and said: 'We believe in the rule of law and treat people decently.'[108] Chief Justice Chandrachud responded: 'I presume we are living in a civilized society. If there is the slightest attempt to harm you, you are free to move the courts.'[109]

After the court's decision, Sanjay Gandhi drove to the Tis Hazari court along with his wife Maneka and a few supporters, and surrendered. He was taken in a police van to Tihar jail. Forty-eight of his supporters were arrested for violating the prohibitory orders which were in force around the Tis Hazari court.[110] Indira Gandhi, who returned to Delhi that evening from Azamgarh, went to Tihar jail and met Sanjay for 50 minutes.[111] Sanjay was allowed better prison facilities by the sessions judge, and he spent his time in jail reading newspapers and books, listening to the radio and watching TV. He got his food from outside.[112] A few weeks later, when his wife Maneka went to Tihar jail to deliver him his food, she was attacked by five persons who snatched the thermos flask in her hand and swung it at her while she was seated in the office of the deputy superintendent of the jail.[113] She was saved by someone who was accompanying her.

Despite the fact that witnesses kept turning hostile in the case[114] and the son of the chief investigating officer of the CBI died under suspicious circumstances,[115] the *Kissa Kursi Ka* trial continued in the sessions court. In February 1979, the sessions court found Sanjay Gandhi and V.C. Shukla guilty.[116] The following day, they were each sentenced to two years' rigorous imprisonment and a fine.[117] The courtroom was packed with Sanjay Gandhi supporters. When the judge finished reading out the sentence, they raised pro-Sanjay and pro-Shukla slogans.[118] The judge, O.N. Vohra, tried to pacify them by saying that he had merely done his duty as a judge, and the two convicts were like a son and brother, respectively, to him. Upon hearing this, Sanjay Gandhi, who was standing in the dock, said: 'I hope what you say you really believe.'[119]

Once the judge retired into his chamber, pandemonium broke loose. Sanjay Gandhi's supporters stood on benches and chairs, hurled abuses at CBI officials, broke court furniture, flung law books towards the dais, raised slogans, hurled stones and damaged two Delhi Transport Corporation (DTC) buses.[120] When Sessions Judge O.N. Vohra was elevated to the Delhi High Court soon thereafter, Shanti Bhushan in

Parliament rejected the suggestion that this was a reward for sentencing Sanjay Gandhi.[121]

Sanjay and Shukla filed an appeal in the Delhi High Court.[122] Their appeals were admitted and their sentences stayed.[123] In the meantime, the Janata government enacted a new law by virtue of which the *Kissa Kursi Ka* appeal in the Delhi High Court was transferred directly to the Supreme Court.[124] On 9 November 1979, Sorabjee then went to the Chief Justice's court and 'mentioned' the case with a view to getting an early hearing. He wanted the court to cancel Sanjay Gandhi's bail, alleging that he had misused his freedom. A war of words ensued between Sorabjee and Sanjay Gandhi. Sanjay called Sorabjee's application 'frivolous' and said that the Janata government always 'steamrolls' the courts. Sorabjee objected to Sanjay's use of such words and reminded him where he was standing. Sanjay said that he never told 'untruths'. Sorabjee replied that Sanjay was the 'personification of untruths'. Chief Justice Chandrachud then intervened and told Sanjay to sit down and to not interrupt Sorabjee.[125]

Four days later, a sensational hearing occurred in the Supreme Court. Chief Justice Chandrachud revealed to a packed courtroom that an advocate had visited his home the previous evening and warned him not to come to court. Chandrachud had gone out to attend a wedding. The advocate came to his residence, met his secretary Mr Luthra, and told him that the Chief Justice should not go to court the next day or take the utmost care while going to court. Chandrachud made this revelation just as the very advocate who had threatened him stood up in court to address him. The advocate, a Congress (I) supporter, swore by his wife and child that he had made no such threat. When he tried to interrupt while Chandrachud was narrating the story, the latter thundered from the dais: 'If you rise again, it would be a contempt of court. Sit down.'

Chandrachud said that people had been coming to him in the name of his friends and telling him to be careful. 'I am not afraid', he said, 'I pay no heed to such warnings. These do not disturb my cool and my poise. I am not going to die many times before I die', he said, quoting a line from Shakespeare's play, *Julius Caesar* ('Cowards die many times before their deaths; The valiant never taste of death but once.').[126] Sorabjee, the Solicitor General, then stood up and said that all this called for firm action from the Chief Justice in order to maintain the sanctity of the judicial system and the Supreme Court.[127] Such reprehensible acts, Sorabjee added, required the utmost condemnation and stern action.[128]

Eventually, the court decided that no case had been made out for cancelling Sanjay Gandhi's bail.[129] By the time the appeal was decided by the Supreme Court, the Janata government had fallen out of power. A bench presided over by Justice S. Murtaza Fazal Ali held that there was insufficient evidence to implicate Sanjay Gandhi and V.C. Shukla in the *Kissa Kursi Ka* case. They were both therefore acquitted.[130] Incidentally, the film *Kissa Kursi Ka* was remade by Nahata, who became a member of Parliament on a Janata ticket.[131] The fact that even under the Janata government, the censor board recommended fifteen cuts to the film,[132] and the state-run Doordarshan refused to show it on television,[133] speaks to how sordid and crude the film's contents might actually have been.

8

A Chief Justice on Trial

In the general election that was held in January 1980,[1] after 33 months out of office,[2] Indira Gandhi's Congress (I) party came back to power with a thumping two-thirds majority.[3] On 10 January, a triumphant party meeting was held in the flood-lit central hall of Parliament to elect Indira as the leader of the Congress (I) party.[4] When Indira's name was proposed for the post of leader of the party, the presiding officer at the meeting jokingly asked, '*Aur koi naam hai*?' (Is there any other name?), evoking peals of laughter in the 'overflowing and applauding hall'.[5] Indira made a speech in which she said that neither she nor her party would indulge in any kind of vendetta against the losing side.[6] 'We are not small people; we are not petty-minded people', she said.[7] Minutes later, President Sanjiva Reddy invited her to form the government.[8] The previous day, spinning his *charkha* (spinning wheel) despondently at his flat in Bombay, the former Prime Minister,[9] Morarji Desai, said that the electorate's verdict was a personal victory for Indira.[10]

Sorabjee resigned as the Solicitor General of India a few days later.[11] Being a law officer in the Janata government had brought him into the national limelight like never before. He had made frequent appearances on television and radio. He had been invited to prestigious ceremonies in the UK and the US. The nature of his law practice had changed both in quantity and quality. His excise practice had taken a back seat as he had been engaged in diverse areas of law, including criminal law. He had appeared in more cases as a law officer than he ever had in his career until then.

In the years immediately following his resignation as Solicitor General, Sorabjee's practice seemed to be busier than ever.[12] In 1980 and 1981, Sorabjee had 28 and 33 reported judgments to his credit respectively—more than he ever had in any previous year in his career. Though the volume of work slowed down for a few years thereafter, it picked up again, such that by 1989, on the eve of his appointment as Attorney General of India, he had 43 reported judgments to his name—more than in any former year in his entire professional life. His tenure as a law officer had helped his private practice. He was a nationally and internationally known name between 1977 and 1980, and people naturally wished to now engage him to appear in their cases against the government.

The nature of Sorabjee's practice after he resigned in January 1980, however, changed in some respects. Between 1980 and 1989, as a private lawyer, Sorabjee now started appearing in a tribunal (the Customs, Excise and Gold [Control] Appellate Tribunal or CEGAT) in New Delhi quite often, something he had hardly done, if at all, as a law officer. Though he still appeared primarily in the Supreme Court (73 per cent of his reported cases were in the Supreme Court), he appeared often in various High Courts in the country (most often, the Delhi High Court[13]) and CEGAT. Sorabjee appeared more often in CEGAT in New Delhi at this time than he even did in the Bombay High Court, which he attended only on rare occasions. Out of around 268 reported judgments in which Sorabjee's name has been recorded between 1980 and 1989, only 2 cases were in the Bombay High Court.

One of these cases was a libel suit filed by a Bollywood actress against *Stardust* magazine. In its April 1987 issue, *Stardust* had alleged that the actress was having a 'torrid' extra-marital affair with her former fiancée.[14] A single judge of the Bombay High Court had directed *Stardust* to reveal its sources. Appearing for *Stardust* in appeal, Sorabjee argued that a legal principle in England called the 'newspaper rule' prevented courts from directing newspapers to reveal their sources before the commencement of the trial.[15] The appellate bench of the Bombay High Court held in Sorabjee's favour and *Stardust* magazine was permitted to keep its sources secret.[16]

In the years after his resignation, Sorabjee went back to being primarily a customs and excise lawyer. Between 1980 and 1989, around 31 per cent of his reported cases were all in customs and excise cases, as compared to 13 per cent in those areas of law when he was a law officer with the Janata government. He now appeared in hardly any criminal cases. Only around 1 per cent of his work was now in criminal law, as against 20 per cent in that area as a Janata law officer. He also had a sizeable indirect tax, labour and service law practice.[17] A large chunk of his cases in the Supreme Court came from Delhi and Bombay. Around 24 per cent of his Supreme Court cases were appeals from courts in Delhi, while 21 per cent were appeals from Bombay. The junior who appeared with him and assisted him most often during this time, between 1980 and 1989, was Harish Salve.

Sorabjee now appeared primarily for private clients. His win–loss record went back to being around what it was before he had become a law officer. As a law officer with the Janata government, he won 70 per cent of the cases in which his name was carried in the law reports. After resigning as Solicitor General, between 1980 and 1989, he won 54.7 per cent of his reported cases in which there was a clear winner and loser. Once again, it is highly doubtful if Sorabjee's advocacy skills diminished dramatically in the years between his being a law officer and resigning as such. This underscores the argument we encountered in the introductory chapter. Among various possible explanations, one reason why Sorabjee's success rate may have fallen as a private lawyer is that courts in India tend to be deferential towards the government, regardless of which party is in power. For instance, whenever a law is challenged for violating the Constitution, the court starts with the presumption that the law is constitutionally sound, and it is for the litigant who assails the law to establish that it breaches the Constitution, regardless of which fundamental right is at stake in the case.

Apart from his law practice, Sorabjee frequently wrote for the *Times of India* on constitutional law subjects like freedom of speech,[18] the right to privacy,[19] the judiciary[20] and the position of the President[21] and Governors[22] in India, apart from other subjects.[23] He was also becoming somewhat of a minor celebrity. In November 1988, the state of Jammu and Kashmir published a full-page advertisement in the *Times of India* promoting tourism in the state. The advertisement carried a prominent quotation by Sorabjee on Kashmir's scenic beauty. It said: 'Courts, cases, arguments—I forget them all on landing in Kashmir and exclaim with the poet, "Earth has not anything to show more fair."'[24]

During this period, Sorabjee appeared in several cases that are considered landmarks even today. What constitutes an appealable 'judgment' in the chartered High Courts (e.g., the Bombay High Court)?[25] Can a dispute between a landlord and tenant be referred to private arbitration?[26] Can an advocate tell an appellate court that he or she never made a concession before a lower court though the judgment of the lower court records such a concession?[27] Can a state Governor repeatedly keep re-promulgating the same ordinance without getting it approved by the state legislature?[28] Can the principles of natural justice be dispensed with if giving the aggrieved party a hearing would be a mere useless formality?[29] Can the followers of Sri Aurobindo be considered a religious denomination?[30] Can the government grant an amnesty to tax-evaders?[31] Can a censor certificate be denied to a film which criticizes the caste-based reservations policy of the government?[32] These were amongst the important questions that the Supreme Court settled during this period in cases in which Sorabjee appeared. A young lawyer would be expected to have the names of many of these cases (e.g., 'Shah Babulal Khimji' or 'Natraj Studios') at the tip of his or her tongue even today.

Two of Sorabjee's cases at this time, however, were particularly interesting. In one, the Chief Justice of India appeared to be on trial. In the second, Sorabjee strongly opposed the viewpoint of a political party for whose government he would eventually become the Attorney General.

. . .

In 1981, Sorabjee appeared in a case at the Supreme Court which had far-reaching implications for India's judicial system. After coming back to power, Indira Gandhi had said that her administration would not be vindictive. However, by the middle of 1980, the union law ministry in her government mooted a plan which substantially threatened the independence of the judiciary. The government had decided that it would undertake a large-scale transfer of judges across the country such that one-third of the judges in each High Court, including the Chief Justices, would come from a different state.[33] Observers feared that this meant that the government would have the power to decide which judge could be transferred and which judge would remain in his or her original High Court—a power which could then potentially be used as a carrot and stick to coerce judges into deciding cases favourably. It was believed that a judge who decided cases against the government would be transferred to a remote backwater, while a judge who decided otherwise would remain untouched.[34] The government, however, argued that its transfer of judges policy was only meant to ensure national integration— if a large number of judges came from outside the state, they would not be influenced by local concerns.[35]

In July 1980, a judge of the Allahabad High Court resigned, saying that he could not reconcile himself with the government's policy on the transfer of judges.[36] Then, on 19 January 1981, Chief Justice K.B.N.

Singh of the Patna High Court, was transferred to Madras, while Chief Justice M.M. Ismail of the Madras High Court was transferred to Kerala.[37] Almost immediately thereafter, an advocate by the name of Lily Thomas filed a petition in the Supreme Court objecting to the transfer of Chief Justice Ismail.[38] The court passed an interim order restraining the transfers of Chief Justices Singh and Ismail.[39]

While this case was pending, on 18 March 1981, the Union Law Minister, P. Shiv Shankar, sent a letter to the Chief Ministers of the states[40] asking them to obtain the consent of all the 'additional' judges in the High Courts in India for being transferred and made 'permanent' judges in other High Courts. 'Additional' judges are temporary judges appointed to a High Court, usually for a period of two years,[41] on the understanding that barring exceptional circumstances, they will be confirmed as regular permanent judges at the end of the two-year term.

Shiv Shankar's letter set off a storm in legal and political circles. Professional organizations like the Bar Council of Maharashtra and the Bombay Bar Association condemned the letter.[42] The Bombay High Court was boycotted by lawyers in protest.[43] Opposition parties in the Maharashtra state legislative assembly staged a walk-out.[44] The Janata party pleaded with additional judges across the country not to give their consent for being transferred.[45] The Chief Justice of the Bombay High Court, however, sent the law minister's letter to all the additional judges of the court.[46] By April 1981, out of 59 additional judges in the country, 11 had given their consent to being transferred.[47] By July, this number had increased to 36.[48] In the meantime, a petition was filed by Iqbal Chagla, an advocate belonging to Kharshedji's chamber, in the Bombay High Court, challenging the law minister's letter. The letter was 'stayed' (or prevented from being acted upon) by a single judge of the Bombay High Court, Justice M.L. Pendse.[49]

At around this time, trouble was brewing at the Delhi High Court. Two additional judges of that court (O.N. Vohra and S.N. Kumar) were not made permanent judges by the government once their two-year terms came to an end.[50] One of these judges, Justice O.N. Vohra, had convicted Sanjay Gandhi in the *Kissa Kursi Ka* case.[51] The other judge, Justice S.N. Kumar, felt that he was being penalized because of false rumours that he had attended RSS *shakhas* in his school days and had, despite being a judge, campaigned for Atal Bihari Vajpayee in the 1980 general election.[52] An advocate at the Delhi High Court, V.M. Tarkunde, who had also been a judge of the Bombay High Court, filed a petition challenging the government's refusal to extend the terms of these two judges. He engaged Sorabjee to appear for him in the Supreme Court.

Eventually, nine cases, including Tarkunde's case, were taken up by a bench of seven judges of the Supreme Court for hearing in August 1981. Sorabjee addressed the court in the second half of August 1981. He argued that since the law minister had not consulted Chief Justice Y.V. Chandrachud before sending his letter to the Chief Ministers, the letter was in violation of the Constitution.[53] He also submitted that the two Delhi judges, O.N. Vohra and S.N. Kumar, had not been given an opportunity by the government to explain why they should be continued in office. The government had thereby violated the principles of natural justice, he suggested.[54]

The court heard arguments for 35 days,[55] until 19 November 1981.[56] Among the various issues that the court decided in the case, three were particularly important: (1) Firstly, was the law minister's letter dated 18 March 1981, which asked the Chief Ministers of the states to get the consent of additional High Court judges to be transferred, valid? (2) Secondly, was the government's decision to refuse to make Justice S.N. Kumar of the Delhi High Court a permanent judge sound? (3) Thirdly, was the government's decision to transfer Chief Justice K.B.N. Singh from Bihar to Madras permissible? O.N. Vohra (the *Kissa Kursi Ka* judge) and M.M. Ismail (the Chief Justice of Madras) decided not to contest the government's decision. The court therefore confined itself to the cases of Justice S.N. Kumar and Chief Justice K.B.N. Singh.

The court pronounced its judgment in a historic sitting at 8.30 a.m. on 30 December 1981 during the winter vacation. The court decided to sit so early, instead of its usual time of 10.30 a.m., since one of the judges on the bench needed to catch a flight.[57] The judgment could not be delivered after the court vacation because one of the members of the bench, Justice A.C. Gupta, was due to retire on 1 January 1982, which would have meant that the case would have had to be reheard.[58] Each of the seven judges delivered a separate judgment. Occupying over 900 pages in the law reports, the court's judgment in that case was its longest one ever.[59]

Each of the three important questions set out above were decided by the court by the narrowest majority of 4–3. Firstly, the court decided that there was nothing wrong with the law minister's letter.[60] Secondly, a majority of judges found that the government's decision to discontinue Justice S.N. Kumar at the Delhi High Court was improper. The government had relied on a letter of the Chief Justice of the Delhi High Court which was never shown to Chief Justice Chandrachud and therefore, the constitutionally-required consultations with the Chief Justice of India had not taken place before the decision to relieve Kumar could have been taken.[61] Thirdly, a majority of the judges found that Chief Justice Chandrachud had recommended the transfer of Chief Justice K.B.N. Singh to Madras after duly consulting all the constitutional functionaries.[62]

During the hearings of the case, however, it seemed as though it was Chief Justice Chandrachud himself who was on trial. The bench presided over by Justice P.N. Bhagwati, who was next in line for appointment as Chief Justice, and who had a long-standing rivalry with Chandrachud,[63] directed[64] Chief Justice Chandrachud to file an affidavit in the case explaining the steps he took before recommending the transfer of Justice K.B.N. Singh to Madras.[65] In his judgment, Bhagwati harshly described a statement in Chandrachud's affidavit as being 'delightfully vague'.[66] The government too seemed to be keen on embarrassing the Chief Justice of India who, after all, was responsible for sending Sanjay Gandhi to Tihar jail only a few years ago. One of the judges hearing the case, Justice V.D. Tulzapurkar, wrote in his judgment how he entertained 'a feeling of uneasiness' at the hearing of Justice K.B.N. Singh's case because of the manner in which it was conducted by the government. 'On more occasions than one', he wrote, 'I was left in doubt whether they were really interested in having the transfer order upheld.'[67]

This was a serious allegation against the government. The government's order transferring Justice K.B.N. Singh to Madras had been challenged in the Supreme Court. If, as Justice Tulzapurkar wrote, the government was not really interested in having that transfer order upheld, then what is it that the government was really after in that case?

In fact, a mysterious turn of events on the last day of the case hearing, left observers at a loss for words. In his affidavit filed in court, Chief Justice Chandrachud had said, on oath, that he had consulted the President of India prior to recommending the transfer of Justice K.B.N. Singh to Madras. He had not said that he had a personal conversation with the President, but that he had consulted him through the official channels. On 19 November 1981, however, the very last date of the hearing at the Supreme Court, the Solicitor General of India, K. Parasaran, stood up and read out a statement prepared by President N. Sanjiva Reddy, in which Reddy said that Chief Justice Chandrachud had not consulted him personally before recommending the transfer of Justice K.B.N. Singh.[68] The impression which was perhaps sought to be created in the court was that Chief Justice Chandrachud had said something in his sworn affidavit which was incorrect. In fact, a few days previously, even the government had tried to say that Chief Justice Chandrachud had not 'discussed' the proposed transfer of Justice K.B.N. Singh with the law minister but merely 'mentioned' the matter to him.[69]

Justice Tulzapurkar thought that there was something fishy about all of this. As he explained in his judgment, Chief Justice Chandrachud, in his affidavit, had not said anything about personally consulting President

Sanjiva Reddy before recommending the transfer. 'I have failed to appreciate the desirability or necessity of the statement made on behalf of the President of India disowning the "personal discussion" with the Chief Justice of India', he wrote in his judgment, 'especially when the [Chief Justice of India] had not raised a whisper about such personal discussion' in his affidavit.[70] He also observed that the voluminous documentary records of the case showed that Chief Justice Chandrachud had 'discussed' the transfer of Justice K.B.N. Singh with the law minister and not merely 'mentioned' it to him. The government's suggestion that Chief Justice Chandrachud had not discussed the transfer with the law minister, thought Justice Tulzapurkar, showed that the government was not keen on having the transfer order sustained.[71]

Reading Justice Tulzapurkar's judgment with the benefit of hindsight today, one gets the feeling that the government wanted to embarrass the Chief Justice, perhaps with a view to forcing him to resign.[72] This purported plan never materialized. 'After all is said and done', wrote Justice Tulzapurkar in his judgment, 'it must be observed that while acting administratively the attitude and behaviour of the Chief Justice of India was befitting the paterfamilias of the Judiciary.' Justice Tulzapurkar felt that the Chief Justice of India had dealt with the cases of Justice S.N. Kumar and Chief Justice K.B.N. Singh in a manner which was both 'objective and judicious'.[73] A majority of the judges of the court agreed.

In high-flown language, the court relaxed the rules of *locus standi* and permitted a group of lawyers, who were not personally involved in the case, to file cases for the betterment of the judicial system. However, the eventual result of the case was that the court had allowed the government to transfer judges as they pleased. When he learned the outcome of the case, Sorabjee remarked that he had never been as bewildered by any other judgment. The rhetoric in the judgment is 'historic', he said, but the 'result is zero'.[74]

. . .

From its slow beginnings in the late 1950s, television in India had come a long way. The first television broadcast began as a small educational experiment in Delhi in 1959.[75] Limited regular television transmissions began in the mid-1960s.[76] By 1974, when Sorabjee was dividing his time between Delhi and Bombay, he would have had very restricted options for watching television. Television broadcasts in Bombay in August 1974, for instance, were divided into three transmissions, adding up to only 4 hours and 20 minutes of television in a day.[77] The first two transmissions, from 11.40 a.m. to 12 p.m. and 2 p.m. to 2.20 p.m., contained an English lesson for Class 5 students. The third transmission was longer, lasting from 6.50 p.m. to 10.30 p.m. Programmes shown in the evening included news in Hindi and Marathi, an instructional Marathi programme for farmers, a Gujarati play, a harmonium recital, and a BBC serial on the six wives of Henry VIII (interrupted for 10 minutes by the English news at 10 p.m.).[78] By 1979, a person with a television set in Bombay could have watched 6 hours and 50 minutes of television in a day if he or she so wished.[79]

Black and white television sets in India were replaced by colour TV around 1982 when the Asian Games were held in Delhi.[80] Things drastically changed, however, with the INSAT-1B satellite being launched in 1983.[81] In 1984, India's first indigenous Hindi serial, *Hum Log*, aired on television at 9.20 p.m., sandwiched between the 9 p.m. Hindi news and 9.50 p.m. English news bulletin.[82] The 22-minute episodes, shown on television between 1984 and 1985, were a huge success.[83] Touching on social themes like alcoholism, domestic abuse, dowry, respect for elders and so on,[84] each episode typically ended with the famous Bollywood actor, Ashok Kumar, explaining the moral of the story to viewers.[85] Some 60 million viewers across the country tuned in to watch *Hum Log*,[86] on around 6 million TV sets.[87] In the commercial break, viewers saw advertisements for a new product called Maggi noodles, now a household brand.[88]

After the last episode of *Hum Log* aired in December 1985, a number of popular Indian serials appeared on television in the coming years. *Buniyad*, which aired between 1986 and 1987, and *Ramayana*, which started in 1987,[89] were crowd favourites.[90] By 1987, India had 80 million television viewers, accounting for around 10 per cent of the population.[91] It was against this silent small-screen revolution which was occurring on Indian television that in August 1987, Govind Nihalani wrapped up the shooting for his much-anticipated new Hindi television serial, *Tamas*.[92] Set in partition-era Lahore,[93] Nihalani's *Tamas* was based on a Hindi novel written by Bhishma Sahni, which had won the Sahitya Akademi Award in 1975,[94] though some details from the novel were changed in the television show.[95] A six-part Hindi series,[96] *Tamas* portrayed scenes of Hindu-Muslim communal violence during India's partition.

The first two episodes of *Tamas* aired on the second and third Saturday of January 1988.[97] They were shown at 9.50 p.m. after the news in English. Viewers at that time could watch television for 13 hours and 15 minutes across two channels offered by Doordarshan.[98] A few days after the second episode had aired on television, the Bharatiya Janata Party (BJP) and the Bharatiya Janata Yuva Morcha (BJYM) held demonstrations at Doordarshan centres to protest against some scenes in *Tamas*.[99] The young president of the BJYM, Pramod Mahajan, held a press conference and demanded that Doordarshan withdraw the serial as it was provocative and would jeopardize communal harmony in India.[100] At a protest held in Amritsar, effigies were burned of the writer and producer of the serial.[101] Hindu political organizations were unhappy over the fact that *Tamas* appeared to portray Hindus in a negative light and as being responsible for partition, though Nihalani denied that this was the message of the series.[102] One scene, in which a Hindu boy killed a Muslim perfume seller saying that his 'Guruji' had directed him to do so, was particularly controversial.[103] Another scene, in which a dead animal was dumped outside a house of worship, also raised eyebrows.[104]

A Muslim businessman filed a writ petition in the Bombay High Court and asked that Doordarshan be directed to stop showing the serial. On 21 January 1988 (Thursday), five days after the second episode had aired on television, and two days before the third episode was due to air that Saturday, a single judge of the Bombay High Court, Justice S.C. Pratap, issued an interim order restraining Doordarshan from showing the serial. He directed the parties to arrange a special screening for him that Saturday, so that he could decide whether the series was fit to be continued on air.[105] Justice Pratap's order was passed at around 1.15 p.m.[106] However, at 2.45 p.m. on the same day,[107] after the lunch break (which lasted between 2 p.m. and 2.45 p.m.) an appeal was filed before a division bench of the Bombay High Court.[108] The appeal bench consisted of Justice B. Lentin and Justice Sujata Manohar, the first female judge of the Bombay High Court (she later went on to become the first female Chief Justice of the Bombay High Court, and a Supreme Court judge).[109] Incidentally, Justice Manohar was the judge who had directed *Stardust* magazine to reveal its sources in the Bollywood actress libel suit—an order which Sorabjee had been successful in overturning on appeal.[110] The bench decided to urgently see the entire *Tamas* series that following day (Friday) in order to decide whether it could be shown on television on Saturday.[111]

On 22 January 1988 (Friday), a court holiday,[112] Justice Lentin and Justice Manohar viewed all six episodes of *Tamas* between 10.45 a.m. and 4.30 p.m. at the 'Blaze Minuet', a high-end preview theater in Colaba, Bombay.[113] The following day, a photograph appeared in the *Times of India* of the two judges 'engrossed in discussion' about the merits of the show at the Blaze Minuet, with Justice Lentin characteristically clutching his tobacco pipe in his right hand.[114] The judgment of the court was delivered later that day at Justice Lentin's residence, as it was a Saturday. The court allowed the appeal and permitted *Tamas* to be shown on television that night. In a powerful judgment, the court wrote: 'Yes, violence has been depicted. But then, such was exactly the tragic past.

Tamas is not entertainment. It is history. And you cannot wish away history simply by brushing it under the carpet.'[115] In a strong passage, the court held that even illiterate people in India, who might see the show, were not devoid of common sense. Even they would be able to understand that the fundamentalists and extremists depicted on screen were wrong to engage in violence.[116]

Though the third episode was shown on television that night, the matter was far from over. Nihalani received two threatening phone calls and was subsequently provided an armed security guard by the Bombay police.[117] The BJYM held a protest at Worli in Bombay, outside the office of Doordarshan.[118] The Shiv Sena threatened to hold processions to protest the airing of the series.[119] The general secretary of the BJP, Krishan Lal Sharma, said that *Tamas* was a 'perverse piece and a distortion of history'.[120] The Delhi police lathi-charged a group of protestors who turned violent outside the Doordarshan office.[121]

In the meantime, tensions simmered at the Bombay High Court when Justice Pratap, whose order had been appealed against, requested the Chief Justice to assign the *Tamas* case to some other judge, when the case came up before him for further directions on 28 January.[122] Pratap felt that Nihalani had abused the process of the court by filing an appeal against his interim order on the same day.[123] He too would have been willing to watch the film on 22 January if the parties had asked him to, he said.[124] 'What was the grave urgency to act in this manner?' he asked in his order, adding, 'Were [the] heavens going to fall in the meanwhile?'[125] In turn, Justice Lentin remarked that they had to see the show because of the urgency of the case, since Justice Pratap was unable to see it on Friday. 'We had no pleasure to waste a Friday (January 22) to see "Tamas"', he said, adding that they had better things to do than 'breaking [one's] backs and ruining [one's] eyes' by watching the series. Each episode was between 50 and 55 minutes in length. 'It was sheer hell', Justice Lentin said.[126] Senior lawyers at the Bombay High Court were divided over the question of whether the appeal court ought to have intervened when Justice Pratap was already seized of the matter.[127]

However, while this tussle was taking place at the Bombay High Court, the matter reached the Supreme Court. Sorabjee was engaged by Nihalani to argue the cause of free speech. The standard for judging the serial, Sorabjee submitted to the bench of two judges of the Supreme Court, was not that of a fanatic.[128] 'If beauty lay in the eyes of the beholder', he argued, 'then smut lay in the eyes of one who was inclined to view things in a distorted manner'.[129] When his opponent argued that truth, in some cases, had to be suppressed as truth was more dangerous than fiction,[130] Sorabjee responded that it was strange that his 'learned friend' (the customary appellation for one's opponent in court) spoke of suppressing the truth though India's national emblem had the motto '*Satyameva Jayate*' or 'the truth always triumphs'.[131] The court dismissed the appeal against the Bombay High Court's judgment, and said that it would issue its reasons later on. The demonstrations against the serial, however, continued. Three days after the Supreme Court's decision, the police in Hyderabad opened fire on BJP demonstrators who were protesting outside Doordarshan's office.[132] The police claimed that the protest had turned violent, though this was denied by the BJP's leadership.[133] Ironically, thousands of people thronged to buy the *Tamas* novel[134]—far more than would have probably even heard about the book had the protests against the television series not taken place.

In the meantime, the sixth and final episode of *Tamas* aired on 13 February 1988.[135] The Supreme Court delivered its judgment in the *Tamas* case a few days later, on 16 February. Accepting Sorabjee's arguments, the court held that the test to be applied in such cases was not whether a fanatic would be unhappy after watching the show. The series had to be 'judged from the standards of reasonable, strong-minded, firm and courageous men, and not those of weak and vacillating minds, nor of those who scent danger in every hostile point of view'.[136] The test in free speech cases, said the court, must be formulated in such a manner that 'we are not reduced to a level where the protection of the least capable and the most depraved amongst us determines what the morally healthy cannot view or read'.[137] The court noted that *Tamas* had been cleared by the censor board.[138] The court relied on the judgment delivered by the Bombay High Court, as the High Court's judges had actually seen the show. Though Justices Lentin and Manohar were 'two experienced Judges of one of the premier High Courts of this country', and though average Indians may not have been 'as sober and experienced' as them, they had seen the film 'from an average, healthy and commonsense point of view', which was the correct yardstick to apply in such cases.[139] Despite the fact that there were protests and scenes of violence occurring in the country, the court found that there was no apprehension that *Tamas* would be 'likely to affect public order' or incite the commission of an offence.[140]

After the *Freedom First* case, decided by the Bombay High Court during the Emergency, Sorabjee had won his first major free speech case at the Supreme Court.[141] Incidentally, the political party which entertained the greatest grievance against the airing of *Tamas* would one day form the government at the Centre and appoint Sorabjee as its Attorney General.

9

'We are being Impeached Every Day'

At 12.15 a.m. on 3 December 1984, workers at a pesticide plant in Bhopal met in the control room for their customary tea break.[1] After some time, one of the workers noticed that pressure was beginning to build up in tank number E610, which contained a chemical called methyl isocyanate (MIC).[2] Soon, a 'torrent of heated gas' started being released into the air. Between 12.30 a.m. and 2 a.m., the entire contents of that tank were emptied out into the atmosphere.[3] The effect on the population was catastrophic. Some 375 were reported dead and 20,000 had to be treated at various hospitals.[4] The death toll later went up to 3,828,[5] making this the 'world's worst industrial disaster'.[6] Some 18,922 people suffered permanent injuries, while 1,73,382 were temporarily injured.[7]

That night, thousands of people left their homes and thronged the streets of Bhopal, 'running, gasping for breath, unable to see' because their eyes were stinging.[8] At the time, Deepchand Yadav, mayor of the municipal corporation of Bhopal, was sleeping at home, with his wife, his one-year-old son, and other family members. He woke up 'coughing violently'. Both his eyes were burning 'as if they [had] been exposed to chilli powder'. There was a burning sensation in his chest. He went outside and saw that people were running on the streets, in a state of shock. He saw 'dead infants being [breastfed] by dead mothers'. He took his family to a nearby village where they waited for six hours until the gas had cleared from Bhopal. His brother's pregnant wife, a healthy woman who had previously given birth to a daughter and son, suffered a miscarriage—a side-effect of exposure to the gas.[9] He and other victims, those who had survived the gas leak, suffered from symptoms like burning and watery eyes, a burning sensation in the chest, loss of memory and exhaustion.[10] In the coming days, thousands fled Bhopal despite assurances from the government that it was now safe to return.[11]

The chemical plant at which the disaster occurred belonged to a company called Union Carbide India Ltd., a subsidiary of an American company, Union Carbide Corporation. In the years leading up to the tragedy, a series of accidents had taken place at the plant in Bhopal in which its workers had been either killed or injured.[12] The chairman of the American company, W.M. Anderson, was soon arrested on his arrival in India,[13] but was released on bail shortly thereafter. He left for the US, never to face trial in an Indian court again.[14]

Ambulance-chasing American lawyers descended on Bhopal[15] and soon, dozens of law suits were filed across the US seeking billions of dollars in damages against Union Carbide Corporation in class action law suits.[16] Most of the suits were consolidated and sent to Judge John F. Keenan, a district judge in the southern district of New York who had been appointed to his post by President Ronald Reagan around two years earlier.[17] In the meantime, the President of India issued an ordinance giving the Indian government the exclusive right to sue on behalf of the victims of the Bhopal Gas Tragedy.[18] The government then filed its own suit before Judge Keenan, claiming compensation in an unspecified amount for the victims of Bhopal from Union Carbide Corporation.[19] At the time, there were already some 65 suits concerning the tragedy pending in that court.[20]

The proceedings in the New York case started in April 1985.[21] Union Carbide contended that the suit ought to be filed in India, not in the US. Expert witnesses then submitted evidence before Judge Keenan on the condition of the judicial system in India, in order to help Keenan decide whether India was an adequate forum for this dispute. On behalf of the victims, Marc Galanter, a professor of law at the University of Wisconsin, told Judge Keenan that the Indian legal profession did not 'presently possess the pool of skills, the fund of experience, or the organizational capacity' to 'effectively and efficiently' pursue 'massive and complex litigation'.[22] On the other hand, on behalf of Union Carbide, Nani Palkhivala submitted an affidavit to Judge Keenan in which he said that Galanter's claim that the Indian bar was 'ill-equipped to deal with the Bhopal cases [was] a slanderous reflection on the legal profession in India'.[23] He suggested that the Indian government's suit in New York was a 'thinly disguised' attempt at getting American foreign aid. He said that the Bhopal victims had claimed, in their suits, more compensation than the $9.5 billion that the US had given in aid to India over the past 35 years.[24]

Keenan tried to get the parties to settle the suit. The Attorney General of India at the time, K. Parasaran, was also of the opinion that the government ought to negotiate a 'substantial and decent amount' from Union Carbide.[25] In the settlement talks, Union Carbide offered a figure of $400 million.[26] The government's American attorneys suggested that a settlement might be struck at $500 million.[27] Eventually, no settlement materialized and Judge Keenan decided the case in favour of Union Carbide, saying that the suit ought to be filed in India.[28]

In two articles written for the *Times of India* thereafter, Sorabjee, who was then a private lawyer in Delhi, praised Keenan's decision to send the case to India. Sorabjee clearly felt offended by what Galanter had written in his affidavit. 'Never has our legal system been more savagely mauled, more vilely maligned before a foreign court', he wrote.[29] 'The

most shocking part', he added, was that 'the Union of India supported
these slanderous arguments, and in the process condemned the Bench
and the Bar of its own country in a foreign court.'[30] In New York,
the government of India had contended that India would not be an
'adequate' forum for the case.[31] '[W]hat was the ultimate purpose of
this exercise in self-denigration? More American dollars from Union
Carbide?' he asked.[32] He felt that Keenan's decision offered India 'the
opportunity to vindicate the suffering of its own people within the
framework of its own legal system'.[33]

The Indian government then filed a suit against Union Carbide,
once again for an unspecified sum of money, in the district court of
Bhopal.[34] The government was very hesitant to quantify the exact claim
of damages. As Attorney General K. Parasaran explained in a confidential
note to the government, if the amount claimed was too small by
American standards, then Union Carbide might have offered to deposit
the sum in court, and people would have said that the amount claimed
by the government was small either because the government was trying
to favour the company or because the government was incompetent.
On the other hand, if the government claimed too large a figure, that
would serve as a precedent for suits to thereafter be filed against Indian
public sector corporations for 'fabulous' amounts.[35] The government
finally quantified its claim at $3.1 billion.[36] The district court then
directed Union Carbide to preserve its unencumbered assets worth $3
billion until the case was finally decided by the court.[37] Sorabjee's former
chamber colleague and rival, Fali Nariman, appeared for Union Carbide
before the district judge.[38]

In the meantime, the *Wall Street Journal* reported that the Indian
government and Union Carbide were close to settling the dispute
between $500 million and $600 million.[39] Many protested, saying that
this was too small an amount. One commentator in the *Times of India*,
for instance, wrote that a settlement of $600 million would mean that
every Bhopal victim would get only around Rs 15,000.[40]

The district judge in Bhopal, Judge Deo, delivered an interim order directing Union Carbide to pay a sum of Rs 350 crores for Bhopal victims as interim compensation.[41] In the Madhya Pradesh High Court, Nariman argued that this interim order amounted to 'a judgment and decree without trial'.[42] The district judge, he said, had been swayed by his emotions and was no longer impartial.[43] The High Court reduced the figure to Rs 250 crores. The matter travelled to the Supreme Court.[44]

Then, all of a sudden, on 14 February 1989, when the Supreme Court was hearing the case regarding the interim compensation which had been awarded in the Bhopal case, the court convinced both sides to settle the dispute at $470 million (Rs 715 crores).[45] It was the 20th day of the hearing of the case in the Supreme Court and there was hardly anyone in the Chief Justice's courtroom, apart from the Union Carbide and government lawyers, a few other lawyers and some security guards.[46] When the court reassembled after the lunch break at 2.15 p.m., Chief Justice R.S. Pathak asked both Nariman and Parasaran whether their clients would be willing to settle the case. After some deliberations, both agreed.[47] Parasaran believed that the sum of $470 million with compound interest over a period of 20 years (the time it would have otherwise taken for the Indian government to get a decree in the Bhopal suit), worked out to $3.1 billion—the amount which had been claimed by the government.[48] However, not merely was the civil suit concluded by the settlement, but even the criminal prosecutions against Union Carbide's management were brought to an end.[49]

The settlement initially met with mixed reactions in the press.[50] Professor Upendra Baxi, for instance, strongly criticized it, saying that the court had obviously not taken into account many factors like the 'cost of loss of lives, . . . costs of medical treatment, compensation for pain and suffering, the cost of governmental rehabilitation schemes, the overall environmental damage' and so on while approving of the settlement.[51] According to Baxi, a multinational corporation had been let off the hook. This was all the more painful, he wrote, because the court had not heard any of the actual Bhopal victims before endorsing the compromise. He believed that a sum of $1 billion would have been a more just figure. Baxi had a point. Union Carbide had willingly undertaken not to transfer its assets worth $3 billion until the suit was decided. It was strange for the government to have settled the dispute for only around 15 per cent of that amount.

Sorabjee and his former client in the Judges case, V.M. Tarkunde, found themselves on opposite sides of this debate. Sorabjee thought that there was something odd about the settlement. 'The manner in which it was handled', he said, 'makes it seem like a cloak-and-dagger affair'.[52] On the other hand, Tarkunde supported the settlement.[53] He believed that the claim of $3.1 billion made by the Indian government in the district court was overvalued, and '[s]uch exaggerated figures are often given in plaints of damages filed in India'. The figure of $470 million, he wrote, was roughly in between what Union Carbide had offered and what the Indian government had asked for in private negotiations. Had the settlement not materialized, the litigation would have taken several years to conclude in India, and a decree of the Bhopal district court would have been difficult to enforce against Union Carbide in the US.[54] He noted that motives were being attributed to the government and even the Supreme Court's judges, which he felt was unfair.[55]

As the Supreme Court commenced its hearings in a petition filed to challenge the Bhopal Act[56] (which had replaced the ordinance), one of the members of the bench, Justice E.S. Venkataramiah, withdrew from the case, accusing the press of 'vilification' and of launching an attack on the Supreme Court which was 'worse than impeachment'.[57] 'You take any newspaper', he said, 'we are being impeached every day.'[58] 'I want to withdraw and live peacefully at this state of my life', he said.[59] A few days later, Atal Bihari Vajpayee decided to lead a procession in Bhopal to protest the settlement, even as hundreds of Bhopal victims demonstrated outside the premises of the Supreme Court.[60]

. . .

In the general election which was held in November 1989, no single party won a clear majority in Parliament—the first time in India's history that this had happened.[61] V.P. Singh's Janata Dal party secured 143 seats in the Lok Sabha (less than the 197 seats obtained by Rajiv Gandhi's Congress) and formed a coalition government, with the BJP supporting it from the outside.[62] Singh was sworn in as Prime Minister on 2 December 1989.[63] A week later, in a small, three-line article published on its first page, the *Times of India* reported that the 59-year-old Sorabjee had been appointed the Attorney General of India.[64] Sorabjee informed the press that as Attorney General, it was his duty to act as a guardian of public interest and not as a 'hatchet-man of the government'.[65]

A few days later, Nani Palkhivala wrote Sorabjee a letter praising him for making that statement. 'The greatest glory of the Attorney General is not to win cases for the government', Palkhivala wrote, 'but to ensure that justice is done to the people.' Palkhivala added that he had initially intended to write to Sorabjee to congratulate him on his appointment as the Attorney General, but after reading his statement, he now wished to 'congratulate India on having you as the highest law officer of the Government'.[66] Palkhivala was not alone in this view. In a speech in Bombay a few weeks later, Fali Nariman said that Sorabjee would restore the importance of the position of Attorney General.[67]

The following month, in a hastily convened press conference, Dinesh Goswami, Union Law Minister, announced that V.P. Singh's National Front government had decided that it would support the review petitions which had been filed in the Supreme Court and challenge the Bhopal settlement.[68] Human life in India, he said, was not 'so cheap' that the world's worst industrial disaster, which had affected lakhs of people, could be compensated for only $470 million.[69] Baxi immediately hailed the announcement as marking the revival of the rule of law in India.[70]

Arguments began in the Bhopal review case in July 1990 and were concluded by the end of August.[71] However, the case had to be re-argued[72] due to the untimely demise of the Chief Justice of India,

Sabyasachi Mukharji.[73] The re-hearing of the case was delayed because the new Chief Justice, Ranga Nath Misra, was hearing the Mandal Commission case[74]—V.P. Singh's government had decided to implement the commission's recommendations for granting reservations to Other Backward Classes (OBCs) in central government jobs. The Mandal Commission had been set up during the Janata government's tenure in office, but its report was never given effect to when Indira Gandhi returned to power. In October 1990, the Supreme Court passed an interim order staying the implementation of the Mandal Commission report, when Sorabjee told the court that the government would take 2–3 months to identify the backward classes who would be entitled to get reserved seats.[75] Pro-Mandal Commission activists then burned an effigy of Sorabjee for 'not effectively arguing the case for the government' in the Supreme Court.[76]

When the Bhopal review case was taken up in November, Sorabjee made several arguments before the bench, as the Attorney General of India. He submitted that it was wrong for the court to have put an end to the criminal prosecutions against Union Carbide's management. According to India's criminal procedure code,[77] certain offences are 'non-compoundable', i.e., they cannot be settled or put to an end by private agreement. The sections of the Indian Penal Code which were invoked against Union Carbide, he said, were non-compoundable, and therefore the criminal case could not be terminated by private agreement.[78] India's code of criminal procedure permits a 'public prosecutor'[79] to withdraw a prosecution with the consent of the court.[80] However, Attorney General Parasaran was not a public prosecutor and therefore had no authority to withdraw the criminal case against Union Carbide, Sorabjee submitted.[81] Justice Venkatachaliah found this argument amusing and wondered how it could be said that the Attorney General of India lacked the powers of a public prosecutor.[82] Justice K.N. Singh added that the National Front government was withdrawing criminal cases nearly every day—how could it now oppose the withdrawal of the Union

Carbide criminal case, he asked Sorabjee. Ten wrongs do not make a right, Sorabjee retorted.[83]

The quashing of the criminal case against Union Carbide, Sorabjee added, had given rise to a 'deep and rankling sense of injustice among the Bhopal gas victims', who were 'left with the feeling that the affluent can escape the consequences of their criminal actions by entering into monetary bargains'.[84] Article 142 of the Constitution, which permits the Supreme Court to do 'complete justice' in any case, said Sorabjee, did not enable the court to 'bend the law and break the constitution'.[85] 'Indeed', he added, 'the judicial oath of office requires that discharge of judicial functions will be to uphold the Constitution and the laws, not to bend or break them.'[86] Sorabjee said that the health of the residents of Bhopal would have to be periodically monitored, since many who were asymptomatic might develop symptoms subsequently, which would affect the settlement amount.[87]

During the case, heated exchanges took place between Union Carbide's counsel, Fali Nariman, and Sorabjee. Sorabjee argued that Union Carbide had hastily deposited the sum of $470 million on 28 February 1989, even though the deadline to do so was 31 March 1989 with a view to foreclosing any possibility of the settlement being set aside. Nariman responded that the government had requested Union Carbide to deposit the amount early, before the budget.[88] On a query from the judges, Sorabjee informed the court that Union Carbide had deposited the amount in the name of the registrar general of the Supreme Court, with the Reserve Bank of India.[89] The figure had been exempted from income tax and was invested by the government in securities.[90] In November 1990, while the case was being heard, the amount had grown, with interest, to Rs 867 crores.[91] Justice K.N. Singh asked Sorabjee how the government could now change its stand, having signed off on the settlement agreement earlier that year.[92] The government of India had not filed any petition challenging the settlement or seeking to resile from it. Walking a tightrope, Sorabjee said that the government was supporting the various petitions which had been filed, on behalf of the victims of the Bhopal tragedy, though it had not instituted any proceedings itself to challenge the settlement.[93]

The court rejected Sorabjee's argument on Article 142 of the Constitution as being 'unsound and erroneous'.[94] It said that it had the power to quash a criminal case under Article 142 even if no case had been made out for compounding,[95] withdrawing[96] or quashing[97] the case under the criminal procedure code. While exercising its powers to do 'complete justice' under Article 142, the Supreme Court had to merely 'take note' of legal statutes like the criminal procedure code, but it was not bound by them.[98] In several places in its judgment, the court expressed its disapproval over the central government changing its stand and opposing the settlement.[99]

However, at the same time, the court acknowledged that in this case, there were insufficient reasons for quashing the criminal case against Union Carbide's management. In this 'terrible and ghastly tragedy', said the court, in which nearly 4,000 lives were lost and tens of thousands of citizens had suffered, an offence of 'such gravity and magnitude' should 'not remain uninvestigated'.[100] Accordingly, the criminal case, which had been quashed in the settlement, was restored.[101] The court agreed with Sorabjee and held that the agreement could not grant immunity to Union Carbide and its officers from any future prosecutions which were not pending at the time of the settlement.[102]

Apart from restoring the criminal case, the court issued some equitable directions. It ordered Union Carbide to pay for a new hospital in Bhopal which would monitor the health of the population for eight years in order to detect cases which were asymptomatic at present but which might arise later on.[103] It directed the Central government to take out a group insurance policy for asymptomatic patients who might develop symptoms within eight years.[104] Though the government was not responsible for the disaster,[105] the court said that it would, as a 'welfare State', be responsible for paying the balance compensation to Bhopal victims in the 'unlikely' event that the sum paid by Union Carbide fell short of what was required.[106] The court agreed that it was wrong not to hear the victims of the Bhopal tragedy before approving the settlement between Union Carbide and the government.[107] However, in view of its equitable directions, it decided that no further hearing was required to be given to the victims. The court also answered a number of other points raised by the parties, some of which the court termed 'hypertechnical'.[108]

. . .

As the Attorney General of India, Sorabjee's High Court and CEGAT work came to a standstill. Like his days as a law officer with the Janata government, Sorabjee now appeared most often in the Supreme Court. Though he attended the odd case before a tribunal or High Court, Sorabjee appeared in the Supreme Court in 92 per cent of his reported cases as the Attorney General. By contrast, as a private lawyer in the 1980s, he had appeared in the Supreme Court in around 73 per cent of his cases. Further, as a private lawyer in the 1980s, only around 9 per cent of Sorabjee's cases were placed before a 'Constitution Bench'—a bench of five or more judges of the Supreme Court, which typically hears cases of far-reaching significance. However, as a law officer in the Janata government, 29 per cent of his cases, and as the Attorney General for the National Front government, 21 per cent of his cases, were before a Constitution Bench. In other words, being a high-ranking law officer for the government meant arguing more important cases in the Supreme Court.

Sorabjee's customs and excise practice went down during his Attorney General term. As a private lawyer in the 1980s, around 31 per cent of Sorabjee's reported cases were in the field of customs and excise. Now, as the Attorney General, his customs and excise practice occupied approximately 20 per cent of his time.[109] In his private practice in the

1980s, around 21 per cent of his cases came to him from Bombay. As a law officer, both under the Janata and National Front governments, a negligible proportion of his work (3 per cent under Janata and 11 per cent under the National Front) came to him from Bombay. In other words, though his Bombay connections helped him to some extent in his private practice, they hardly mattered when he was a law officer.

Unsurprisingly, after becoming the Attorney General, Sorabjee's win–loss record once again went up. As a private lawyer in the 1980s, Sorabjee won around 54 per cent of his cases that were published in the law reports in which there was a clear winner and loser. As the Attorney General, on the other hand, he won 68 per cent of those cases—a proportion very similar to the 70 per cent cases that he won as a law officer with the Janata government. There appeared to be an unmistakable trend in Sorabjee's career—Sorabjee was more successful, he won more cases, when he was a law officer, rather than when he was a private lawyer. Once again, it is highly unlikely that Sorabjee's advocacy skills substantially improved each time he was appointed a law officer.

One of the high-profile cases he won as Attorney General was the case of Devi Lal, the astute 75-year-old Deputy Prime Minister and former Chief Minister of Haryana.[110] The petitioner in that case said that Devi Lal had taken an oath of office which was not sanctioned by the Constitution—there was no prescribed oath for any Deputy Prime Minister. Sorabjee informed the court that though Lal had, in his oath, described himself as the 'Deputy Prime Minister' of India, the oath that he had taken was otherwise in the required format. '[F]or all purposes', Sorabjee said, Devi Lal was only a minister in the government as there was 'no constitutional sanction for the post of Deputy Prime Minister as such'.[111] The court agreed with him and dismissed the case.

Apart from the Devi Lal case, many important judgments were delivered by the Supreme Court in cases in which Sorabjee appeared as Attorney General during this time. Several interesting questions came before the court in this period: When there is a conflict between two statutes, which statute prevails?[112] In what cases would the court be justified in issuing a 'mandatory' (as opposed to a 'prohibitory') interim injunction?[113] Can the Supreme Court hold somebody in contempt of a subordinate court?[114] These and other questions were answered by the Supreme Court during Sorabjee's tenure as Attorney General in cases in which he appeared.

'Year 1990', wrote Sorabjee in the *Times of India* that December, 'was one of my most memorable: Never-ending files, court appearances in the momentous Bhopal gas tragedy and Mandal cases, opinions on sensitive constitutional issues required overnight...'[115] As the Attorney General, Sorabjee had to constantly remind government officials to promptly comply with court orders. He soon realized 'the power of the bureaucracy' and its 'ingenuity in stalling proposals not to its liking'.[116] He also met 'some bureaucrats', however, of 'high calibre and integrity'.[117]

Sorabjee stopped writing newspaper articles after becoming the Attorney General in the National Front government (a tradition he would not maintain in his next term in office). He found no time to do the things he enjoyed—spend time with his children, read poetry, meet local musicians and dear friends.[118] He was unable to visit his favourite holiday destination at the time, Matheran.[119] However, though he was busy, he was sidelined by the National Front government and not consulted on the important constitutional issues of the day.[120] It is doubtful if he was consulted by the government on the implementation of the Mandal Commission report.

As L.K. Advani 'thundered on'[121] in his Rath Yatra to Ayodhya, irreconcilable differences emerged between two of the key supporters of the National Front government—the BJP and Left.[122] On 23 October 1990, Atal Bihari Vajpayee informed President Venkataraman that his party had withdrawn its support to the National Front government.[123] Over the next 24 hours, President Venkataraman consulted several constitutional experts, including Sorabjee.[124] 'Discussions with the

President in response to his request were stimulating', Sorabjee wrote.[125] On 7 November 1990, the National Front government lost its trust vote in the Lok Sabha after an 11-hour-long debate,[126] at which Sorabjee was present. It was a 'historic occasion', he wrote, though 'somewhat marred by noisy interruptions and unseemly gestures'. The debate was not televised in those days. 'Doordarshan should have been there', Sorabjee wished.[127]

On 10 November 1990, Chandra Shekhar, leading a faction of the split Janata Dal, was sworn in as the Prime Minister.[128] Sorabjee resigned shortly thereafter.[129] The four additional solicitors general of India, including Arun Jaitley and Kapil Sibal, had resigned a little earlier.[130] When he was appointed Attorney General, Sorabjee had started receiving 'courtesy calls' from people he hardly knew and was 'flooded with flattery and flowers' by people who thought that he could appoint them to some 'panel or post'. After he ceased to hold that office, all this went away. 'No more flowers and cakes now. And thank god for that', he wrote.[131] With a little more time on his hands, Sorabjee now looked forward to 'a long reading holiday far from the madding crowd, with all the time in the world to stand and stare and reflect on the meaning of it all'.[132]

10

'Sack Bommai, Advises Governor'

In his year spent as the Attorney General with the National Front government, Sorabjee appeared in very select cases. The volume of his work, compared to what it had been when he was in private practice, substantially went down. For instance, in 1989, on the eve of his appointment as Attorney General, his name was recorded in 43 cases that were published in the law reports—the highest number of appearances in any single year of his career until then. However, the following year, in 1990, his name appeared in only 20 cases in the law reports, which was his poorest show since 1983. As the Attorney General of India, he obviously seems to have taken up fewer cases—the more important ones in which his presence was necessary.

After resigning as the Attorney General though, it took the 60-year-old Sorabjee a few more years to get back to his roaring private practice. Between 1991 and 1993, Sorabjee appeared in fewer cases on average than he had in his private practice in the 1980s. In 1992, for example, his name was recorded in only 7 cases that were carried in the law reports—this was the lowest number of reported cases he had appeared in since 1973. Perhaps Sorabjee took a break and decided to be a bit more selective in terms of the cases he took up between 1991 and 1993. However, soon enough, Sorabjee was back to his usual self. Between 1994 and 1998, his volume of work was comparable with what it had been in the 1980s. In 1996, when he had crossed the age of 65—the age at which Supreme Court judges retire in India—Sorabjee appeared in a record 53 reported cases, the highest in his professional career.

In his private practice in the 1980s, though Sorabjee was primarily a Supreme Court lawyer, he had often argued cases in the High Courts and tribunals. During that time, around 73 per cent of his cases were in the Supreme Court, while the rest were in the High Courts and tribunals (most often, the customs and excise tribunal). Now, however, in private practice in the 1990s, Sorabjee confined himself more to the Supreme Court than he had before. Around 84 per cent of his cases as a private lawyer in the 1990s were in the Supreme Court—which is comparable with how he restricted himself to the Supreme Court as a law officer in the Janata period. As a private lawyer in the 1990s, he hardly ever went to the Bombay High Court—only 1 out of 222 cases in which Sorabjee's name was recorded in the law reports during this period was in the Bombay High Court. He argued more cases in the customs and excise tribunal (CEGAT) in Delhi than he did at the Bombay High Court at this time.

After resigning as the Attorney General, Sorabjee moved away from customs and excise work. A substantial proportion of Sorabjee's practice had been in the field of customs and excise before he had become a law officer in the Janata government. Around 26 per cent of his work between 1953 and 1977 was in that area of law. Once he became the Additional Solicitor General (and later, Solicitor General) with the Janata government, however, customs and excise had taken a back seat and fallen to 13 per cent of his practice. Once Sorabjee resumed his private practice in the 1980s, he got back into his comfort zone with customs and excise—around 31 per cent of his private work in the 1980s was in that field. Predictably, after Sorabjee became the Attorney

General with the National Front government, his customs and excise work fell again, as it had with the Janata government, accounting for around 20 per cent of his work. However, after resigning as the Attorney General, Sorabjee's customs and excise work continued to remain at this level—only 20 per cent of his work as a private lawyer in the 1990s was in this field of law. Perhaps Sorabjee was now getting tired of customs and excise and branching out into other fields—constitutional and commercial law.

With Sorabjee ceasing to be the Attorney General, however, some predictable changes took place in his private practice. His win–loss ratio went down once again. As a private lawyer in the 1990s, he won 51 per cent of his reported cases in which there was a clear, discernible winner and loser. He had won 70 per cent of his cases as a law officer with the Janata government and 68 per cent of his cases as the Attorney General with the National Front government. Another predictable change was that his dependence on Bombay increased once again. As a law officer, appeals from Bombay accounted for a negligible proportion of Sorabjee's cases in the Supreme Court. Now, as a private lawyer in the 1990s, 27 per cent of Sorabjee's work came from Bombay. The old Bombay connections played an important part in Sorabjee's professional career in Delhi. Advocates who Sorabjee often appeared with during this period were S. Ganesh, Nisha Bagchi, Harish Salve and Ravinder Narain.

Another predictable change to Sorabjee's private practice in the 1990s was that the proportion of 'Constitution Bench' judgments he argued now went back to the level it had been when he was a private lawyer in the 1980s. In private practice in the 1990s, only 8 per cent of his reported cases were before a 'Constitution Bench' of the Supreme Court (a bench of five judges or more). This was similar to the proportion of Constitution Bench cases he handled as a private lawyer in the 1980s (9 per cent), but substantially lower than the Constitution Bench judgments he featured in when he was a law officer with the Janata (29 per cent) and National Front (21 per cent) governments. Being a private lawyer meant taking up cases that were less significant.

That is not to say that the cases Sorabjee participated in at this time were trivial. As a private lawyer in the 1990s, Sorabjee appeared in a number of cases which are now considered classics. In these cases, the Supreme Court asked itself many interesting questions: Does the right to live include the right to die?[1] Is the practice of offering prayers in a mosque essential to Islam?[2] What is the scope of judicial review in 'tender' cases (i.e., cases where the government floats a tender and invites bids from private parties)?[3] Is the constitutional amendment that prohibited 'defection' (members of a party in a legislature switching sides) valid?[4] Does an arbitrator have the power to award interest during the pendency of the case?[5] Can tenancy rights be inherited through a will?[6] These and many other questions were decided by the Supreme Court in cases in which Sorabjee appeared in this period.

Sorabjee's public speeches were reported in the press. For this, he had his brush with the law. In 1997, he delivered a lecture in which he spoke about judicial appointments and the service conditions of judges. The speech was reported in the *Statesman*, though with some inaccuracies. An advocate then filed a petition in the Calcutta High Court alleging that Sorabjee had committed contempt of court by making that speech. Sorabjee appeared before the High Court and submitted that his views were expressed without any malice. The court dismissed the case, holding that it was not offended by Sorabjee's speech.[7]

The juniors in Sorabjee's chamber were taught important lessons.[8] When they were given a brief, they were expected to prepare a detailed list of dates, setting out the facts of the case.[9] They had to identify the legal issues that arose in the case. Sorabjee often prepared a list of 'things to do' which he called 'TTD . . .',[10] and sometimes gave his juniors a copy.[11] In conferences with clients, Sorabjee liked to play the devil's advocate—he would want to look at the case from the opponent's point of view in order to predict the questions that the court might ask him. In court, Sorabjee never raised his voice and was always respectful towards the judges. He taught his juniors that they must pay close attention to questions that the judges asked in court, always answering those first before moving on to anything else. He did not like pleadings to be drafted in an aggressive manner—the language had to be toned down.[12] If a junior's work impressed him, he would acknowledge that junior's efforts during his arguments in court.[13]

Though he was out of public office, Sorabjee remained in the public eye. In 1993, he was appointed by the UN as a prosecutor to the War Crimes Tribunal at the Hague.[14] He continued to write frequently on legal and non-legal topics in the *Times of India* and occasionally in the *Indian Express*, reaching a broader audience. He remained a minor celebrity of sorts—in their full-page advertisement in the *Times of India* in 1994, Jet Airways, then a successful airline, published the following testimonial from Sorabjee: 'Of all private airlines Jet Airways leads the way in terms of comfort, courtesy and service.'[15] In 1995, he publicly expressed his shock over the Supreme Court's decision to dismiss an appeal against a judgment of the Bombay High Court.[16] The High Court had refused to direct the police to prosecute Bal Thackeray, the leader of the Shiv Sena, for writing allegedly inflammatory articles against Muslims in the *Saamna* newspaper.[17] Later that year, he signed a statement appealing to the voters of Maharashtra to defeat the BJP– Shiv Sena alliance in the state assembly elections.[18] He would not, of course, have known then that three years later, he would be the Attorney General of their coalition government at the Centre.

. . .

The story of one of the most important cases that Sorabjee argued in the Supreme Court as a private lawyer in the 1990s began in Karnataka in 1983. In the elections which were held for the Karnataka state legislature that year, a non-Congress government came to power for the first time in the state's history. It was a Janata coalition[19] government headed by the bearded Chief Minister Ramakrishna Hegde[20] who promised to follow a new kind of 'value-based' politics in public office.[21] When the Janata government suffered a defeat in the national election in 1984, Hegde's state ministry resigned on moral grounds, but was re-elected to power.[22] In 1986, the Karnataka High Court struck down arrack bottling contracts awarded by his government to eight companies, observing that the allotment was 'unlawful, arbitrary and capricious' and had shocked its judicial conscience.[23] Hegde resigned on moral grounds once again, but his party-men insisted that he remain in office.[24] However, in 1988, a scandal broke out that the Karnataka state police had tapped the telephones of 51 people, including members of Parliament and the state legislature.[25] This time, Hegde quit and handed his position over to his revenue minister, a bespectacled,[26] non-practicing lawyer by the name of S.R. Bommai.[27]

In the meantime, opposition parties began to unite with a view to unseating the Congress in the upcoming elections.[28] In October 1988, a new national political party was formally inaugurated when the Jan Morcha, Janata and Lok Dal parties were merged to form the Janata Dal.[29] V.P. Singh was elected the president of the party.[30] In an editorial published the next day, the *Times of India* wrote that through this new party, the 'other backward castes' in India were 'making a bid for dominance at the Centre' though V.P. Singh himself was 'a non-OBC leader'.[31] In Karnataka, the ruling Janata party was renamed the Janata Dal in January 1989.[32] However, rebel groups within the merged parties were unhappy over the formation of the Janata Dal.[33] In Karnataka, the irrigation minister and future Prime Minister of India, H.D. Deve Gowda, resigned from Chief Minister S.R. Bommai's cabinet protesting the merger.[34] Two groups formed within the Janata party in the state—the 'pro-mergerists', loyal to former Chief Minister Ramakrishna Hegde, and dissident 'anti-mergerists' who sided with Gowda.[35]

Given that it was an election year, Bommai kept inducting new ministers into his cabinet[36] with a view towards satisfying various power centres within his party. By 15 April 1989, Bommai's 'airbus' ministry had 34 members in it.[37] Many were unhappy over their exclusion from the new cabinet and there were murmurs that some members of the party might resign.[38] Then, all of a sudden, on 18 April 1989, Kalyanarao Molakeri, a member of Bommai's party, withdrew his support to the Janata Dal government in Karnataka, along with several others.[39] The party leadership 'was not unduly alarmed' by this and thought that Deve Gowda was up to his old tricks.[40] However, two days later, the Governor of Karnataka, P. Venkatasubbiah, sent a communication to President R. Venkataraman recommending that the Karnataka legislature be dissolved as Bommai's government had been reduced to a minority—19 MLAs had withdrawn their support.[41] Bommai now had only 109 MLAs on his side, in a legislature which consisted of around 225 members.[42] On its front page the next day, the *Times of India* carried the headline: 'Sack Bommai, advises Governor'.[43]

Even before the Molakeri fiasco, Governor Venkatasubbiah had been under immense pressure from the Congress central leadership to dissolve the state legislature.[44] The Governor did not give Chief Minister Bommai the chance to prove himself in a 'floor-test', i.e., by showing that he had a majority in the state legislature in a no-confidence motion. Bommai called this an 'arbitrary, dictatorial', 'a most undemocratic' and 'politically-motivated decision'.[45] Justice Krishna Iyer who had, by this time, retired from the Supreme Court, told the press that Governor Venkatasubbiah's decision not to follow the floor-test was 'subversive' of the Constitution.[46] In fact, many[47] of the rebel MLAs wrote to the Governor retracting their letters and telling him that they now wished to continue supporting the government.[48] Molakeri, on the other hand, alleged that the rebel MLAs were being offered large sums of money to recant.[49]

On 21 April 1989, without giving Bommai the chance to prove his strength in the house through a floor-test, President Venkataraman dissolved the legislature and imposed President's Rule in the state of Karnataka.[50] When Home Minister Buta Singh made the announcement in the Lok Sabha later that day, opposition MPs accused the government of murdering democracy. '[D]emocracy is being traded on the streets of Bangalore', Buta Singh retorted,[51] referring to the alleged horse-trading in which legislators were being offered sums of money to support the government. On the other hand, V.P. Singh, not yet the Prime Minister, said that they would teach the Congress a lesson.[52]

Bommai filed a petition in the Karnataka High Court challenging the decision of the President to dissolve the assembly. He engaged Sorabjee who went to Bangalore in order to argue the case at the High Court.[53] Though Sorabjee, at this time, was primarily a private Supreme Court lawyer, devoting 73 per cent of his time to cases in the apex court, he spent the rest of his time in the High Courts and the central excise tribunal. He appeared most often in the Delhi High Court, but also toured the country, appearing in the High Courts in Andhra Pradesh, Uttar Pradesh, Punjab and Haryana, Jammu and Kashmir, Kerala, Orissa, Bihar, West Bengal and Rajasthan.

In July 1989, several months before the National Front government came to power at the Centre and he became the Attorney General, Sorabjee argued the Bommai case for four consecutive days before a special 3-judge bench of the Karnataka High Court.[54] He submitted that the Central government must disclose the materials on the basis of which the President had been advised to dissolve the state legislature.[55] True, Article 74(2) of the Constitution says that a court cannot inquire into whether the council of ministers gave any advice to the President and, if so, what that advice was. However, Sorabjee argued that the government could nonetheless be called upon to disclose the material on the basis of which the President was advised to impose President's Rule in Karnataka.[56] He said that if the Governor had allowed a floor-test to take place, the legislators who had withdrawn their support would have been disqualified under the Anti-defection Act.[57] He also added that many of the 19 MLAs might have changed their minds and decided to support the government had a floor-test taken place.[58] In this high-profile encounter in the High Court, Sorabjee was opposed by Attorney General Parasaran[59] who had, only a few months before, endorsed a settlement in the Bhopal case. On 4 August 1989, the Karnataka High Court delivered its judgment and held against Bommai and Sorabjee.[60] Among other things, the High Court found that a floor-test was 'neither compulsory nor obligatory'.[61]

The wheels of justice in India move slowly but surely. An appeal against the Karnataka High Court's Bommai judgment was filed in the Supreme Court. By the time the court took up the case, however, the entire dispute had blown over. In the November 1989 elections, the Congress party came back to power in the Karnataka state legislature with a two-thirds majority, winning a record number of seats.[62] The Bommai government had been irreversibly dissolved and now the Supreme Court could not unscramble a scrambled egg.

When the court finally decided Bommai's case in March 1994, the issue had become academic. In the Bommai case, the Supreme Court was really laying down guidelines for the future. Apart from Karnataka, President's Rule had been imposed in Madhya Pradesh, Himachal Pradesh and Rajasthan in December 1992 because of the role played by these governments in contributing to the *kar seva* at Ayodhya which had led to the demolition of the Babri Masjid.[63] The court was also considering the legality of President's Rule which had been imposed in Nagaland and Meghalaya in 1988 and 1991, respectively.

The nine judges who sat in the Supreme Court to decide the Bommai case wrote six different judgments. In view of this 'curious admixture' of divergent opinions, wrote Sorabjee later on, it was 'beyond the capacity of ordinary mortals' to say exactly what the court had decided in the case.[64] A majority of the court had agreed, however, that the test laid down by the Supreme Court in the *State of Rajasthan* case decided after the Janata government had come to power in 1977 was correct.[65] In other words, the decision to impose President's Rule on a state under Article 356 of the Constitution could be interfered with by the courts if it was wholly extraneous, grossly perverse or mala fide. However, the court now added a new ground on the basis of which President's Rule could be set aside. If there was no material at all on the strength of which the President had decided to invoke Article 356, or the material was not 'relevant' to the decision, then the court could also intervene.[66]

The Supreme Court agreed with Sorabjee and held that Article 74(2) of the Constitution did not bar the court from looking at the materials which were examined by the President before invoking Article 356,[67] though it prohibited the court from examining whether the council of ministers gave any advice to the President and, if so, what that advice was. The Central government could, of course, claim that the materials on the basis of which the President decided to impose President's Rule are privileged—but it then ran the risk that the court might hold that the decision to invoke Article 356 was made without any reasons.[68] When a prima facie case is made out that the imposition of President's Rule was unlawful, the burden is on the government to show that there was 'relevant material' on the basis of which it had decided to take the step.[69]

The Supreme Court in Bommai's case decided that in the future, no person could come to court and seek interim orders preventing the President from imposing President's Rule under Article 356 of the Constitution.[70] However, once the President issued a proclamation imposing President's Rule on a state, the court could issue interim orders restraining fresh elections from being held to the state legislative assembly pending the hearing of the case.[71] If the President's decision were found to be illegal, the court could then restore the status quo and revive the legislature and the ministry.[72] The President would not be entitled to dissolve the legislative assembly or take other such irreversible steps until his decision to invoke Article 356 was approved by both houses of Parliament.[73] The court agreed that secularism is a part of the basic structure of the Constitution and the President would be entitled to dissolve a state legislature if it 'subverted or sabotaged' secularism.[74] After the decision of the Supreme Court in Bommai's case, it is very doubtful if the President can recommend the dissolution of state legislatures following a change of regime in a general election,[75] which is what had happened after the Janata government came to power in 1977.

Perhaps most importantly, as Sorabjee opined later on,[76] a majority of the judges of the court had agreed that if a situation were to arise in the future, as it had in Karnataka in 1989, where legislators withdrew their support from the government, the Governor was barred from recommending the imposition of President's Rule without a floor-test being conducted.[77] On this reasoning, the decision of Governor Venkatasubbiah to recommend the invocation of Article 356 of the Constitution in 1989, merely after getting letters from 19 legislators who had withdrawn their support from the Bommai government, was clearly wrong. After five long years, Bommai had won his case but lost his government.

. . .

The story of another significant case Sorabjee participated in as a private lawyer in the 1990s also began in the year 1983. In February 1983, the *New York Times* reported that the 'bandit queen' of the Chambal valley had surrendered in 'an elaborately staged ceremony witnessed by several thousand cheering peasant admirers'.[78] At a college campus in Madhya Pradesh, wearing 'blue jeans', 'a stolen police officer's blouse' and a 'belt of cartridges' across her chest, the 27-year-old Phoolan Devi laid down her .315-mm Mauser rifle at the feet of Chief Minister Arjun Singh.[79] So much had been written about the story of her life, wrote the *New York Times*, that it was 'difficult to separate fact from fiction'.[80] Driven to a life of crime by desperate circumstances, she was said to be involved in several murder cases,[81] including an alleged massacre of 22 people in Behmai, Uttar Pradesh in 1982.[82]

In 1994, after eleven years in prison, Mulayam Singh Yadav's government in Uttar Pradesh decided to withdraw all the cases which were being tried against her in that state.[83] In February that year, the Supreme Court released her on parole in view of the time she had already spent behind bars.[84] Shortly thereafter, a film based on her life directed by the talented filmmaker Shekhar Kapur, was shown at the Cannes Film Festival in France.[85] Phoolan Devi, however, threatened to set herself on fire if the film, entitled *Bandit Queen*, was approved by the censor board without showing it to her first. She was upset over the many factual inaccuracies about her life and the many graphic scenes which were shown in the film.[86] She approached her lawyers and in September 1994, the Delhi High Court issued an interim order banning the film.[87] Her advocate in court objected to the depiction of nudity in the film and to the fact that she had been shown as guilty of crimes for which cases were still pending against her.[88]

In November, after being permitted to watch the movie, the Film Federation of India nominated *Bandit Queen* as India's entry to the Oscars.[89] However, the Delhi High Court then passed an order prohibiting the Oscar committee from viewing the film in Los Angeles,[90] and it was withdrawn from the Oscar race.[91] Though the film was banned in India because of the Delhi High Court order, pirated video prints were circulating freely in Bombay, Delhi, Madras, Bangalore and Jaipur.[92] In Delhi, a pirated copy of the film could be rented out for Rs 50 or purchased outright for Rs 350–500.[93] In March 1995, however, Phoolan Devi and the producers of the film reached an agreement. The Delhi High Court lifted the ban after the producers agreed to delete four scenes in the film and to pay Phoolan a sum of 40,000 pounds.[94] The film would no longer say that it was a true story.[95]

However, *Bandit Queen's* troubles were only beginning. Unhappy with the censor board's decision to make several cuts to the film, director Shekhar Kapur said, 'This is not the film I made—I don't stand by this film.'[96] Just as it was being readied for release in January 1996, a man called Om Pal Singh Hoon filed a petition in the Delhi High Court asking the court to stay the film on the ground that it was obscene and that his community had been depicted in a depraved manner in it.[97] A case against the distributor of the film was also filed in the National Human Rights Commission.[98] Legislators belonging to the BJP in the Karnataka assembly and women's organizations in Mumbai[99] demanded that the film be banned.[100] A member of the censor board resigned, upset over the fact that his plea that *Bandit Queen* should not be cleared by the censor had fallen on deaf ears.[101]

This time, however, the film was not initially barred from being shown in theatres, and it opened to house-full audiences, some of whom might have been there for the wrong reasons—not to see Shekhar Kapur's technical brilliance, but to watch nudity, violence and profanity in a mainstream movie on the big-screen like never before.[102] At Metro cinema in Mumbai, Shekhar Kapur noticed five people whistling during a serious scene when the protagonist was 'paraded nude in the village square'.[103] However, Kapur made the point that there were only five such perverts in a packed cinema hall. The four million people who had already seen the film were not all perverts. This was a serious film, unlike the many soft-porn films which were readily available at theatres in Mumbai.[104]

After watching the film,[105] in March 1996, Justice Anil Dev Singh of the Delhi High Court passed an order directing the producers to stop screening it until the censor board had reviewed the film once again.[106] The court was particularly unhappy over scenes where the 'frontal nudity'[107] of a female character and the 'naked posterior'[108] of a male character had been shown, apart from the abusive language which was used in the film.[109] India's youth, said the court, must not be 'fed on sex and violence in the films'.[110]

The matter travelled in appeal to a bench of two judges of the Delhi High Court. Sorabjee was engaged to appear on behalf of a distributor before the bench. He explained to the court that 'frontal nudity', as the judge had described it, was not, in all cases, akin to 'hard-core' pornography. Hard-core pornography, he said, was meant to 'provoke sheer lust'. 'It depicts sex for the sake of sex', he said. That was not the objective of *Bandit Queen*.[111] However, the appeal bench of the Delhi High Court upheld the judgment of Justice Singh.[112] The court was worried that viewers would hear the expletives in the film and try to emulate and use them in real life.[113]

The appeal bench of the Delhi High Court also issued a notice to the *Times of India* for contempt[114] when one of its writers suggested that *Bandit Queen* had been banned for 'political' rather than 'moral' reasons.[115] The newspaper later published an unconditional apology for carrying that article.[116]

The matter soon travelled to the Supreme Court.[117] Sorabjee asked the court to immediately stay the Delhi High Court's judgment and permit the screening of the film to continue. His client's profits from 38 cinema halls in Delhi and Uttar Pradesh, as a distributor of the film, he said, amounted to Rs 20 lakhs per week. He submitted that this was an example of how 'oppressive' a public interest litigation could become 'in a matter concerning a work of art'.[118] He pointed out that even the government of India supported his stand.[119] The court declined his request for a stay order, but said that it would decide the case on the next date itself.[120]

In May 1996, however, the Supreme Court reversed the Delhi High Court. In its judgment, the court said that the 'frontal nudity' scene was not obscene. In the film, the protagonist was 'humiliated, stripped naked, paraded, made to draw water from the well, within the circle of a hundred men'.[121] The object of showing the protagonist naked was 'not to titillate the cinemagoer's lust' but to 'arouse in him sympathy for the victim and disgust for the perpetrators'.[122] Nudity in films is not necessarily obscene. 'Nakedness', said the court, 'does not always arouse the baser instinct.'[123] The court gave the example of the film *Schindler's List* which had been approved for screening in India. The film showed 'rows of naked men and women . . . being led into the gas chambers of a Nazi concentration camp.'[124] Watching the scene, most viewers would be moved to tears, said the court, except the odd pervert 'who might be aroused'.[125] However, in a powerful line, the court explained the objective of the law of obscenity in India. It said: 'We do not censor to protect the pervert or to assuage the susceptibilities of the over-sensitive.'[126] In other words, a work of art must be judged from the point of view of a reasonable person. Merely because some pervert or hypersensitive person might derive pleasure from or object to a nude scene does not mean that it is obscene.

The court disagreed with the Delhi High Court's view and suggested that it had made '[t]oo much' of 'a few swear words' in the film which were of a kind 'which can be heard everyday in every city, town and village street'. 'No adult', the Supreme Court added, 'would be tempted to use [the swear words] because they are used in this film.'[127]

The court noted the fact that the tribunal which had cleared the film in the censor process was chaired by Justice Lentin[128]—the same judge who had allowed *Tamas* to be shown on Doordarshan in 1988. The tribunal had three women on it.[129] The film had been approved for viewing only by adults.[130] The film was based on a book which had been in the market since 1991 'without objection'.[131] 'Adult Indian citizens', said the court, could be trusted to intelligently comprehend the message of a nude scene.[132] A film that denounces a social evil, said the court, 'necessarily must show that social evil'.[133] Interestingly, the court did not view the film and relied on how it had been described by the Delhi High Court.[134] The court lifted the ban on the film, but allowed it to be shown only after the elections were concluded as Phoolan Devi was contesting a Lok Sabha seat in Uttar Pradesh.[135] Several lawyers apart from Sorabjee appeared in the case, including Sorabjee's junior, Harish Salve.

The following year, *Bandit Queen* won three Filmfare awards, including best director, best female debutante and best cinematography.[136] Deprived of an Oscar for *Bandit Queen*, Shekhar

Kapur went on to make *Elizabeth* which was nominated for several Oscars.[137] Phoolan Devi became a member of Parliament[138] but was later shot dead at her home in Delhi in 2001.[139]

A few days after the Supreme Court had delivered its judgment, in his regular column called 'Out of Court' in the *Times of India*, Sorabjee hailed the court's judgment in the *Bandit Queen* case as 'a resounding vindication' of the 'cherished' fundamental right to freedom of expression and 'a rebuff to prudery'.[140] Of course, no one had the right, he wrote, 'to peddle in hard-core pornography'.[141] At a personal level, however, though Sorabjee was opposed to censorship, he did not like to read books which indiscriminately used 'sexually explicit language'.[142] One of his favourite books, Charles Dickens's *The Pickwick Papers*, 'an inexhaustible source of joy and entertainment' for him, had been a resounding success without the use of any such language, he pointed out to his readers.[143] 'Today's teenagers', he wrote, 'spout four-letter words as if without these expletives their freedom of expression is impaired.'[144]

11
Coalition Dharma

The 1990s were a decade of fragile political alliances and short-lived governments. In November 1990, Sorabjee had to resign as the Attorney General of India when the V.P. Singh-led National Front government lost power after the BJP withdrew its support.[1] Chandra Shekhar, who came to power with outside support from the Congress, resigned a few months thereafter.[2] P.V. Narasimha Rao's Congress party formed a minority government after the 1991 elections,[3] riding a sympathy wave after the assassination of Rajiv Gandhi.[4] Though Narasimha Rao survived a full five-year term, an era of political uncertainty soon followed. In May 1996, Atal Bihari Vajpayee was sworn in as the Prime Minister of India.[5] With its 161 seats in the Lok Sabha, his BJP, the single-largest party, fell substantially short of a majority of the house which had 543 seats.[6] Vajpayee resigned less than two weeks later, before the confidence motion could be put to vote in the Lok Sabha,[7] and his 13-day government was the shortest ever in India's history.[8] Vajpayee's Law Minister, the famous criminal lawyer, Ram Jethmalani,[9] had to resign as well.

Sorabjee, however, was quite impressed with Vajpayee's performance in the Lok Sabha during the confidence motion. 'The redeeming feature' of the entire episode in Parliament, which was shown on live television,[10] Sorabjee wrote, 'was the heroic performance of Vajpayee'. 'Today he is the most popular political leader', Sorabjee added, 'and is perceived by many as the prime minister of our country but without the BJP, which is like expecting [a] performance of Hamlet without the Prince of Denmark.'[11] Among other things, Sorabjee hinted that the BJP needed to 'shed its obsession with demolishing mosques' and replace 'Hindutva' with 'Indianness or Bharatva' in order to survive.[12] Sorabjee was not alone in entertaining his view on Vajpayee. A few weeks before, Nani Palkhivala had praised Vajpayee and said that he had been an excellent foreign minister during the Janata regime, he was a 'figure known throughout the world' and that India would play a much larger role in world affairs under his leadership.[13]

H.D. Deve Gowda was sworn in as the Prime Minister next[14]—the same Deve Gowda who was suspected of having caused trouble for the Bommai government in Karnataka in 1988, which had led to Sorabjee arguing Bommai's case in the Karnataka High Court over several days. Gowda headed an alliance of thirteen parties which had recently been renamed the 'United Front' (after being called various names like the 'National Front-Left Front'[15] and 'Third Front'[16]). The United Front government was supported by the Congress which, with its 140 seats, was the second-largest party in the Lok Sabha.[17] The love affair between the Congress and United Front, however, was short-lived. As Sitaram Kesri took the reins of the Congress party in 1997,[18] a rift began to develop between the United Front and Congress. The Congress complained that it was not being consulted on important government decisions.[19] The Central Bureau of Investigation conducted a probe against Kesri.[20]

In March 1997, barely a year into the United Front's tenure in office, the Congress withdrew its support and staked its own claim to form the government,[21] even as reports began to emerge of infighting within the Congress.[22] The deadlock was broken when another candidate within the United Front, foreign minister I.K. Gujral, was made the new Prime Minister, with the approval of the Congress.[23] However, even this was not to last. In November 1997, the Jain Commission, headed by a retired Chief Justice of the Delhi High Court,[24] opined that the DMK—a party which was a coalition partner in the United Front government—had abetted the LTTE, which was believed to be responsible for the assassination of Rajiv Gandhi.[25] With this, the Gujral government's days were numbered. The Congress withdrew its support a few weeks later,[26] and President K.R. Narayanan dissolved the Lok Sabha the following month.[27]

In the general election which was held in 1998, the BJP once again emerged as the single-largest party in the Lok Sabha. However, with only 182 seats[28]—a marginal improvement over its performance in 1996—it still fell substantially short of a majority in the house. This time, however, Vajpayee won the trust vote by a narrow margin.[29] Around a week later, Sorabjee was appointed the Attorney General of India once again.[30] Many in the legal fraternity praised the government for choosing Sorabjee. V.M. Tarkunde, Sorabjee's former client in the Judges case, said that it was 'nice' of Sorabjee to have accepted the position, and that the 'present coalition led by the BJP' was 'the only viable choice'.[31]

In that climate of political uncertainty, who knew how long the government would last? Between 1990 and 1998, India had seen six different Prime Ministers.[32] However, Sorabjee probably felt that he had nothing to lose by accepting the position. His previous term with the National Front government had lasted only around a year. At 68 years of age, Sorabjee had already crossed the age of retirement for a Supreme Court judge (65). In fact, a case was filed against him in the Allahabad High Court for this reason. Article 76 of the Constitution says that the Attorney General must be 'qualified to be appointed a Judge of the Supreme Court'.[33] The petitioner in the case against Sorabjee contended that since Sorabjee had crossed 65, he was no longer 'qualified' to be appointed a judge of the Supreme Court. The case was dismissed with costs after the Allahabad High Court held that the age of a Supreme Court judge had nothing to do with his or her qualifications.[34]

. . .

In his first year in office as the Attorney General, Sorabjee had to defend one of the BJP government's dubious attempts at wooing its most powerful[35] coalition ally—the AIADMK headed by J. Jayalalitha in Tamil Nadu. With 18 seats in the Lok Sabha,[36] the AIADMK was the largest party, apart from the BJP itself, in the alliance. Jayalalitha had been the Chief Minister of Tamil Nadu between 1991 and 1996, but was replaced by M. Karunanidhi (DMK) in 1996.[37] After the DMK came to power in the state, some 38 criminal cases (the number thereafter increased) were filed against Jayalalitha alleging corruption and disproportionate assets.[38]

One of these cases, for instance, was the Pleasant Stay Hotel case.[39] The allegation against her was that as the Chief Minister, she had approved the construction of a seven-storey hotel in the scenic town of Kodaikanal, in violation of building safety and environmental regulations, for which she had allegedly received a bribe.[40] Another case against her was that she owned property worth Rs 15 crores, which was allegedly 'disproportionate to her known sources of income'.[41] In December 1996, Jayalalitha was arrested in connection with some of these cases, taken away from her Poes Garden residence and imprisoned in a separate cell in the women's enclosure at the central jail in Chennai.[42] With no special privileges, her jailers gave her two bedsheets, a pillow, and a prison diet.[43] She was released on bail nearly a month later, in January 1997.[44]

Criminal cases in India take a long time to decide. The cases against Jayalalitha had hundreds of witnesses and were so complex that they would have ordinarily taken around ten years to reach their end.[45] With a view to fast-tracking the process against their political opponent, in

April 1997, the DMK government decided to set up three special courts, headed by special judges, who would almost exclusively hear the cases against Jayalalitha.[46] Jayalalitha challenged this move, and the case travelled to the Supreme Court. In the meantime, however, in the general election in 1998, her party won 18 seats in the Lok Sabha and joined the BJP-led coalition government at the Centre. In December that year, when Jayalalitha's case came up before the Supreme Court, Sorabjee, as the Attorney General, informed the court that it was the Central government which had the power to transfer cases to special judges under the Prevention of Corruption Act, not the state government.[47]

The following year, in February 1999, the Central government issued a notification transferring Jayalilatha's corruption cases back to the regular criminal courts in Tamil Nadu.[48] This was done only a few days after Jayalalitha had threatened to withdraw from the government.[49] The Central government's move meant that Jayalalitha's corruption cases would now be heard by the ordinary criminal courts, which would have taken much longer to decide the cases. Ram Jethmalani, a minister in the government, later alleged that the notification to transfer the cases was issued by the Law Minister, M. Thambidurai, who was a member of the AIADMK, without informing the cabinet.[50] Lawyers belonging to the DMK and other opposition parties burned copies of the Central government notification in protest.[51] The DMK government challenged the notification in the Supreme Court and engaged Fali Nariman, who pointed out that in the Madras High Court, the Central government had supported the DMK government's decision to transfer Jayalalitha's cases to special judges.[52]

On the other hand, Sorabjee informed the Supreme Court that the BJP-led Central government did not wish to delay the hearing of Jayalalitha's cases and that the Supreme Court could issue directions for her cases to be heard speedily if required.[53] In 1997, a year before becoming the Attorney General, Sorabjee had appeared in the Madras High Court for Jayalalitha in a case against one of her former party members,[54] though this would not have been considered a conflict of interest as a counsel who does not receive a retainer from a client is usually free to appear against that client in an unrelated case.

Despite the transfer of cases, Jayalalitha seemed to be in a sort of love–hate relationship with the BJP coalition government. On some occasions, she would pledge her support to the government.[55] At other times, she would express her unhappiness with its decisions. For instance, in February 1999, only a few weeks after the Central government transferred her cases to the regular courts, she voiced her displeasure over the Union railway budget, pointing out that it had not done enough for her state.[56] When Vajpayee visited Tiruchi in Tamil Nadu, Jayalalitha decided not to attend the event.[57] She openly criticized the government's foreign policy.[58]

However, things became more serious when India's Defence Minister, George Fernandes (the same George Fernandes who had orchestrated the railway strike before the Emergency in the 1970s), decided to sack Admiral Vishnu Bhagwat from the Indian Navy for allegedly leaking sensitive information about India's nuclear submarine project to the press.[59] Jayalalitha threatened to withdraw support from the BJP coalition unless three demands were met: remove George Fernandes from the defence ministry, reinstate Admiral Bhagwat, and set up a joint parliamentary committee to probe why he was sacked.[60] The BJP stood its ground and refused to do any of these things. Jayalalitha then started the process of withdrawing from the government. AIADMK ministers in the Union cabinet resigned.[61]

In the Supreme Court, however, Sorabjee continued defending the Central government's decision to transfer Jayalalitha's corruption cases to the regular courts. 'I do not wish to add or subtract a jot from what I had submitted previously', he informed the court.[62] However, he admitted that the Central government had only minimally consulted the Chief Justice of the Madras High Court before transferring Jayalalitha's cases to the regular courts, which might have rendered the Central government's notification illegal.[63] As the Supreme Court reserved its order in the case concerning the transfer of Jayalalitha's corruption cases,[64] the BJP was faced with the prospect of having to endure another trust vote in Parliament. In a surprising turn of events, the DMK now pledged its support to the BJP coalition.[65] In April 1999, however, Vajpayee lost the confidence motion in the Lok Sabha by only one vote (269–270), when the Chief Minister of Orissa, Giridhar Gamang, voted against the government.[66]

Unlike in his first tenure as Attorney General with the National Front government, Sorabjee continued writing articles, especially his column 'Out of Court' in the *Times of India*, even after becoming the Attorney General in the BJP-led coalition government. In April 1999, after the Supreme Court had reserved its orders in the Jayalalitha case but not yet delivered its judgment, Sorabjee wrote an article on corruption and Jayalalitha. In politics, he wrote, 'there are no permanent friends and enemies'.[67] Subramanian Swamy, he added, who was once an ardent rival of Jayalalitha, who had 'been instrumental in launching criminal prosecutions against' her and had described her as the 'fountain of corruption' was now 'ostensibly her staunchest ally'. Jayalalitha had once told Swamy, whose wife, Roxna, was a junior in Sorabjee's chamber, that he would meet his Waterloo. To this, Swamy had retorted, much to Sorabjee's disgust, that he would 'send her to the loo without water'.[68]

In his article, Sorabjee wrote that the 'most effective way to combat corruption' was to 'prevent the corrupt person from enjoying the fruits of his or her misdeeds'.[69] Imposing a sentence of imprisonment and a fine were not effective deterrents. Those who were found guilty of corruption, he added, ought to have their property forfeited. Otherwise, their families, he wrote, would 'continue with their foreign travels and lavish shopping in London, Paris or New York'.[70]

In May 1999, the BJP and its coalition allies formed a new front called the 'National Democratic Alliance' (NDA) with a joint manifesto.[71] In the meantime, the Supreme Court decided Jayalalitha's case. It approved of the DMK government's decision to transfer her corruption cases to special judges.[72] The regular courts, even the existing special courts under the Prevention of Corruption Act, said the Supreme Court, were overburdened, and there was good reason to have Jayalalitha's cases tried by a newly constituted special court.[73] On the other hand, the court rejected the BJP government's February 1999 decision to transfer her cases back to the regular criminal courts, saying that there was absolutely no reason for it to have done so.[74]

In the elections which were held that year, though the BJP failed to improve on its past year's performance and ended up with 182 seats in the Lok Sabha,[75] Jayalalitha's party suffered losses and fell from 18 seats to 10.[76] The National Democratic Alliance formed the government and unanimously elected Vajpayee as its leader.[77] To the surprise of many, a young lawyer who was not a member of either house of Parliament, was now inducted as a minister. It was Arun Jaitley, who had assisted Sorabjee as the Additional Solicitor General for India with the National Front government, who was now made the minister of state with independent charge of the information and broadcasting ministry.[78] The following month, Sorabjee was appointed as the Attorney General once again.[79]

Jayalalitha was eventually acquitted of any wrongdoing in the Pleasant Stay Hotel case by the Madras High Court in 2001.[80] However, the disproportionate assets corruption case against her was finally decided by the Supreme Court only after she had died in 2016. In 2017, the court found that though the case against her had come to an end because of her death, her associates were guilty of corruption.[81]

. . .

In 1999, the government used Sorabjee in order to push through a controversial decision to bail out private telecom companies in India. The telecommunications industry had been opened up to the private sector in the 1990s.[82] Private companies were given licences to operate in the industry after a competitive bidding process. As part of their contract, they had to pay the government a fixed licence fee. By 1999, there were 8.73 million telephone lines in India, one public call office (PCO) booth for every 522 people in urban India and a telephone network available in 3.1 lakh Indian villages.[83] Though there were only 51 cell phones in India (all of them in Delhi) in 1986,[84] with the liberalization of the sector in the 1990s, especially after the new national telecom policy of 1994, this number increased such that by 1998, there were around 0.8 million cell phone subscribers in India.[85] Of course, the cell phone revolution, which would begin in the 2000s, had not yet occurred in India. Even so, Nokia 5110,[86] Samsung SPH-6310[87] and Ericsson I-888,[88] were among the cell phone models which were becoming available for sale in India between 1998 and 1999.

The problem, however, was that Indian telecom companies were in dire straits. They had been far too optimistic in their earnings projections during the competitive bidding process for telecom licences and now owed the government around Rs 48,000 crores in licence fees payable over the next 10–15 years,[89] which they were not in any position to pay. Almost all of them had defaulted on the licence fees they were supposed to hand over to the government.[90] They started lobbying the government and asking for a bailout. They no longer wanted to pay a fixed licence fee and hoped that they could move to a revenue-sharing model in which they would only have to pay the government a small percentage of the revenues they earned.[91] Around January 1999, Sorabjee was asked by the government to give an opinion as to whether this would be legally permissible. In a written opinion, Sorabjee advised the government against this move.[92] The department of telecommunications in the government then took steps to invoke the bank guarantees which had been given by the telecom companies that were unable to pay their licence fees.[93]

However, the government soon announced its 'New Telecom Policy' of 1999.[94] In it, the government said that existing telecom

An advertisement published by Sorabjee's grandfather's firm, Hormasjee Sorabjee & Sons in the *Bombay Chronicle* in 1920, for selling the American car known as 'Oldsmobile' at their Queen's Road showroom in Bombay.

Jehangir Sorabjee (Soli Sorabjee's father)

Khorshed Sorabjee (Soli Sorabjee's mother)

Maneckbai Dubash (Soli Sorabjee's maternal grandmother)

Ardeshir Dubash (Soli Sorabjee's
maternal grandfather)

A certificate from Bombay Municipality dated 16 January 1899,
recognizing that Sorabjee's grandfather, Hormasjee Sorabjee, was
rendering services towards the suppression of the plague.

Sorabjee (top row, standing fifth from right)
at the Bharda New High School.

Young Sorabjee with
his dog. As the only
child of his parents,
his two dogs were his
constant companions.

Young Sorabjee (standing on the right) 'leading in' his father's horse,
Doodal Dandy, after it won a race in 1945.

Young Sorabjee on a bicycle.

Mr. & Mrs. Jehangir Hormusjee Sorabjee
request the pleasure of

_____'s

company to Dinner on the occasion of the
"Navjote" (Thread Ceremony) of their son,

Sohrab

at All6less Baug, Charni Road,
on Thursday, 18th February, 1937, at 6 p.m.

R. S. V. P.,
Dubash Bungalow,
27, Nepean Sea Road,
Malabar Hill,
Bombay.

Indian Dramatic Entertainment
6-15 to 7-30 p. m.
Dinner 7-45 p. m.

Sorabjee as a teenager.

An invitation card to Sorabjee's 'Navjote' (thread ceremony) in 1937.

Sorabjee (standing, first from the right, third row from the bottom) as a student at St. Xavier's School in January 1944.

Sorabjee as a law student at Government Law College in 1951.

Sorabjee as a fellow at Government
Law College in 1953.

The Kinloch Forbes Gold Medal in
Roman Law and Jurisprudence won by
Sorabjee as a student at Government
Law College in his first year LLB
examination in 1951.

Sorabjee (standing,
second row, fourth
from the right) as
a member of the
magazine committee
at Government Law
College in 1953. Seated
in the photograph,
third from the right,
was his good friend,
J.S. Khambata.

Sorabjee
(seated, center,
in robes), as the
elected speaker
of the student
parliament at
Government
Law College
in 1953.

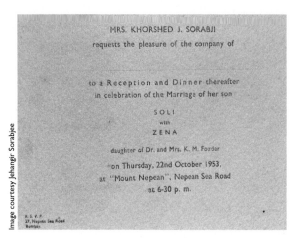

MRS. KHORSHED J. SORABJI

requests the pleasure of the company of

to a Reception and Dinner thereafter
in celebration of the Marriage of her son

SOLI

with

ZENA

daughter of Dr. and Mrs. K. M. Fozdar

on Thursday, 22nd October 1953,
at "Mount Nepean", Nepean Sea Road
at 6-30 p. m.

R. S. V. P.
27, Nepean Sea Road
Bombay.

An invitation card to a reception and dinner held to celebrate Sorabjee's marriage to Zena in October 1953.

Sorabjee and Zena after they were married in October 1953.

Sorabjee as a young man.

Sorabjee playing the clarinet.

Sorabjee (second from the right) with his first juniors, Avinash Rana (first from the right) and Obed Chinoy (third from the right).

Sorabjee (right) with Jayprakash Narayan (centre) and Acharya J.B. Kripalani (left).

Sorabjee with his daughter, Zia.

Sorabjee with his son, Jehangir. Sorabjee was initially keen on naming his son 'Hamlet' (after Shakespeare's famous play).

Sorabjee, Zena, and their daughter, Zia.

Sorabjee, Zena, and their four children (from left to right: Jehangir, Hormazd, Jamshed, and Zia), on the verandah in Sorabjee's grandfather's bungalow at Mahabaleshwar, Valley View.

Sorabjee, Zena and their daughter, Zia.

Sorabjee on the clarinet.

Sorabjee playing charades.

Sorabjee, seated on his Dodge, outside Valley
View.

Sorabjee on holiday in the UK.

Sorabjee and his son Hormazd getting
ready to go on a trip in his Dodge.

Sorabjee on the phone.

Sorabjee on the phone again.

Sorabjee and Zena.

Sorabjee and Zena.

Sorabjee reading a biography of Justice Thurgood Marshall at Valley View.

Sorabjee (left) with Justice V.D. Tulzapurkar (second from left).

Sorabjee (right) with Nani Palkhivala (centre) and Justice M.C. Chagla (left).

Sorabjee (centre) with J.R. Gagrat (left)
and Justice M.C. Chagla (right).

Sorabjee with Justice H.R. Khanna.

Sorabjee with President Bill Clinton (the photograph has been
signed by Clinton).

Sorabjee (centre) with Justice A.S. Anand (left) and Justice
J.S. Verma (right).

Sorabjee with Justice V.R. Krishna Iyer.

Sorabjee with Nani Palkhivala.

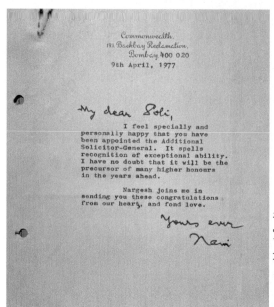

Commonwealth,
131. Backbay Reclamation,
Bombay 400 020
9th April, 1977

My dear Soli,

I feel specially and
personally happy that you have
been appointed the Additional
Solicitor-General. It spells
recognition of exceptional ability.
I have no doubt that it will be the
precursor of many higher honours
in the years ahead.

Nargesh joins me in
sending you these congratulations
from our heart, and fond love.

Yours ever
Nani

A letter dated 9 April 1977 from Nani Palkhivala to
Sorabjee congratulating the latter on his appointment
as the Additional Solicitor General.

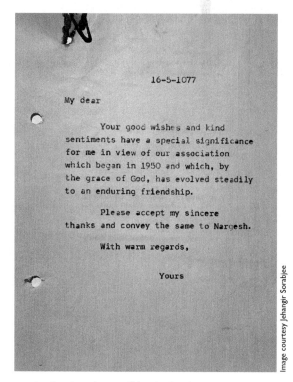

16-5-1077

My dear

Your good wishes and kind
sentiments have a special significance
for me in view of our association
which began in 1950 and which, by
the grace of God, has evolved steadily
to an enduring friendship.

Please accept my sincere
thanks and convey the same to Nargesh.

With warm regards,

Yours

Sorabjee's reply to Palkhivala dated 16 May 1977.

Sorabjee and President Barack Obama.

Sorabjee as a UN Special Country Rapporteur in Nigeria in 1998.

Sorabjee receiving his Padma Vibhushan from President K.R. Narayanan in 2002.

Sorabjee with L.K. Advani.

Sorabjee with the Emperor and Empress of Japan.

Sorabjee with President Xi Jinping

Photographs of Sorabjee

projects were 'facing problems' because the 'actual revenues' realized by telecom companies had fallen 'far short of the projections' and they were therefore 'unable to arrange financing for their projects'.[95] With this in mind, the policy announced that the government intended to move from a fixed licence-fee model to a revenue-sharing model.[96] The government decided to ask Sorabjee whether he would be willing to change his previous opinion on the legality of this move.

In the meantime, by June 1999, Vajpayee, who had already lost his trust vote after Jayalalitha withdrew her support, was now heading a caretaker government pending the forthcoming elections. However, during this period, Prime Minister Vajpayee changed the portfolio of the communications minister, Jagmohan.[97] Jagmohan was known to have expressed views against allowing telecom companies to migrate from licence fees to revenue-sharing.[98] At this time, Sorabjee was on vacation abroad during the court holidays. He was summoned back to India by the government. On 16 June 1999, Sorabjee then changed his previously given opinion and said that it would now be okay to allow existing telecom companies to migrate from a fixed licence-fee arrangement to a revenue-sharing arrangement.[99] However, he said that these companies must first be required to pay all their outstanding licence fee arrears by 31 December 1999.[100] He gave several reasons why he had changed his mind: If telecom licences were cancelled, this would have an adverse effect on the banks which had lent them money. Cancelling their licences would entail long-drawn out litigation. A revenue-sharing model was in the larger public interest as it would revive and grow the telecom sector.[101]

Did Sorabjee do the right thing in changing his opinion? We do not have enough information to make a judgment one way or the other. A lawyer will ordinarily not change his or her opinion of a case unless the facts which were shown to the lawyer have changed or unless the lawyer admits that he or she made a mistake in the original opinion. Since the government's files concerning this opinion are not available with us, it would be unfair of us to express an opinion on whether Sorabjee was right or wrong to have changed his opinion.

The comptroller and auditor general of India (CAG) reportedly opined that the government should not have taken such a decision based only on a legal opinion and that it ought to have taken the advice of an expert financial body.[102] In other words, the CAG felt that it was not Sorabjee who was at fault but the government, to have relied so heavily on a legal opinion to take what was essentially a financial decision. On the other hand, Law Minister Ram Jethmalani, with whom Sorabjee later had a very public falling-out, agreed that Sorabjee's opinion was being misused by the government,[103] but he also crudely accused Sorabjee of overcharging for the second opinion.[104] When President K.R. Narayanan raised concerns and said that such a drastic step should not be taken by a caretaker government,[105] Prime Minister Vajpayee told him, among other things, that the move had been recommended by Sorabjee.[106]

After the opinion, the government acted swiftly. The day after Sorabjee's revised opinion was written, the Prime Minister's office sent a note to the Department of Telecommunications asking it to urgently refer the matter to the cabinet.[107] The cabinet approved of the decision the following month, on 6 July 1999.[108] Telecom companies thereafter had to pay the government a share of 15 per cent of their revenue (the figure went down later on), rather than a fixed licence fee.[109]

A public interest case was thereafter filed in the Delhi High Court challenging the government's decision. Sorabjee appeared in the case and defended the policy change.[110] The court then passed an interim order which said that the migration of telecom companies to revenue-sharing would be allowed subject to the decision of the new cabinet after the election. In October 1999, Vajpayee's newly constituted cabinet ratified the decision after the elections were over.[111] Though a joint parliamentary committee later opined that this decision had cost the exchequer Rs 42,080.34 crores,[112] the telecom regulatory authority of

India noted, on the other hand, that it was responsible for huge growth in the telecom sector.[113]

. . .

In the year 2000, Sorabjee was involved in a sordid war of words with outgoing Law Minister Ram Jethmalani. The story of their tussle began in December 1992. For two blood-soaked months, communal riots shook the city of Bombay. The *Times of India* alleged that the Shiv Sena was responsible for inciting the riots and some of its members even participated in them, though things got out of hand when 'anti-social elements' got involved.[114] Around 1,500 people were reported to have lost their lives in the carnage.[115] When things calmed down the following month, a one-man commission headed by Justice B.N. Srikrishna of the Bombay High Court was set up to inquire into what the causes of the riots were.[116] Three years later, the Shiv Sena government had the commission disbanded, only to have it restored when Prime Minister Vajpayee intervened.[117]

After five years of hearing around 503 witnesses and parsing through some 150,000 pages of evidence,[118] Justice Srikrishna finally submitted his report in February 1998.[119] For some time, nobody really knew what he had concluded, and opposition parties demanded that the report be made public.[120] By August 1998, however, it was clear that Justice Srikrishna had found the Shiv Sena guilty of instigating the riots. 'The communal violence and the rioting triggered off by the Shiv Sena', Justice Srikrishna wrote, 'was hijacked by local criminal elements who saw in it an opportunity to make quick gains.'[121] The report also pointed fingers at the indecisive Congress leadership of the time and the 'biased' police force.[122] However, communal feelings had been greatly incited, the report concluded, by articles which were written in the *Saamna*,[123] the Shiv Sena mouthpiece. In fact, as we saw in the previous chapter, in 1995, Sorabjee had issued a public statement along with other lawyers condemning the Supreme Court's decision to dismiss an appeal filed against a Bombay High Court judgment exonerating Bal Thackeray for his articles in the *Saamna*.[124] The Shiv Sena–BJP government in Maharashtra, however, swiftly rejected the Srikrishna Commission report,[125] calling it anti-majority community and pro-minority.[126]

A petition was filed in the Supreme Court seeking directions to implement the report. The court issued a notice to the Central government, asking it to respond.[127] Among other things, Justice Srikrishna had recommended that compensation be paid to riot victims' families, prosecutions be launched against errant policemen, and investigations in riot-related cases be reopened.[128] In the meantime, with a change in the ruling dispensation, the Congress–NCP (Nationalist Congress Party) coalition government in Maharashtra promised to enforce Justice Srikrishna's recommendations, but failed to do so.[129]

Then, the Deputy Chief Minister of Maharashtra, Chhagan Bhujbal, sanctioned the prosecution of Bal Thackeray under Section 153A of the Indian Penal Code (promoting enmity between different groups), a non-bailable offence.[130] The atmosphere in the state was tense. The police were worried that violence would break out if Thackeray were to be arrested.[131] Against this backdrop, Union Law Minister Ram Jethmalani spoke to the press and said that the threatened prosecution of Thackeray was 'much ado over nothing'[132] as it was a time-barred case[133] (i.e., the statutory period of limitation[134] for a court to take cognizance of a criminal case had expired). He even hinted that the Central government could dissolve the Maharashtra state legislature under Article 356 of the Constitution if the need arose.[135] In fact, it was Prime Minister Vajpayee himself who had asked Jethmalani to ensure that Thackeray was not arrested.[136] Another union minister defended Thackeray on television.[137]

As all this was going on, the Central government had filed an affidavit in the Supreme Court stating that it had nothing to do with the prosecution of Bal Thackeray since law and order was a state subject.

In its affidavit, the Central government had said that it therefore could not implement the findings of the Srikrishna Commission, conduct the prosecution or direct the state government to do so.[138]

When the case to implement the Srikrishna Commission report came up for hearing before the Supreme Court on 21 July 2000,[139] Chief Justice A.S. Anand was visibly upset. 'It is distressing', he said to Sorabjee, 'that comments are made by cabinet ministers while a petition seeking implementation of the commission's report is pending before the highest court of the land.'[140] The judge was particularly upset over how the government had said one thing in its affidavit in court, but the ministers had said something entirely different in the press. 'Is there something like collective responsibility or not?', Chief Justice Anand asked,[141] adding: 'Is [this] the way to run a civilised government? Telling the court something and playing to the gallery by saying something else to the public . . .'[142]

Sorabjee said nothing in defence of the two ministers.[143] He was absolutely right to have done so. The ministers were wrong to have contradicted their own government's affidavit filed in the Supreme Court. Sorabjee told the court that he shared the court's concern over what the ministers had said.[144] Ram Jethmalani, however, reacted sharply.[145] 'The learned Chief Justice should at least have realised', he said to the press, 'that he was making comments about a minister who knows his law as well as anyone else.'[146] He wished that the Chief Justice had asked him for an explanation over his comments. He had not expressed any opinion on the Srikrishna Commission report, said Jethmalani, but only pointed out what the 'correct legal position' was 'as a citizen, as an experienced lawyer and as the minister of law and justice'.[147] He hinted that the other judges on the bench perhaps did not share Chief Justice Anand's views.[148]

Soon after making these comments, Jethmalani received a phone call from external affairs minister, Jaswant Singh, who told him that Prime Minister Vajpayee wanted him to resign.[149] He did so, and he was replaced by Arun Jaitley.[150] Livid over what had happened, Jethmalani gave interviews to the media and wrote a book in which he made several allegations against Sorabjee and Chief Justice Anand. In the book, which bore the title *Big Egos, Small Men*, Jethmalani crudely said of Sorabjee that he had been too cautious during the Emergency,[151] that he had been handpicked by Jayalalitha for the post of Attorney General with a view to getting her cases transferred,[152] that he had a 'cosy, quasi-paternal relationship' with Arun Jaitley[153] and that he had been conspiring to have Jethmalani removed from the law ministry.[154] Jethmalani was unhappy over the fact that Sorabjee had not stood up for him in court when Chief Justice Anand had said all those things about him.[155] He alleged that Prime Minister Vajpayee had picked 'a pliant attorney general' over a 'no-[nonsense] law minister.'[156]

Jethmalani pointed fingers at Sorabjee for giving an opinion to the Hinduja brothers despite being the Attorney General of India. One[157] of the Hinduja brothers was implicated in the Bofors scandal—in which a Swedish company, AB Bofors, was alleged to have paid kickbacks to top Indian politicians to secure a contract to sell weapons to the Indian army.[158] However, Sorabjee's opinion had nothing to do with the Bofors case. It concerned a power project that the Hindujas had set up in Andhra Pradesh.[159] Sorabjee had specifically taken permission from the union law minister to give that opinion.[160] Further, though it was being crassly hinted in the press that Sorabjee had received his fees in cash from the Hindujas for the opinion,[161] this was not true. Jethmalani admitted all of this in his own book. However, Jethmalani's grievance with Sorabjee's Hinduja opinion was that the decision to allow Sorabjee to give that opinion should have been taken by the entire cabinet, not just the law minister.[162] He also felt that the Attorney General should not have done any private work at all, especially when it was against the government.[163]

Sorabjee defended himself in the press and pointed out that Jethmalani had only raised all these grievances after being sacked as the law minister.[164] Having entered public life, Sorabjee added, he was prepared for criticism but not vilification.[165]

In the meantime, in July 2000, Bal Thackeray was arrested in connection with the case. When he was taken to the chief metropolitan magistrate, the judge threw out the entire case, saying that it was time-barred—the government had acted too late.[166] The Bombay High Court later agreed with this decision.[167] In 2020, the Supreme Court asked the Maharashtra government what steps it had taken to implement the Srikrishna Commission report.[168]

A few months after his war of words with Jethmalani, in October 2000, Sorabjee had a knee joint replacement surgery at Breach Candy Hospital in Mumbai, where he was operated upon by Dr Chitranjan S. Ranawat from the US. Dr Ranawat had also operated on Vajpayee, whom Sorabjee fondly called 'Atalji', earlier that day.[169] After Sorabjee's right knee had been fractured in the motorcycle accident in 1948, the fracture had not been set correctly, due to which the right knee bore more weight than the left.[170] The cartilage had worn off and the knee had developed osteoarthritis over the years.[171] L.K. Advani had come to see Vajpayee at the hospital and he dropped in to see how Sorabjee was doing as well.

. . .

Sorabjee's tenure as the Attorney General in the BJP-led coalition government, between 1998 and 2004,[172] was perhaps one of the most difficult and contentious phases of his career. Among 192 reported cases that carried his name during that period, 84 per cent were in the Supreme Court. He appeared in the High Courts (mostly in the Delhi High Court, but also in the Karnataka, Bombay, Andhra Pradesh, Madhya Pradesh and Madras High Courts) as the Attorney General for this government more often than he had as a law officer with the Janata or National Front governments. He did a fair amount of customs and excise work during this period as well—around 25 per cent of his cases were in this field of law.

Around 12 per cent of his cases as the Attorney General this time around were 'Constitution Bench' decisions—much lower than the proportion of Constitution Bench cases he had argued as a law officer with the Janata and National Front governments. The number of Constitution Benches which were set up by the Chief Justice of India remained around the same when he was a law officer in the three regimes. Between 1975 and 1979, 15 per cent of the Supreme Court's cases per year were decided by Constitution Benches. Between 2000 and 2004, the proportion of such benches was around the same, i.e., 14 per cent.[173] As the Attorney General for the BJP-led coalition government, Sorabjee clearly had to do a lot of the firefighting and could not devote himself exclusively to appearing in lengthy cases involving important questions of constitutional law.

That is not to say that Sorabjee had no significant cases in his tenure as the Attorney General this time around. During his term as the Attorney General, the Supreme Court decided a number of fascinating questions: How many judges should be a part of the 'collegium' (i.e., the body that decides which judges to appoint to constitutional courts in India)?[174] Should the Supreme Court issue directions banning cigarette smoking in public places?[175] Can writ petitions be filed against non-governmental bodies which discharge public functions?[176] Should prisoners be paid for their labour?[177] Should persons with disabilities be entitled to get concessional fares on Indian Airlines?[178] How must the government identify which educational institutions have 'minority' status?[179] Do lawyers have a right to strike?[180] Are the Prevention of Terrorism Act[181] and the Securitization act[182] constitutionally valid? These and many other questions were answered by the Supreme Court in cases in which Sorabjee appeared as the Attorney General during this time.

Once again, predictably, Sorabjee's win–loss ratio went up substantially when he became the Attorney General. As a private lawyer in the 1990s, Sorabjee won 51 per cent of his cases. As the Attorney General between 1998 and 2004, he won 69 per cent of his cases. Once again, this does not suggest that Sorabjee's advocacy skills improved as a law officer. Perhaps the government was a more responsible client than his private clients were and chose to contest only those cases where the odds of winning were greater. Perhaps as the Attorney General, Sorabjee had greater flexibility in deciding which cases to contest, and only picked those cases where the chances of winning were higher. Or perhaps courts in India tend to be more deferential towards the government, regardless of which dispensation is in power. After all, when a law is challenged in court, the court begins by presuming that the law is constitutionally valid, and it is for the petitioner to establish that it is not, even when violations of very important fundamental rights are involved.

On 8 January 1999, the post of Solicitor General of India fell vacant when the incumbent, Santosh Hegde, became a judge of the Supreme Court.[183] Law minister Ram Jethmalani initiated the appointment of his junior,[184] S.B. Jaisinghani, to the position[185]—the same lawyer who had appeared along with Jethmalani in the trial of Sanjay Gandhi in the *Kissa Kursi Ka* case and whom Sanjay Gandhi had arrogantly called a 'scoundrel' in open court. Sorabjee opposed the appointment as he wanted his own junior, the brilliant lawyer Harish Salve, to be appointed to the position, so that he could have a 'congenial team'.[186] In choosing Salve, Sorabjee rejected another outstanding lawyer from Bombay[187]— Iqbal Chagla, his colleague in the chambers of Kharshedji Bhabha and Chief Justice M.C. Chagla's son. Jaisinghani was eventually appointed as the Additional Solicitor General for India at the Bombay High Court.[188]

Over the years, however, a noticeable unpleasantness[189] began to develop between senior and junior, Sorabjee and Salve. In April 1999, Sorabjee had openly said that he wished to retire the following year at the age of 70 so that he could move to a hill station and read to his seven grandchildren.[190] However, Sorabjee never retired. Perhaps Salve was disappointed that Sorabjee did not keep his word, since Salve would

ABHINAV CHANDRACHUD   162

naturally have been the candidate to replace Sorabjee as the Attorney General. Thereafter, unlike Sorabjee's other juniors, Salve did not attend Sorabjee's birthday parties or respond to invitations for social events. Salve gave credit, for his rise in the profession, to Nani Palkhivala, and not to Sorabjee. This hurt Sorabjee, though he never admitted it. In public, however, Sorabjee maintained that Salve was one of his best juniors and that they were good friends at the Bar, though they may have disagreed on what line to adopt in some cases. In 2002, for instance, in the Minority Educational Institutions case, Sorabjee and Salve took contradictory positions in their arguments.[191] When Salve was asked about this, he reportedly said: 'I am arguing the case for the government of India and not for Sorabjee'.[192] Many years later, Salve delivered a touching tribute to Sorabjee at a prayer meeting held in Sorabjee's honor after Sorabjee passed away in 2021.

In 2002, another controversy erupted in the Ayodhya case when Sorabjee told the Supreme Court that allowing between 50 and 70[193] Hindu priests to perform a 3-hour-long prayer ceremony at the disputed land would not violate the Supreme Court's status quo order. Around 1,000 *kar sevaks* ought to be permitted to watch the ceremony from afar, in batches of 25, he had requested the court.[194] After a sharp exchange of views between the judges and Sorabjee, the court rejected his request.[195] Justice G.B. Pattanaik asked him whether the government would permit a prayer ceremony at Rashtrapati Bhavan as well. 'The Rashtrapati Bhavan belongs to you, so [does] the acquired land', the judge added.[196] 'This is not Rashtrapati Bhavan', Sorabjee replied. 'The object is not to rake up the past', he submitted. However, one of the judges then retorted, 'We cannot forget the past. We do not want to repeat the past.'[197] One of the judges also asked him: 'If you allow puja today, will you allow "namaz" there tomorrow?'[198]

Sorabjee's arguments in the Ayodhya case upset many of the coalition allies in the NDA government,[199] though BJP leaders like Vajpayee, Advani and Jaitley supported him.[200] Possibly to save the government some embarrassment and to ensure that the coalition does not break up because of what he had argued, Sorabjee informed news reporters that he had taken his own independent view in the Ayodhya case, and nobody in the government had given him instructions on what to argue.[201]

Sorabjee remained an internationally acclaimed jurist in his years as the Attorney General with the BJP-led coalition government. In 1998, as a UN Special Country Rapporteur,[202] Sorabjee visited Nigeria for 10 days in order to determine the extent of the human rights abuses that had taken place there.[203] The following year, he was appointed as a personal envoy to the UN High Commissioner for East Timor.[204] However, in 2001, as a member of the UN sub-commission on the prevention of discrimination, he opposed caste-based discrimination from being discussed at a UN conference on racism in South Africa.[205] He was awarded the Padma Vibhushan in 2002.[206] In 2003, Sorabjee wrote a letter to the government asking them to release Pakistani prisoners who had served out their sentences in India. Using them as 'hostages' or 'levers for bargaining', he wrote, was 'legally untenable'.[207]

12

The Sunset Years

Sorabjee's career graph tells a very interesting story. After finishing his fellowship at Government Law College in Bombay in 1953, his career went through ups and downs until 1968, when he got his own chamber. The following year, in 1969, Sorabjee featured in the highest number of reported cases that he had ever appeared in until then, i.e., 14 cases in a single year. The best, of course, was yet to come. There were four peaks in Sorabjee's career: when he became the additional solicitor general with the Janata government in 1977, when he practised as a private lawyer in the late 1980s, when he resumed his private practice in the 1990s after ceasing to be the Attorney General with the National Front government, and as the Attorney General of India with the BJP-led coalition government in 1998. In each of these four phases of his life, his career scaled impressive heights. For instance, in the year 1996, when Sorabjee was a private lawyer, his name appeared in a staggering 53 reported judgments in a single year—many lawyers will be content to appear in around 5 to 7 reported cases in a year.

After resigning as the Attorney General of India in May 2004[1] with the fall of the NDA government, the 74-year-old Sorabjee entered the final stages of his career. In terms of the volume of work he did, never again would he scale the same peaks that he had in his younger days.

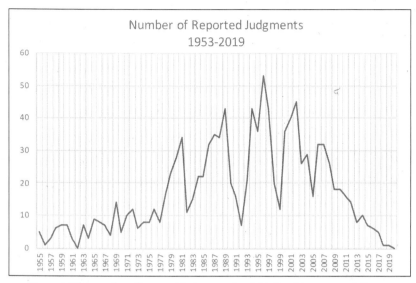

Figure 1: The number of reported judgments in which Sorabjee appeared between 1953 and 2019

However, he still did a fair amount of work. For instance, at the age of 76, in 2006, he appeared in 32 reported cases—more reported cases than he had appeared in during any single year from 1953 to 1980. However, after 2007, his work began to gradually decline. He was plagued by several health problems towards the end of his life—strokes, diabetes, prostate issues, paralyzed vocal chords, and respiratory failure.

In this final stage of his career, he appeared in the Supreme Court in 72 per cent of his cases, around the same proportion that he had appeared in as a private lawyer in the 1980s.

In the early stages of his career, Sorabjee appeared in a very high number of 'Constitution Bench' cases (i.e., cases decided by five or more judges of the Supreme Court, usually on an important point of law). For instance, between 1953 and 1975, around 48 per cent of Sorabjee's reported Supreme Court cases were decided by a 'Constitution Bench'. This tells us that when he ventured out of Bombay to appear in a case in Delhi (Sorabjee was staying in Bombay in those days), the case was often a very important one. However, as Sorabjee relocated his practice to Delhi and started appearing in the Supreme Court more often, the proportion of 'Constitution Bench' judgments that he participated in fell. As a law officer with the Janata government, 29.7 per cent of Sorabjee's cases in the Supreme Court were before a Constitution Bench. However, in his sunset years, Sorabjee appeared in a relatively smaller proportion (10 per cent) of Constitution Bench decisions, which was comparable with the proportion of such cases that he had appeared in as a private lawyer in the 1980s and 1990s.

Once again, that is not to say that Sorabjee appeared in only insignificant cases in his final years as a lawyer. Between 2004 and 2019, the Supreme Court decided fascinating questions in cases in which Sorabjee appeared: Can a writ petition under the Constitution be filed against the Board of Control for Cricket in India?[2] Can the members of the Parsi community be permitted to have a housing society exclusively for Parsis?[3] Can the government reserve seats in private minority and non-minority educational institutions?[4] Can the government totally ban the slaughter of cows and other cattle?[5] To what extent can a court review the decision of the President of India to dissolve state legislatures?[6] Under what circumstances can a court prevent an unconditional bank guarantee from being honoured?[7] Can a law which is inserted into the 9th schedule of the Constitution be challenged for violating the basic structure of the Constitution?[8] Is it considered hate speech for a historian to write a bona fide revisionist history of a beloved historical figure?[9] Must a suit to evict a gratuitous licensee be filed only in the Small Cause Court?[10] And perhaps most importantly—does the Constitution give us all a right to privacy?[11] The Supreme Court answered these and many other questions of enormous significance in cases in which Sorabjee appeared at this time.

However, in his sunset years, Sorabjee's career underwent one important change. Throughout his life, Sorabjee had done a substantial amount of customs and excise work. As a private lawyer in the 1980s, for instance, around 31.3 per cent of his practice consisted of customs and excise work. Even as the Attorney General between 1998 and

2004, around 25 per cent of Sorabjee's practice was in this field of law. However, after stepping down as the Attorney General in 2004, Sorabjee did less customs and excise work than he ever had in his life. Now, only 4.5 per cent of his practice was in this field of law. He now did a vast amount of work involving the interpretation of the Constitution.

Sorabjee was never heavily dependent on his Bombay connections in order to sustain his law practice in the Supreme Court. In his early years, between 1953 and 1975, around 52 per cent of Sorabjee's work in the Supreme Court involved an appeal which had been filed against a judgment delivered by a court in Bombay. However, as the years rolled on, his dependence on Bombay went down. As a law officer, he hardly had any appeals from Bombay. For instance, as the Attorney General with the National Front government, around 11 per cent of his Supreme Court cases were appeals from Bombay. In his sunset years, around 18 per cent of his Supreme Court appeals came from Bombay. In other words, his Bombay connections only gave him his initial foothold in the Supreme Court. Once his merit was recognized, cases came to him from all over the country and not from Bombay alone.

Sorabjee's win–loss record raises a very interesting question about the legal system in India. As a private lawyer (when he very rarely appeared for the government), Sorabjee won between 51 per cent and 59 per cent of the cases he contested—cases in which there was a clear, discernible winner and loser, not those in which the court passed a nuanced order which benefitted nobody or everybody. As a government lawyer (when he hardly did any private work), however, Sorabjee's proportion of cases won increased and ranged between 68 per cent and 70 per cent. Why is it that Sorabjee did better when he was a government lawyer as against when he was a private lawyer? Three possible answers have been offered in this book. Perhaps the Central government was more responsible than his private clients were, and only chose to contest those cases which were worth fighting. Perhaps Sorabjee had greater discretion in deciding to settle cases for the Central government which were not worth contesting than he did as a private lawyer. Or perhaps courts in India tend to be deferential towards the government, regardless of which political party is in power. As this book has repeatedly pointed out, in a case in which the constitutional validity of a law is challenged, the court will begin with the presumption that the law is constitutionally sound, regardless of the importance of the fundamental right which is at stake.

	Proportion of Supreme Court Cases Argued (%)	Constitution Bench Cases Participated in (%)	Sorabjee's Customs/ Excise Cases (%)	Bombay Appeals (%)	Cases Won (%)
Early Years (1953–75)	19	48	26.5	52.63	59.8
Emergency Years (1975–77)	31.6	33.3	42.11	20	56.3
ASG / SG, Janata Government (1977–80)	87.04	29.7	13	3.03	70.2
Private Lawyer (1980s)	73.51	9.6	31.3	21.67	54.7
Attorney General, National Front Government (1989–90)	92	21.7	21.74	11.8	68.4
Private Lawyer (1990s)	84.23	8	20.27	27.7	51.66
Attorney General, BJP Coalition (1998–2004)	84.9	12.2	25	13.48	69.6
Sunset Years (2004–2019)	72.07	10	4.5	18.48	58

Table 1: Sorabjee's career at a glance

In his sunset years, Sorabjee often gave quotes to the media on the latest legal happenings of the day. For instance, when Hollywood actress Angelina Jolie's bodyguards were arrested in 2006 for allegedly saying 'bloody Indians', Sorabjee told the *Times of India* that though their words were uttered 'in very bad taste', 'much should not be made of this incident' as they had committed, at the most, a minor bailable offence.[12] The following year, when a court in India found that the Hollywood actor, Richard Gere, had kissed a Bollywood actress on her cheek in a 'sexually erotic' manner in full public view, Sorabjee opined that the court's pronouncement was reminiscent of the 'Taliban moral police'.[13] In 2006, Sorabjee headed a government panel to reform the police administration in the country.[14] When the terror attack took place in Mumbai in 2008, Sorabjee filed a PIL in the Supreme Court, seeking directions to have the Central government arm and train police officers in Mumbai.[15] In 2009, after a 40-year-old legal battle, the Sorabjee family lost the porch and lawn of their ancestral home in Mumbai, Hill Side Villa in Nepean Sea Road, to a road-widening project.[16] The longstanding rivalry between Sorabjee and his colleague in Kharshedji's chamber, Fali Nariman, dissolved into friendship soon thereafter.[17] For many years, Sorabjee was the president of his beloved India International Centre in Delhi (IIC), where he would often be seen having lunch. During his term as the president, IIC took the controversial decision of denying membership to the politician Lalu Prasad Yadav.[18] For many years after resigning as the Attorney General, Sorabjee regularly wrote his column 'Soli Loquies' in the *Indian Express*. He remained an internationally renowned figure. He was a life president of the Commonwealth Lawyers Association, and in 2006, Sorabjee was appointed an honorary member in the General Division of the Order of Australia.

On 30 April 2021, Sorabjee succumbed to Covid-19. Many years before, when he was asked what he would like to be remembered for, he said two things in particular. The assistance that he gave 'to victims of the spurious 1975 Emergency to retrieve and preserve their freedoms when they were abandoned by others' and the 'training and encouragement' that he had given 'to the juniors in my chambers, who have made their mark in the profession'.[19] Several members of the Sorabjee chamber went on to become giants in the legal profession: Harish Salve, Gopal Subramanium, Justice U.U. Lalit, and many others. The poet Percy Shelley once wrote that 'music, when soft voices die, vibrates in the memory'. Despite his few shortcomings and human failings, Sorabjee's powerfully independent voice—the voice of reason, the voice of liberty, the voice of balance, the voice of the rule of law, never its client's mouthpiece—will forever resonate in the corridors of India's courts and in public life.

Appendix

EXCERPTS FROM SOLI SORABJEE'S FAVOURITE POEMS AND QUOTES

In the columns he wrote in the *Times of India* and the *Indian Express*, Sorabjee often fondly recalled the lines which have been reproduced below. Apart from jazz, poetry was Sorabjee's 'constant and most dependable companion(. . .).'[1] Sorabjee had wished to put together a dictionary of quotations.[2]

If I can stop one heart from breaking
I shall not live in vain
If I can ease one life the aching
Or cool one pain
Or help one fainting robin
Unto his nest again
I shall not live in vain.[3]

—Emily Dickinson

When, in disgrace with fortune and men's eyes,
I all alone beweep my outcaste state,
. . .
Haply I think on thee, and then my state,
(Like to the lark at break of day arising
From sullen earth) sings hymns at heaven's gate;
For thy sweet love remember'd such wealth brings
That then I scorn to change my state with kings.[4]

     —William Shakespeare, 'Sonnet 29'

Love some one—in God's name
love some one—for this is
the bread of the inner life, without
which a part of you will
starve and die; and though you
feel you must be stern,
even hard, in your life of affairs,
make for yourself at least
a little corner, somewhere in the
great world, where you may
unbosom and be kind.[5]

    —Max Ehrmann, 'Love Some One'

Let me not to the marriage of true minds
Admit impediments. Love is not love
Which alters when it alteration finds,
Or bends with the remover to remove.
O no! it is an ever-fixed mark
That looks on tempests and is never shaken;

    —William Shakespeare, 'Sonnet 116'

My name is Ozymandias, King of Kings;
Look on my Works, ye Mighty, and despair!

Nothing beside remains. Round the decay
Of that colossal Wreck, boundless and bare
The lone and level sands stretch far away.[6]

—P.B. Shelley, 'Ozymandias'

What is this life if, full of care,
We have no time to stand and stare.

. . .

A poor life this if, full of care,
We have no time to stand and stare.[7]

—W.H. Davies, 'Leisure'

From quiet homes and first beginning,
Out to the undiscovered ends,
There's nothing worth the wear of winning,
But laughter and the love of friends.[8]

—Hilaire Belloc, 'Dedicatory Ode'

For who would bear the whips and scorns of time,
The oppressor's wrong, the proud man's contumely,
The pangs of despised love, the law's delay,
The insolence of office and the spurns,
That patient merit of the unworthy takes,
When he himself might his quietus make
With a bare bodkin?[9]

—William Shakespeare, *Hamlet*

The first and indispensable requisite of happiness is [a] clear conscience,
unsullied by the reproach or remembrance of an unworthy action.[10]

—Edward Gibbon

All great poetry is dipped in the dyes of the heart.[11]

—Edith Sitwell

A map of the world that does not include Utopia is not worth even glancing at, for it leaves out the one country at which Humanity is always landing . . . Progress is the realisation of Utopias.[12]

—Oscar Wilde, 'The Soul Of Man Under Socialism'

'Question not, but live and labour
Till yon goal be won,
Helping every feeble neighbour,
Seeking help from none;
Life is mostly froth and bubble,
Two things stand like stone,
Kindness in another's trouble,
Courage in your own.'[13]

—Adam Lindsay Gordon, 'Ye Wearie Wayfarer'

Whither is fled the visionary gleam?
Where is it now, the glory and the dream?[14]

—William Wordsworth, 'Ode: Intimations of
Immortality from Recollections of Early Childhood'

Those who apply themselves too much to little things often become incapable of great ones.[15]

—Francois de La Rochefoucauld

'When I use a word,' Humpty Dumpty said, in rather a scornful tone, 'it means just what I choose it to mean, neither more nor less.'

'The question is,' said Alice, 'whether you *can* make words mean so many different things.'

'The question is,' said Humpty Dumpty, 'which is to be master—that's all.'[16]

—Lewis Carroll, *Through the Looking-Glass*

A man cannot always be estimated by what he does. He may keep the law, and yet be worthless. He may break the law, and yet be fine . . . There are as many perfections as there are imperfect men.[17]

—Oscar Wilde , 'The Soul Of Man Under Socialism'

Blow, blow, thou winter wind,
Thou are not so unkind
As man's ingratitude.[18]

—William Shakespeare, *As You Like It*

Oh sleep! It is a gentle thing
Beloved from pole to pole![19]

—Samuel Taylor Coleridge, 'The Rime of the Ancient Mariner'

There ain't no way to find out why a snorer can't hear himself snore.[20]

—Mark Twain

No man is an island entire of itself. Every man is a piece of the continent, part of the main . . . And therefore never send to know for whom the bell tolls; it tolls for thee.[21]

—John Donne, 'No Man Is an Island'

The unholy feast in which the West revels every moment, growing more and more bloated and red and dangerously delirious . . . Not for us this mad orgy of midnight, with lighted torches, but awakenment in the serene light of the morning.[22]

—Rabindranath Tagore

The road to hell is paved with good intentions.[23]

—Robert Lynd, 'The Book of This and That'

The exhaustion of passions is the beginning of wisdom.[24]

—James Hilton, *Lost Horizon*

Men fear silence as they fear solitude because both give them a glimpse of the terror of life's nothingness.[25]

—André Maurois

Silence is not merely an absence of noise. Real silence begins when a reasonable being withdraws from the noise in order to find peace and order in his inner sanctuary.[26]

—Peter Minard

Man is a moment in astronomic time, a transient guest of the earth, a spore of his species, a scion of his race.[27]

—Will and Ariel Durant, *The Lessons of History*

The purity of language is defiled, the meanings have turned traitor in the night.[28]

—Anonymous

Give me a kiss, and to that kiss a score ;
Then to that twenty add a hundred more :
A thousand to that hundred : so kiss on,[29]

—Robert Herrick, 'To Anthea'

[A] kiss's strength, I think, it must be reckoned by its length.[30]

—Lord Byron, 'Love on the Island', *Don Juan*

Logicians have but ill defined as rational the human mind.[31]

—Oliver Goldsmith

Think twice before you open your mouth.[32]

> —Father Bonet (Sorabjee's professor at St Xavier's)

Recession is worse than a divorce. You lose half your fortune and still have your wife.[33]

> —Anonymous

The difference between communism and capitalism is that in communism we nationalise the banks and then push them to bankruptcy. In capitalism we push the banks to bankruptcy and then nationalise them.[34]

> —Anonymous

We look before and after,
and pine for what is not.[35]

> —P.B. Shelley, 'To a Skylark'

[The assessment of judges by lawyers]: If a judge decides in their favour, he is a good judge. If against them, he is a bad judge or he has an off day.[36]

> —Lord Denning

The unexamined life is not worth living.[37]

> —Socrates

And not by eastern windows only
When daylight comes, comes in the light;
In front the sun climbs slow, how slowly!
But westward, look, the land is bright![38]

> —Arthur Hugh Clough, 'Say not the Struggle nought Availeth'

Good fences make good neighbours.[39]

> —Robert Frost, 'Mending Wall'

Glad to meet you as the gentleman said to the five pound note.[40]
> —Charles Dickens, *Pickwick Papers* (Sam Weller's unusual simile)

Quite enough to get, Sir, as the soldier said when they ordered him 350 lashes.[41]
> —Charles Dickens, *Pickwick Papers* (Sam Weller's unusual simile)

What's in a name?
That which we call a rose,
By any other name would smell as sweet.[42]
> —William Shakespeare, *Romeo and Juliet*

Our dreams are tales
Told in dim Eden
By Eve's nightingales.[43]
> —Walter de la Mare, 'All That's Past'

Time present and time past
Are both perhaps present in time future,
And time future contained in time past.
If all time is eternally present
All time is unredeemable.[44]
> —T.S. Eliot, *Four Quartets* (Burnt Norton)

Taking a leaf out of the prayer of Saint Francis of Assisi,
let our New Year resolution be to sow love where there is hatred;
to pardon where there is injury;
to kindle hope where there is despair;
to spread joy where there is sadness and to strive ceaselessly for peace and harmony.[45]
> —Soli Sorabjee

Sweet sounds, oh, beautiful music, do not cease!
Reject me not into the world again.
With you alone is excellence and peace,
Mankind made plausible, his purpose plain.[46]
> —Edna Millay, 'On hearing a Symphony of Beethoven'

My friend, you would not tell with such high zest
To children ardent for some desperate glory,
The old Lie: Dulce et decorum est
Pro patria mori[47]
['It is sweet and fitting to die for one's country.'[48]]
> —Wilfred Owen, 'Dulce et Decorum Est'

The English have lost sight of the fact that poetry exists to speak the spiritual law.[49]
> —Ralph Waldo Emerson

Let us be crowned with roses,
let us drink wine,
and break up the tiresome old roof of heaven into new forms.[50]
> —Hafiz

This above all:
to thine own self be true,
And it must follow as the night the day,
Thou canst not then be false to any man.[51]
> —William Shakespeare, *Hamlet*

Hath not a Jew hands, organs, dimensions, senses, affections, passions? Fed with the same food, hurt with the same weapons . . . if you prick us, do we not bleed? If you tickle us, do we not laugh? If you poison us, do we not die?[52]
> —William Shakespeare, *The Merchant of Venice* (Shylock)

Once sent out a word takes wing irrevocably.[53]

—Horace

The most important thing we do is not doing.[54]

—Louis D. Brandeis

If you can wait and not be tired by waiting,
Or, being lied about, don't deal in lies,
Or being hated don't give way to hating,
And yet don't look too good, nor talk too wise.[55]

—Rudyard Kipling, 'If'

None shall be turned away
From the shore of this vast sea of humanity
That is India.[56]

—Rabindranath Tagore

The boast of heraldry, the pomp of [power],
And all that beauty, all that wealth [ever] gave,
Awaits alike [the] inevitable hour.
The paths of glory lead but to the grave.[57]

—Thomas Gray, 'Elegy Written in a Country Churchyard'

Only the actions of the just
Smell sweet and blossom in their dust.[58]

—James Shirley

Shut up in a lonely mansion, with police night and day
Patrolling the gardens to keep assassins away,
He got down to work, to the task of settling the fate
Of millions. The maps at his disposal were out of date
And the Census Returns almost certainly incorrect,

But there was no time to check them, no time to inspect
Contested areas. The weather was frightfully hot,
And a bout of dysentery kept him constantly on the trot,
But in seven weeks it was done, the frontiers decided,
A continent for better or worse divided.
The next day he sailed for England, where he quickly forgot
The case, as a good lawyer must. Return he would not,
Afraid, as he told his Club, that he might get shot.[59]

      —W.H. Auden, *Partition* (On Cyril Radcliffe)

Hogamous, higamous
Man is polygamous
Higamous, hogamous
Woman monogamous.[60]

           —William James

Just as fish moving under water cannot possibly be found out either as
drinking or not drinking water, so government servants cannot be found
out while taking money for themselves.[61]

         —Kautilya, *Arthashastra*

Words strain,
Crack and sometimes break, under the burden,
Under the tension, slip, slide, perish,
Decay with imprecision, will not stay in place,
Will not stay still . . .
So here I am, in the middle way, having had twenty years . . .
Trying to learn to use words, and every attempt
Is a wholly new start, and a different kind of failure
Because one has only learnt to get the better of words
For the thing one no longer has to say, or the way in which
One is no longer disposed to say it.[62]

      —T.S. Eliot, *Four Quartets*, East Coker

Then felt I like some watcher of the skies
When a new planet swims into his ken;
Or like stout Cortez when with eagle eyes
He star'd at the Pacific—and all his men
Look'd at each other with a wild surmise—
Silent, upon a peak in Darien.[63]

　　　　　　—John Keats, 'On First Looking Into Chapman's Homer'

Water, water, every where,
And all the boards did shrink;
Water, water, every where,
Nor any drop to drink.[64]

　　　　　　—Samuel Taylor Coleridge, 'The Rime of the Ancient Mariner'

The violin after the organ is tackled
the flute, oboe and trumpet too,
the gamba follows along in the bass,
only with here and there a trill.
No, no, it is not enough
that the notes just sound
that you know only how to take your wares
to market.
Give each instrument
what it can bear,
so the player has pleasure
and you have enjoyment from it.[65]

　　　　　　—Georg Philipp Telemann

The dead keep their secrets, and in a while we shall be as wise as they—
and as taciturn.[66]

　　　　　　—Alexander Smith, *Dreamthorp*

I am not resigned to the shutting away of loving hearts in the hard ground.
So it is, and so it will be, for so it has been, time out of mind:
Into the darkness they go, the wise and the lovely. Crowned
With lilies and with laurel they go; but I am not resigned.[67]

—Edna St. Vincent Millay, 'Dirge Without Music'

Yet many a man is making friends with death
Even as I speak, for lack of love alone[68]

—Edna St. Vincent Millay, 'Love Is Not All'

Acknowledgements

I owe an immense debt of gratitude to the Sorabjee family, without whom this book could never have been written. Many thanks to Zena, Zia, Jehangir and Hormazd for speaking to me in connection with this book. I benefitted a great deal from insights offered by my senior, Darius Khambata, to whom I am deeply grateful. Thank you, Avinash Rana, Obed Chinoy, Varun Bhabha, Jimmy Avasia, Upendra Baxi, Nisha Bagchi, Shridhar Mama, Sibobey Sagar, and Ujwal Rana for speaking to me in connection with this book. Thank you, Uma Narayan, Chetan Arora, Fernan Restrepo, Unnati Ghia, and Pranit Kulkarni for providing reading materials to me for this book. I am grateful to Vaidehi Thakar and the *Indian Express* for giving me their archive of Sorabjee's articles. Thanks are due to Saanchi Dhulla, Rhea Rao, and Ameya Pratap Singh for giving me access to the archives of the Government Law College Magazine and St Xavier's College Magazine. I owe an intellectual debt to professor Leandra Zarnow, whose course at Stanford University in 2013, 'History Through a Life: The Allure of American Biography', taught me a great deal. Saanchi Dhulla was very kind to proofread the manuscript and spot errors. Thank you Meru and Premanka for the faith that you have shown in me and my writing. Lastly, many thanks to my family—Aai, Baba, Dad, and Kalpana.

Notes

Chapter 1: The Last Soliloquy

1 See Soli Sorabjee, 'Repression in Myanmar', *Indian Express*, 30 September 2007, page 7; Soli Sorabjee, 'Memories of the First Independence Day', *Indian Express*, 16 August 2009, page 9; Soli J. Sorabjee, 'In Nehru's Judgment', *Times of India*, 30 April 1989, page A1.

2 Soli J. Sorabjee, 'Intolerance, Auden and Names', *Times of India*, 7 May 1998, page 11.

3 Soli Sorabjee, 'New Year Literary Musings', *Indian Express*, 1 January 2006, page 6; Soli Sorabjee, 'Favourite Poems', *Indian Express*, 12 October 2003, page 7. Sorabjee used the word 'despised' instead of 'disprized' in Hamlet's soliloquy. See Cedric Watts (ed.), *Hamlet: William Shakespeare* (Hertfordshire: Wordsworth Classics, 2002 edition), page 87.

4 Soli Sorabjee, 'Conventional Lies', *Indian Express*, 18 January 2004, page 7.

5 Ibid.

6 Readers must, therefore, recognize the shortcomings of the source material. In this book, history has been recreated by relying partly on newspaper articles. Readers must go through the endnotes and understand that relying on newspaper reports has its limitations as newspaper reports may contain inaccuracies.

7 I used various permutations and combinations in order to find these cases, looking for the following key words: 'Sorabjee', 'Soli J. Sorabji', 'Soli Sorabji', 'S.J. Sorabji', 'Soli Sohrabjee', 'Soli Sohrabji', 'Soli J. Sohrabji', 'S.J. Sohrabji'. Towards the later years, I had to exclude cases in which one F. Sorabjee appeared.

8 Soli J. Sorabjee, 'Affirmative Action & Views of Attorneys General', *Times of India*, 27 October 2002, page 8.

Chapter 2: Hormasjee Sorabjee & Sons

1 This name was spelled differently in various sources, e.g., as 'Horm*a*sjee' (with an 'a'), 'Horm*u*sjee' (with a 'u'), or 'Hormasj*i*' (with an 'i'). The name Sorabjee was often spelled as either 'Sorabji' or 'Sorabjee'. Here, the spelling 'Hormasjee Sorabjee' has been uniformly used for the sake of consistency.

2 'Death of Mr. Hormasji Sorabji', *Times of India*, 18 May 1931, page 4.

3 'The Late Cummoo Sulliman's Property in Dispute', *Times of India*, 5 February 1889, page 3; 'Obituary', *Times of India*, 25 May 1886, page 4.

4 'Obituary', *Times of India*, 25 May 1886, page 4.

5 'The Late Cummoo Sulliman's Property in Dispute', *Times of India*, 5 February 1889, page 3.

6 See 'Turkish Compassionate Fund', *Times of India*, 9 March 1880, page 2.

7 'Classified Ad 1', *Times of India*, 13 August 1861, page 1.

8 Ibid.

9 'Classified Ad 1', *Times of India*, 6 June 1872, page 1.

10 'Classified Ad 3', *Times of India*, 15 February 1872, page 4; 'Bombay Races', *Times of India*, 4 March 1872, page 3; 'Bombay Races', *Times of India*, 4 March 1874, page 3; 'Bombay Races, 1876', *Times of India*, 14 February 1876, page 3; 'Bombay Races, 1877', *Times of India*, 12 February 1877, page 3.

11 'Bombay Races, 1871', *Times of India*, 7 March 1871, page 2.

12 'Classified Ad 1', *Times of India*, 27 March 1872, page 1.

13 'Classified Ad 1', *Times of India*, 6 June 1872, page 1.

14 'Obituary', *Times of India*, 25 May 1886, page 4.

15 'New Dharamsalas in Cutch', *Times of India*, 5 June 1885, page 5.

16 'Medical Women for India Fund', *Times of India*, 10 December 1883, page 6. See further 'Mr. Kittredge on the Medical Women for India Fund', *Times of India*, 2 May 1889, page 5.

17 'Women Doctors for the Women of India', *Times of India*, 31 March 1885, page 8 (quoting from the speech of Justice Scott).

18 Ibid.

19 Ibid.

20 'Opening of the Jaffer Sulliman Dispensary', *Times of India*, 30 March 1886, page 5.

21 Pestonji Cama & Albless Hospital & Jaffer Suleman Dispensary. See http://www.camahospital.org/ (last visited 9 July 2021).

22 Pestonjee Cama, who donated the sum of Rs 1,69,000. 'Women Doctors for the Women of India', *Times of India*, 31 March 1885, page 8 (quoting from the speech of Justice Scott).

23 'Obituary', *Times of India*, 25 May 1886, page 4; 'Article 14 – No Title', *Times of India*, 27 March 1878, page 3.

24 'Bombay Corporation: Municipal Address to the Viceroy', *Times of India*, 13 December 1876, page 3.

25 'Meeting of Justices of the Peace', *Times of India*, 14 May 1881, page 3.

26 'Obituary', *Times of India*, 25 May 1886, page 4; 'The Late Cummoo Sulliman's Property in Dispute', *Times of India*, 5 February 1889, page 3.

27 'Death of Mr. Hormasji Sorabji', *Times of India*, 18 May 1931, page 4.

28 See 'Cummoo Suleman's Charities', *Times of India*, 19 December 1913, page 7.

29 'Classified Ad 7', *Times of India*, 6 April 1889, page 2.

30 'Death of Mr. Hormasji Sorabji', *Times of India*, 18 May 1931, page 4.

31 'Classified Ad 9', *Times of India*, 15 October 1900, page 3.

32 Letter from Charles Sargent to Hormasjee Sorabjee dated 2 May 1894, Sorabjee family archive.

33 Letter from E.C.K. Ollivant to Hormasjee Sorabjee dated 27 June 1892. At the time, Ollivant was the Political Agent and Collector of Stamp Revenue in Kathiawar. 'Sir Charles Ollivant', *Times of India*, 25 April 1902, page 4.

34   National Bank of India Ltd. passbook, December 1890–January 1891, Sorabjee family archive.

35   See 'Bombay High Court: Litigation over Durbar Tents', *Times of India*, 25 September 1906, page 5; 'Litigation over Durbar Tents', *Times of India*, 26 September 1906, page 10.

36   'The Ichhapur Relief Fund', *Times of India*, 24 April 1888, page 5.

37   'The Ichhapur Relief Fund', *Times of India*, 19 April 1888, page 3.

38   See Lieutenant Colonel W.B. Bannerman, *Plague in India, Past and Present: A Contrast*, 16 August 1910, available at: https://archive.org/details/b22432073/mode/2up/search/%22plague+in+india%22?q=%22plague+in+india%22 (last visited 20 March 2020), at page 6; J.M. Eager, *The Present Pandemic of Plague* (Washington: Government Printing Office, 1908), available at: https://archive.org/details/presentpandemico00unit/page/n3/mode/2up/search/%22plague+in+india%22?q=%22plague+in+india%22 (last visited 20 March 2020), at pages 16–17.

39   'Death of Mr. Hormasji Sorabji', *Times of India*, 18 May 1931, page 4.

40   Ibid.

41   'His Highness the Nizam', *Times of India*, 27 January 1903, page 4.

42   'Classified Ad 11', *Times of India*, 27 February 1902, page 2.

43   Hormasjee Sorabjee had four children: Mehra (a daughter who pre-deceased Hormasjee), Jehangir (Sorabjee's father), Behram (who also pre-deceased Hormasjee), and Maneck. Maneck later became insolvent. See 'Public Notices', *Times of India*, 22 June 1942, page 10.

44   'Classified Ad 11', *Times of India*, 27 February 1902, page 2.

45   Preeti Chopra, *The City and Its Fragments: Colonial Bombay, 1854–1918* (DPhil dissertation, University of California, Berkeley, Fall 2003) page 487.

46   'Classified Ad 18', *Times of India*, 29 February 1908, page 16.

47   'Special Short Advts.', *Times of India*, 9 April 1909, page 4.

48   'The Health Camp Fire Fund', *Times of India*, 29 May 1908, page 8.

49   'Classified Ad 12', *Times of India*, 18 February 1911, page 5.

50   'Indian Industries & Power: Incorporating "Indian Motor News"', vol. 7, September 1909–August 1910, page xxxviii, available at: https://

www.google.co.in/books/edition/Indian_Industries_and_Power/ cJQ7AQAAMAAJ?hl=en&gbpv=0 (last visited 10 May 2021).

51 'Classified Ad 3', *Times of India*, 18 August 1917, page 4.

52 *Bombay Chronicle*, 14 June 1920, page 16.

53 'Classified Ad 21', *Times of India*, 3 June 1930, page 2.

54 'Display Ad 7', *Times of India*, 15 August 1925, page 16.

55 'Classified Ad 16', *Times of India*, 10 April 1916, page 3.

56 'Classified Advts.', *Times of India*, 22 April 1929, page 4.

57 See 'Ralph Mulford', website of the Vanderbilt Cup Races, available at: https://www.vanderbiltcupraces.com/drivers/bio/ralph_mulford (last visited 2 November 2021).

58 'Death of Mr. Hormasji Sorabji', *Times of India*, 18 May 1931, page 4.

59 'Classified Ad 18', *Times of India*, 7 April 1927, page 2.

60 'Death of Mr. Hormasji Sorabji', *Times of India*, 18 May 1931, page 4.

61 'Classified Ad 24', *Times of India*, 17 October 1936, page 3.

62 See 'Classified Ad 20', *Times of India*, 18 October 1935, page 2.

63 See 'Death of Mr. Hormasji Sorabji', *Times of India*, 18 May 1931, page 4.

64 'Classified Ad 40', *Times of India*, 20 October 1938, page 2.

65 See 'Other Courts', *Times of India*, 11 December 1908, page 7; 'The Late Mr. G.I. Griffiths', *Times of India*, 2 October 1935, page 6.

66 'Governor Entertained by Honorary Presidency Magistrates', *Times of India*, 14 November 1928, page 10.

67 'Toute-de-Suite Annexes the Shri Shivaji Commemoration Cup', *Times of India*, 10 April 1935, page 5.

68 'Colombo Races', *Times of India*, 7 August 1935, page 13.

69 'Company Meetings', *Times of India*, 18 March 1921, page 7.

70 'Company Meetings', *Times of India*, 4 September 1924, page 5.

71 Andrew Yule & Co. v. Ardeshir Bomenji Dubash, (1913) SCC Online Bom 44.

72 A firm called A.M. Jivanji and Company claimed to be a mortgagee of the vessel. It filed a suit in the Bombay High Court against the owner of the vessel and obtained a consent decree allowing them to sell the ship.

73 'Bombay Law Courts', *Times of India*, 18 January 1913, page 10; 'Bombay Law Courts', *Times of India*, 26 March 1913, page 8; 'Bombay Law

Courts', *Times of India*, 23 September 1913, page 10; 'Appellate Court', *Times of India*, 3 October 1913, page 5; 'Bombay Law Courts', *Times of India*, 11 October 1913, page 7; 'Bombay Law Courts', *Times of India*, 31 March 1914, page 5.

74 Abhinav Chandrachud, *An Independent, Colonial Judiciary: A History of the Bombay High Court During the British Raj, 1862–1947* (New Delhi: Oxford University Press, 2015), page 103.

75 See 'I.N.A. Court Martial At Delhi', *Times of India*, 8 November 1945, page 1; 'I.N.A. Officers on Trial', *Times of India*, 6 November 1945, page 1.

76 See 'Inauguration of the Frontier Mail', *Times of India*, 3 September 1928, page 12.

77 Soli Sorabjee, 'Varying Eccentricities', *Indian Express*, 29 August 2004, page 6.

78 'Sport East and West', *Times of India*, 2 September 1903, page 5.

79 See 'Viceroy at Races', *Times of India*, 23 January 1939, page 9.

80 'Death of Mr. Hormasji Sorabji', *Times of India*, 18 May 1931, page 4.

81 See 'Sporting News', *Times of India*, 14 February 1907, page 9; 'Viceroy at Races', *Times of India*, 23 January 1939, page 9.

82 'Bombay Race-Course: Question of Lease to Turf Club', *Times of India*, 11 June 1913, page 5.

83 See 'Bombay Race-Course', *Times of India*, 10 December 1913, page 5.

84 'Success of Photo-Finish Camera at Mahalaxmi', *Times of India*, 6 November 1949, page 5.

85 See 'Dress at the Races', *Times of India*, 21 December 1903, page 5; 'Seen on the Racecourse at Poona', *Times of India*, 4 September 1934, page 15; 'Fashion on the Racecourse', *Times of India*, 6 August 1935, page 13; 'Fashions at the Racecourse', *Times of India*, 19 November 1935, page 12; 'Fashion on the Racecourse', *Times of India*, 4 February 1936, page 13; 'Frocks on the Bombay Racecourse', *Times of India*, 3 March 1936, page 14; 'Little Jackets on the Racecourse', *Times of India*, 30 August 1937, page 12; 'Fashion on the Racecourse', *Times of India*, 27 December 1938, page 18; 'Fashion on the Poona Racecourse', *Times of India*, 19 September 1938, page 13.

86 See 'Huge Attendance at Poona on Governor's Cup Day', *Times of India*, 23 September 1935, page 12.

87 See 'Kolhapur Races', *Times of India*, 29 October 1923, page 15.

88 See 'Prospectus–Ahmednuggur Sky Races', *Times of India*, 8 July 1885, page 3.

89 See 'Mahableshwur Gymkhana Races', *Times of India*, 15 May 1886, page 4.

90 'Race Specials from Poona to Bombay', *Times of India*, 14 November 1931, page 17.

91 'Race Course Pick-Pockets', *Times of India*, 1 September 1923, page 15; 'Alleged Pickpocket on Poona Racecourse', *Times of India*, 5 August 1930, page 3.

92 'Thefts on the Bombay Race Course', *Times of India*, 1 February 1927, page 4; 'Alleged Cheating on Racecourse', *Times of India*, 3 March 1936, page 7.

93 See 'Taking Bets on the Race Course', *Times of India*, 19 December 1928, page 8.

94 See 'Racing: The Bombay Edict', *Times of India*, 1 July 1911, page 7; 'Racing in Bombay', *Times of India*, 22 August 1911, page 6; 'The Turf and the "Ring"', *Times of India*, 6 June 1911, page 6; 'The Stewards and the Turf', *Times of India*, 5 July 1911, page 6; 'Racing in Bombay', *Times of India*, 8 September 1911, page 7; 'Racing in Bombay', *Times of India*, 21 September 1911, page 6; 'Bombay Council: The New Racing Bill', *Times of India*, 15 March 1912, page 7; 'Racing in Bombay', *Times of India*, 24 February 1912, page 8; 'Racing in Bombay: Licensing of Race-Courses', *Times of India*, 24 February 1912, page 9.

95 See 'Rules', *Times of India*, 15 November 1881, page 3; 'W.I.T.C.', *Times of India*, 18 June 1887, page 5; 'Racing in Bombay: Need for Reform', *Times of India*, 12 March 1912, page 7.

96 'Tote or Bookie', *Times of India*, 9 December 1926, page 7.

97 See 'Sporting News: Bombay Sixth Extra Race Meeting', *The Bombay Gazette*, 3 February 1913, available at: https://archive.org/details/dli.granth.22788/page/5/mode/2up?q=totalizator (last visited 2 November 2021).

98 See John I. Day, 'Horse Racing and the Pari-mutuel', *The Annals of the American Academy* (1950), vol. 269, from page 55 at pages 58–59; 'Pari-mutuel', *Encyclopaedia Britannica*, available at: https://www.britannica.com/topic/pari-mutuel (last visited 12 May 2021).

99 'Racing in England', *Times of India*, 29 October 1927, page 13.

100 John I. Day, 'Horse Racing and the Pari-mutuel', *The Annals of the American Academy* (1950), vol. 269, from page 55 at page 59.

101 See 'Racing in Bombay', *Times of India*, 24 June 1911, page 7.

102 See 'The Turf and the "Ring"', *Times of India*, 6 June 1911, page 6; 'Racing in Bombay', *Times of India*, 22 August 1911, page 6.

103 'The Racecourse: Abolition of Third Enclosure Urged', *Times of India*, 3 February 1925, page 10; 'Third Enclosure', *Times of India*, 11 July 1925, page 10; 'Bombay Racecourse', *Times of India*, 5 February 1934, page 12.

104 'Mr. Gandhi's Views on Racing', *Times of India*, 19 August 1946, page 9.

105 Soli J. Sorabjee, 'A diary's Entries and Some Exits', *Times of India*, 29 January 1996, page 11.

106 Sorabjee himself informed the author that the name of the horse was 'Yankee Doodle'. Interview with Soli Sorabjee dated 26 May 2018. However, his son, Jehangir, later informed the author that the name of the horse was 'Doodal Dandy'. Interview with Jehangir Sorabjee dated 12 November 2021. Incidentally, in 1943, there was an American film by the name of 'Yankee Doodle Dandy' which was playing at Metro cinema in Bombay. See 'On the Bombay Screens', *Times of India*, 5 March 1943, page 8.

107 Soli J. Sorabjee, 'A diary's Entries and Some Exits', *Times of India*, 29 January 1996, page 11. 'Neglected Horses Score on Final Day at Mahalaxmi', *Times of India*, 2 April 1945, page 9.

Chapter 3: Sorabjee, 'SJ'

1 'New High School', *Times of India*, 20 January 1916, page 9.

2 See 'The New High School', *Times of India*, 27 December 1890, page 4.

3 Ibid.

4 'Late Mr. Bharda', *Times of India*, 15 August 1921, page 5.

5 'The Late Mr. K.B. Marzban', *Times of India*, 11 August 1933, page 14. The earliest public reference to the Bharda New High School was in a classified advertisement carried in the *Times of India* in January 1922. 'Classified Ad 11', *Times of India*, 11 January 1922, page 4.

6 'Bombay Govt. Gazette', *Times of India*, 23 September 1921, page 2.

7 *Cameos from the Plays of Shakespeare* (Bombay: J.B. Marzban and Co., 1909, 2nd edition); 'Books Received', *Times of India*, 13 October 1909, page 9; 'Shakespeare Selections', *Times of India*, 29 December 1909, page 11.

8 'Bombay Engagements', *Times of India*, 22 September 1922, page 3.

9 'Bombay Law Courts', *Times of India*, 26 November 1912, page 10.

10 'Bombay's New Justices of the Peace', *Times of India*, 21 March 1927, page 15.

11 'The Late Mr. K.B. Marzban', *Times of India*, 11 August 1933, page 14.

12 'Parsi Central Association: List of Office-Bearers', *Times of India*, 2 April 1924, page 7.

13 'Parsi Central Association', *Times of India*, 9 July 1919, page 7.

14 'The Late Mr. K.B. Marzban', *Times of India*, 11 August 1933, page 14.

15 Ibid.

16 See *Administration Report of the King Edward VII Memorial Hospital and the Seth Gordhandas Sunderdas Medical College for the year 1940–41* (Bombay: Municipal Printing Press, 1941?), page 14, available at: https://archive.org/details/b31833032/page/14/mode/2up?q=%22Bharda+New+High+School%22 (last visited 10 May 2021).

17 S.F. Markham, *A Report to the Sir Ratan Tata Trustees on Problems Affecting the Parsee Community* (Bombay: Commercial Printing Press, 1933), p. xi, available at: https://archive.org/details/dli.granth.91909/page/5/mode/2up?q=%22Bharda+New+High+School%22 (last visited 10 May 2021).

18 Ibid.

19 Ibid.

20 See 'Parsi', *Encyclopaedia Britannica*, available at: https://www.britannica.com/topic/Parsi (last visited 3 November 2021); Mitra Sharafi,

Law and Identity in Colonial South Asia: Parsi Legal Culture, 1772–1947 (Ranikhet: Permanent Black, 2014), pages 16–17; Ellen McDonald Gumperz, *English Education and Social Change in Late Nineteenth Century Bombay, 1858–1898* (PhD dissertation, University of California, Berkeley, 1965), page 200.

21 S.F. Markham, *A Report to the Sir Ratan Tata Trustees on Problems Affecting the Parsee Community* (Bombay: Commercial Printing Press, 1933), page 14, available at: https://archive.org/details/dli.granth.91909/page/5/mode/2up?q=%22Bharda+New+High+School%22 (last visited 10 May 2021).

22 Ellen McDonald Gumperz, *English Education and Social Change in Late Nineteenth Century Bombay, 1858–1898* (PhD dissertation, University of California, Berkeley, 1965), pages 200–201.

23 S.F. Markham, *A Report to the Sir Ratan Tata Trustees on Problems Affecting the Parsee Community* (Bombay: Commercial Printing Press, 1933), page 9, available at: https://archive.org/details/dli.granth.91909/page/5/mode/2up?q=%22Bharda+New+High+School%22 (last visited 10 May 2021).

24 Ellen McDonald Gumperz, *English Education and Social Change in Late Nineteenth Century Bombay, 1858–1898* (PhD dissertation, University of California, Berkeley, 1965), page 101.

25 Ibid.

26 S.F. Markham, *A Report to the Sir Ratan Tata Trustees on Problems Affecting the Parsee Community* (Bombay: Commercial Printing Press, 1933), page 22, available at: https://archive.org/details/dli.granth.91909/page/5/mode/2up?q=%22Bharda+New+High+School%22 (last visited 10 May 2021).

27 Ibid., page 19.

28 Ibid., page 19.

29 Sir Stanley Reed (ed.), *The Times of India Directory of Bombay (City & Presidency): 1937* (Bombay: Bennett, Coleman & Co. Ltd. 1938?), page 142, available at: https://archive.org/details/in.ernet.dli.2015.83757/page/n187/mode/2up?q=bharda (last visited 3 November 2021); 'New High School', *Times of India*, 20 January 1916, page 9.

30 See 'New High School', *Times of India*, 17 January 1916, page 6 (Bharda's speech).

31 See 'The New High School', *Times of India*, 27 December 1890, page 4.

32 'New High School', *Times of India*, 17 January 1916, page 6.

33 Ibid.

34 Ibid.

35 'New High School', *Times of India*, 20 January 1916, page 9.

36 Sir Stanley Reed (ed.), *The Times of India Directory of Bombay (City & Presidency): 1937* (Bombay: Bennett, Coleman & Co. Ltd., 1938?), page 142, available at: https://archive.org/details/in.ernet.dli.2015.83757/page/n187/mode/2up?q=bharda (last visited 3 November 2021).

37 'New High School', *Times of India*, 17 January 1916, page 6.

38 Sir Stanley Reed (ed.), *The Times of India Directory of Bombay (City & Presidency): 1937* (Bombay: Bennett, Coleman & Co. Ltd., 1938?), page 142, available at: https://archive.org/details/in.ernet.dli.2015.83757/page/n187/mode/2up?q=bharda (last visited 3 November 2021).

39 See *Administration Report of the King Edward VII Memorial Hospital and the Seth Gordhandas Sunderdas Medical College for the year 1940–41* (Bombay: Municipal Printing Press, 1941?), page 14, available at: https://archive.org/details/b31833032/page/14/mode/2up?q=%22Bharda+New+High+School%22 (last visited 10 May 2021).

40 S.F. Markham, *A Report to the Sir Ratan Tata Trustees on Problems Affecting the Parsee Community* (Bombay: Commercial Printing Press, 1933), pages 6–7, available at: https://archive.org/details/dli.granth.91909/page/5/mode/2up?q=%22Bharda+New+High+School%22 (last visited 10 May 2021).

41 'New High School', *Times of India*, 17 January 1916, page 6.

42 *Administration Report of the King Edward VII Memorial Hospital and the Seth Gordhandas Sunderdas Medical College for the year 1940–41* (Bombay: Municipal Printing Press, 1941?), page 14, available at: https://archive.org/details/b31833032/page/14/mode/2up?q=%22Bharda+New+High+School%22 (last visited 10 May 2021).

43 'The New High School', *Times of India*, 27 December 1890, page 4.

44 See Dewan Bahadur Manibhai Jasbhai, *A Memorandum on Our Vernaculars as Media of Elementary Instruction* (Bombay: Bombay Gazette Steam Printing Works, 1899), page 4 (available on Google Books). See further Austen John Roberts, *Education and Society in the Bombay Presidency 1840-58* (PhD dissertation, School of Oriental and African Studies, London, 1974), page 110, available at: https://eprints.soas.ac.uk/33959/ (last visited 3 November 2021); Ibid.; J.C. Powell-Price, 'The Present State of Indian Education', *Journal of the Royal Society of Arts*, p. 534 (1945), page 535; *Report of the Committee on University Reform* (1924–25), page 108, available at: https://archive.org/details/dli.granth.117745/page/1/mode/2up?q=%22Bharda+New+High+School%22 (last visited 10 May 2021), Ellen McDonald Gumperz, *English Education and Social Change in Late Nineteenth Century Bombay, 1858-1898* (PhD dissertation, University of California, Berkeley, 1965), pages 101–102.

45 'English in Schools', *Times of India*, 17 April 1912, page 5.

46 See *Report of the Committee on University Reform* (1924–25), page 106, available at: https://archive.org/details/dli.granth.117745/page/1/mode/2up?q=%22Bharda+New+High+School%22 (last visited 10 May 2021).

47 'Bombay Teachers' Association', *Times of India*, 24 April 1912, page 8.

48 'The Reception at St. Xavier's College', *Times of India*, 20 December 1884, page 6.

49 'The Roman Catholic College, Bombay', *Times of India*, 25 October 1869, page 3; 'Article 12', *Times of India*, 25 October 1869, page 3; 'Further Liberality of Cowasjee Jehangier, C.S.I.', *Times of India*, 15 November 1869, page 3; 'St. Xavier's College', *Times of India*, 11 July 1871, page 3; 'The Reception at St. Xavier's College', *Times of India*, 20 December 1884, page 6.

50 'St. Xavier's College', *Times of India*, 11 July 1871, page 3.

51 Preeti Chopra, *The City and Its Fragments: Colonial Bombay, 1854–1918* (DPhil dissertation, University of California, Berkeley, Fall 2003), pages 21, 54, 482.

52 'St. Xavier's School', *Times of India*, 28 November 1908, page 6.

53 'St. Xavier's School', *Times of India*, 1 December 1909, page 5.

54 'The Reception at St. Xavier's College', *Times of India*, 20 December 1884, page 6.

55 'St. Xavier's High School', *Times of India*, 14 February 1903, page 7.

56 Ibid.

57 'St. Xavier's High School', *Times of India*, 14 February 1903, page 7. See further 'Prize Distribution at St. Xavier's College', *Times of India*, 7 December 1886, page 3; 'Distribution of Prizes at the St. Xavier's College', *Times of India*, 2 December 1891, page 3.

58 'Cosmopolitanism in Schools', *Times of India*, 24 April 1937, page 16.

59 'St. Xavier's School', *Times of India*, 28 November 1908, page 6.

60 'Prize Distribution at St. Xavier's College', *Times of India*, 7 December 1886, page 3.

61 'St. Xavier's School', *Times of India*, 24 April 1928, page 5.

62 'Prize Distribution at St. Xavier's College', *Times of India*, 29 November 1895, page 6.

63 Soli Sorabjee, 'Cricket Blues', *Indian Express*, 15 April 2007, page 7.

64 'Death of the Rev. Father J.A. Willy, S.J.', *Times of India*, 24 April 1897, page 6.

65 'St. Xavier's School, Bombay', *Times of India*, 30 November 1905, page 6.

66 'Prize Distribution at St. Xavier's College', *Times of India*, 29 November 1895, page 6.

67 See 'The German Fathers', *Times of India*, 8 December 1914, page 5.

68 See 'The German Jesuits', *Times of India*, 10 August 1915, page 9.

69 'New Cathedral Collegiate School for Bombay', *Times of India*, 6 April 1878, page 3.

70 See 'Findings of April 14 Bombay Docks Explosions Inquiry Commission', *Times of India*, 12 September 1944, page 6; 'Explosions Cause Fires in Bombay', *Times of India*, 15 April 1944, page 1; 'The Day It Rained Gold and Death in Bombay: Rare Footage of the 1944 Dock Explosion', Scroll.in, available at: https://scroll.in/article/661674/the-day-it-rained-gold-and-death-in-bombay-rare-footage-of-the-1944-dock-explosion (last visited 28 May 2018).

71 Soli Sorabjee, 'Pakistan Supreme Court, Lawyers Immunity and Swearing', *Times of India*, 17 September 2000, page 10.

72 Soli J. Sorabjee, 'The Rhythm of Poetry in All That Jazz', *Times of India*, 8 July 1989, page 13.

73 Austen John Roberts, *Education and Society in the Bombay Presidency 1840–58* (PhD dissertation, School of Oriental and African Studies, London, 1974), page 361.

74 Nina Martyris, 'I was not converted, I was transformed', *Times of India*, 25 November 2001, page 4.

75 'Prize Distribution at St. Xavier's College', *Times of India*, 29 November 1895, page 6.

76 See 'H.E. The Viceroy at St. Francis Xavier's College', *Times of India*, 1 December 1880, page 2; 'Prize Distribution at St. Xavier's College', *Times of India*, 29 November 1895, page 6.

77 'Prize Distribution at St. Xavier's College', *Times of India*, 29 November 1895, page 6.

78 Soli J. Sorabjee, 'The Rhythm of Poetry in All That Jazz', *Times of India*, 8 July 1989, page 13.

79 Soli Sorabjee, 'Playing Favourites', *Indian Express*, 9 November 2008, page 7.

80 'Mr. Soli Sorabji', undated newspaper clipping from the Sorabjee family archive; 'Sorabjee Named Additional Solicitor-General', *Times of India*, 12 April 1977, page 4.

81 Soli Sorabjee, 'Varying Eccentricities', *Indian Express*, 29 August 2004, page 6; Soli Sorabjee, 'Hijacking & a Tryst with Millennium', *Times of India*, 2 January 2000, page 14; Soli J. Sorabjee, 'My First Clash with the Secrecy Syndrome', *Times of India*, 5 August 1989, page 11.

82 See Soli J. Sorabjee, 'Judges Must Be Expensive', *Illustrated Weekly of India*, 22 August 1971, page 14; Soli Sorabjee, 'Preserve the Courts', *Illustrated Weekly of India*, 8 February 1976, page 26; Soli J. Sorabjee, 'Role of the Judiciary—Boon or Bane?', *India International Centre Quarterly*, vol. 20 (1993), pages 1–17, at page 2.

83 Soli J. Sorabjee, 'The Rhythm of Poetry in All That Jazz', *Times of India*, 8 July 1989, page 13.

84 Ibid.

85 Soli Sorabjee, 'Flowers as Presents', *Indian Express*, 18 March 2007, page 7.

86 However, Sorabjee got a first class in the First Year Arts certificate examination in 1947. St Xavier's College Magazine, vol. xl, November 1947, page 25.

87 St Xavier's College Magazine, vol. xli, November 1948, page 15.

88 Sorabjee's name was not recorded in the St Xavier's College Magazine between 1949 and 1951 as having received a first class or second class in the BA programme.

89 'Prize Distribution at St. Xavier's College', *Times of India*, 29 November 1895, page 6.

90 'St. Xavier's College', *Times of India*, 30 November 1900, page 6.

91 Soli Sorabjee, 'Social Sins', *Indian Express*, 27 April 2008, page 7.

92 Soli J. Sorabjee, 'The Rhythm of Poetry in All That Jazz', *Times of India*, 8 July 1989, page 13.

93 Ibid. Sorabjee's client, Bennett, Coleman & Co. Ltd., contended in court that its crossword puzzle prize competition did not constitute gambling.

Chapter 4: Chamber No. 1

1   One Cedric A. Santos was enrolled at St Xavier's College and obtained a second class in the BA examination in 1949. See St Xavier's College Magazine, vol. 42 (1949), page 18. This was probably the same Cedric Santos.

2   See 'Convocation of the University of Bombay', *Times of India*, 12 January 1871, page 3; 'The University of Bombay', *Times of India*, 19 February 1874, page 3; 'Bombay University: The Convocation', *Times of India*, 17 January 1877, page 3; 'Convocation of the University of Bombay', *Times of India*, 22 January 1880, page 3; 'Convocation of the University of Bombay', *Times of India*, 3 February 1881, page 3; 'The University Convocation', *Times of India*, 21 January 1885, page 5; 'University Convocation', *Times of India*, 19 January 1887, page 3; 'Bombay University Convocation', *Times of India*, 22 February 1893, page 5; 'Bombay University Senate',

Times of India, 6 April 1897, page 3; 'Bombay University Convocation', *Times of India*, 16 February 1898, page 5; 'Bombay University: Annual Convocation', *Times of India*, 19 February 1902, page 7; 'Education in India', *Times of India*, 18 February 1903, page 7. There is no reason to believe that this trend changed in subsequent decades.

3   Abhinav Chandrachud, *An Independent, Colonial Judiciary: A History of the Bombay High Court During the British Raj, 1862–1947* (New Delhi: Oxford University Press, 2015), page 65 (footnote 217).

4   See 'Bombay Law School: The Principal and Staff', *Times of India*, 5 May 1915, page 5; 'Government Law School: Reorganisation Scheme', *Times of India*, 30 August 1916, page 7; 'Legal Education', *Times of India*, 1 September 1934, page 12.

5   See 'Elphinstone College: A Government Inquiry', *Times of India*, 16 July 1907, page 7.

6   See 'To Peter Peterson...', *Times of India*, 20 September 1888, page 6; 'Government Law School', *Times of India*, 14 March 1914, page 11; 'Government Law School: Reorganisation Scheme', *Times of India*, 30 August 1916, page 7; 'Proceedings in Detail', *Times of India*, 15 March 1918, page 7; 'Bombay Council', *Times of India*, 11 December 1919, page 10; 'State Hostel at Bandra', *Times of India*, 14 June 1950, page 9; 'Bombay Law Classes', *Times of India*, 24 July 1926, page 4.

7   'Government Law School: Reorganisation Scheme', *Times of India*, 30 August 1916, page 7.

8   'University of Bombay', *Times of India*, 21 September 1888, page 5.

9   See 'Government Law School: The Proposed Reforms', *Times of India*, 7 September 1916, page 10; 'Indian Pleaders', *Times of India*, 1 December 1923, page 14.

10 See 'The Status of Pleaders and Vakils in Bombay', *Times of India*, 17 December 1883, page 6; 'Grievances of Law Graduates', *Times of India*, 22 February 1902, page 7; 'To the editor...', *Times of India*, 7 September 1916, page 10; Abhinav Chandrachud, *An Independent, Colonial Judiciary: A History of the Bombay High Court During the British Raj, 1862–1947* (New Delhi: Oxford University Press, 2015), page 30.

11 Editorial Article 1, *Times of India*, 11 August 1888, page 4.

12 'Needy Students', *Times of India*, 14 August 1923, page 11.

13 See 'Government Law School: Reorganisation Scheme', *Times of India*, 30 August 1916, page 7.

14 Abhinav Chandrachud, *An Independent, Colonial Judiciary: A History of the Bombay High Court During the British Raj, 1862–1947* (New Delhi: Oxford University Press, 2015), page 65 (footnote 229).

15 Ibid., page 42.

16 See 'University of Bombay', *Times of India*, 21 September 1888, page 5.

17 'Indian Pleaders', *Times of India*, 1 December 1923, page 14.

18 Abhinav Chandrachud, *An Independent, Colonial Judiciary: A History of the Bombay High Court During the British Raj, 1862–1947* (New Delhi: Oxford University Press, 2015), page 42.

19 Ibid., page 66 (footnote 237).

20 'State Hostel at Bandra', *Times of India*, 14 June 1950, page 9.

21 Chitale ceased to be the principal of the college in 1952, when he left for the US as a Fulbright scholar. The Law College Magazine, vol. xxii, March–May 1953, nos. 1–2, page 126; 'Engagements for Today', *Times of India*, 10 September 1952, page 7.

22 See 'Classified Ad 5', *Times of India*, 3 June 1950, page 12; 'New Principal of Law College', *Times of India*, 3 June 1948, page 3; 'Engagements for Today', *Times of India*, 10 September 1952, page 7.

23 The Law College Magazine, vol. xix, November 1950, no. 1, page 68.

24 See 'Bombay Law College: Additional Divisions', *Times of India*, 22 June 1950, page 11; 'Indian Pleaders', *Times of India*, 1 December 1923, page 14.

25 The Law College Magazine, vol. xix, November 1950, no. 1, page 68.

26 Ibid., page 74.

27 The Law College Magazine, vol. xx, November–December 1951, no. 1, page 79.

28 Ibid., pages 73–74.

29 The Law College Magazine, vol. xxii, March–May 1953, nos. 1–2, page 122.

30 The Law College Magazine, vol. xx, November–December 1951, no. 1, page 79.

31 'Kania Memorial Fund', *Times of India*, 15 April 1952, page 4; 'Oil Portrait Unveiled', *Times of India*, 24 September 1952, page 5.

32 See further The Law College Magazine, vol. xix, November 1950, no. 1, page 68.

33 Gagrat attended St Xavier's College. However, he did not obtain a BA degree. Emails dated 5 November 2021 from Jeh Gagrat to the author.

34 The Law College Magazine, vol. xxii, March–May 1953, nos. 1–2, photographs between pages 40 and 41.

35 Sorabjee's bar council certificate, Sorabjee family archive.

36 The Law College Magazine, vol. xxii, March–May 1953, nos. 1–2, page 122.

37 'Do Not Make Money a God', *Times of India*, 9 February 1929, page 8.

38 Ibid.

39 Ibid.

40 'Oil Portrait Unveiled', *Times of India*, 24 September 1952, page 5.

41 'How to be a Good Advocate: Mr. Jayakar's Advice', *Times of India*, 16 February 1934, page 16.

42 'Government Law School: Annual Social Gathering', *Times of India*, 11 February 1918, page 8.

43 'Mr. Justice Bhagwati Felicitated', *Times of India*, 17 August 1952, page 16.

44 See 'Government Law School: Annual Social Gathering', *Times of India*, 11 February 1918, page 8.

45 Soli J. Sorabjee, 'Judicial Activism—Boon or Bane?', (2008) 3 SCC Journal 24.

46 The Law College Magazine, vol. xxii, March–May 1953, nos. 1–2, page 126.

47 In 1951, Gagrat won the MN Banaji Scholarship for Equity and was elected the deputy speaker of the student parliament. The Law College Magazine, vol. xx, November–December 1951, no. 1, page 78 and the photographs in between pages 32 and 33.

48 In 1949, Nariman won the Sir John Heaton prize and the Alpaiwala Prize. In 1950, he was one of only three students of Government Law College who passed their second LLB examination in the first class. He was a

college fellow for the academic year 1950–51. He was also elected the speaker of the student parliament. The Law College Magazine, vol. xix, November 1950, no. 1, pages 70, 71, 73.

49 The Law College Magazine, vol. xxii, March–May 1953, nos. 1–2, page 122.

50 The Law College Magazine, vol. xx, November–December 1951, nos. 1–2, page 78.

51 The Law College Magazine, vol. xxii, March–May 1953, nos. 1–2, page 126.

52 In 1950, Divan won the Kinloch Forbes Gold Medal and the Arunaditya Vishnu K. Dhurandhar Gold Medal. He was elected the prime minister in the student parliament that year. The Law College Magazine, vol. xix, November 1950, no. 1, pages 70, 73. The following year, he won the Arnould Scholarship, obtained a first class in the 2nd LLB examination, and was elected the speaker of the student parliament. The Law College Magazine, vol. xx, November–December 1951, no. 1, page 78 and the photographs in between pages 32 and 33.

53 See The Law College Magazine, vol. xx, November–December 1951, nos. 1–2, photographs in between pages 32 and 33.

54 'Bombay University First LL.B.: Examination Results', *Times of India*, 16 June 1936, page 6. Kharshedji had stood first in the entire university in the first year LLB examination.

55 Interview with Avinash Rana dated 13 May 2021.

56 Soli J. Sorabjee, 'Judicial Activism—Boon or Bane?', (2008) 3 SCC Journal 24.

57 Interview with Varun Bhabha dated 18 May 2021. Kharshedji Bhabha was born on 8 August 1915. He passed away on 24 May 2004.

58 The data for this section have been collected by the author from SCC Online, Manupatra, and the Proquest Times of India database.

59 Among 104 reported cases in which K.H. Bhabha's name was recorded, collected by the author from SCC Online, Manupatra, and Proquest Times of India, between 1942 and 1969, Bhabha appeared 52 per cent of the time before a single judge and 39 per cent of the time before a division bench.

60 Among 104 reported cases in which K.H. Bhabha's name was recorded, collected by the author from SCC Online, Manupatra, and Proquest Times of India, between 1942 and 1969, Bhabha appeared before Chagla 26 times and before Coyajee 19 times.

61 'Excommunication Act Held Valid', *Times of India*, 18 March 1952, page 7. The decision was affirmed in appeal in Syedna Taher Saifuddin v. Tyebbhai Moosaji Koicha, (1952) SCC Online Bom 81 (paragraph 21).

62 Sardar Syedna Taher Saifuddin Saheb v. State of Bombay, AIR 1962 SC 853 (SCC Online version) (paragraphs 45, 62).

63 'Loss of Gold Parcel', *Times of India*, 4 October 1952, page 3.

64 'Writ to Quash Govt. Order', *Times of India*, 9 December 1953, page 3.

65 As we shall see in the next chapter, however, Sorabjee was on the board of directors of the company that owned the *Statesman* newspaper during the Emergency.

66 'Management's Role', *Times of India*, 9 April 1968, page 4.

67 See 'Classified Ad 11', *Times of India*, 18 January 1967, page 5. He was also a director of Camphor & Allied Products Ltd. See 'Display Ad 9', *Times of India*, 3 May 1982, page 12.

68 Interview with Avinash Rana dated 13 May 2021.

69 Ibid.

Chapter 5: 'Judges Must be Expensive'

1 Between 1953 and 1975, Sorabjee had 55 reported judgments to his credit before a single judge and 46 reported judgments to his credit before a division bench.

2 Kamala Nair v. Narayana Pillai, (1957) SCC Online Bom 50 (paragraph 4).

3 Interview with Avinash Rana dated 13 May 2021.

4 Dr Gopalkrishna K. Salelkar v. Union of India, (1969) SCC Online GDD 28 (paragraph 8).

5 See e.g., Navnitlal M. Shah v. Atul Drug House, (1971) SCC Online Guj 61 (paragraph 2).

6 S.N. Srikantia and Co. v. Union of India, (1965) SCC Online Bom 133 (paragraph 3).

7   See S.N. Srikantia and Co. v. Union of India, (1965) SCC Online Bom
     133; Indian Express Newspapers (Bombay) Ltd. v. Basumati Pvt. Ltd.,
     MANU/MH/0039/1969; Marketing and Advertising Associates Pvt.
     Ltd. v. Telerad Pvt. Ltd., MANU/MH/0004/1969; In re: British India
     General Insurance Co. Ltd., MANU/MH/0076/1970; Framroze
     Rustomji Paymaster v. British Burmah Petroleum Co. Ltd., MANU/
     MH/0069/1971; Bennett Coleman & Co. Ltd. v. Union of India, (1972)
     2 SCC 788: MANU/SC/0038/1972.

8   See Section 3, Central Excises and Salt Act, 1944, available at: https://
     legislative.gov.in/sites/default/files/legislative_references/1944.pdf   (last
     visited 24 May 2021).

9   See Section 174, Central Goods and Services Tax Act, 2017. See further
     Godway Furnicrafts v. State of Andhra Pradesh, (2020) SCC Online AP
     2050 (paragraph 5).

10   See 'JAL Allowed to Inspect ILS', *Times of India*, 19 September 1972,
     page 9.

11   See Daulatram Lachhmandas Nayar v. State of Bombay, MANU/
     MH/0310/1959.

12   Yusuf Abdulla Patel v. R.N. Shukla, MANU/MH/0159/1969.

13   'No Excise Duty on Polymer Chips', *Times of India*, 17 September 1970,
     page 6.

14   AIR 1973 SC 1461.

15   Soli J. Sorabjee, 'Judicial Activism—Boon or Bane?', (2008) 3 SCC Journal
     24.

16   Ibid.

17   Interview with Avinash Rana dated 13 May 2021.

18   Mayer Hans George v. State of Maharashtra, (1963) SCC Online Bom 62
     (paragraphs 23, 37).

19   State of Maharashtra v. Mayer Hans George, AIR 1965 SC 722 (SCC
     Online version).

20   Sorabjee had appeared in Ranchhoddas Atmarain v. Union of India, AIR
     1961 SC 935. However, he was led by Porus A. Mehta in that case.

21   Paragraphs 38, 43–44.

22   Paragraph 39.

23 Paragraph 48.

24 Paragraphs 18, 23.

25 See Union of India v. Ganesh Das Bhojraj, (2000) 9 SCC 461 (paragraph 11).

26 Bhagat Raja v. Union of India, AIR 1967 SC 1606; Shah and Co. v. State of Maharashtra, AIR 1967 SC 1877; Satwant Singh Sawhney v. D. Ramarathnam, AIR 1967 SC 1836.

27 AIR 1967 SC 1836 (SCC Online version).

28 Choithram Verhomal Jethwani v. A.G. Kazi, (1965) SCC Online Bom 38.

29 A.G. Kazi v. C.V. Jethwani, MANU/MH/0098/1967.

30 See Satwant Singh Sawhney v. D. Ramarathnam, AIR 1967 SC 1836 (SCC Online version) (paragraph 31).

31 Interview with Avinash Rana dated 13 May 2021.

32 Paragraph 31.

33 Paragraph 12.

34 Paragraph 32.

35 According to *Illustrated Weekly of India*, he was designated a senior in 1970. One of the earliest reported judgments in which Sorabjee was recorded as being a senior advocate was delivered in December 1971: Barium Chemicals v. A.J. Rana, (1972) 1 SCC 240.

36 See Section 16, Advocates Act, 1961; *Report of the All-India Bar Committee* (Delhi: President's Press, 1953), pages 25–26.

37 *Illustrated Weekly of India*, 22 August 1971, page 14.

38 Ibid., page 15.

39 Ibid., page 16.

40 Ibid, page 16.

41 Ibid., page 16.

42 Ibid., page 15.

43 Ibid., page 16.

44 Ibid., page 15.

45 Ibid., page 15.

46 Ibid., page 15.

47 Ibid., page 14.

48 See Soli Sorabjee, 'Preserve the Courts', *Illustrated Weekly of India*, 8 February 1976, page 26.

49 Soli J. Sorabjee, 'Judges Must be Expensive', *Illustrated Weekly of India*, 22 August 1971, page 15.

50 Ibid., page 15.

51 See Abhinav Chandrachud, *An Independent, Colonial Judiciary: A History of the Bombay High Court During the British Raj, 1862–1947* (New Delhi: Oxford University Press, 2015), page 37.

52 'H.R. Gokhale Resigns', *Times of India*, 11 June 1966, page 1; 'A Judge Deserves a Better Deal, Says Justice Gokhale', *Times of India*, 15 June 1966, page 1.

53 Soli J. Sorabjee, 'Judges Must be Expensive', *Illustrated Weekly of India*, 22 August 1971, page 16.

54 Ibid., page 16.

55 Ibid., page 15.

56 Ibid., page 15.

57 Ibid., pages 15–16.

58 N.A. Palkhivala, 'Justice Is Costly', *Times of India*, 25 June 1966, page 6.

59 'Sir A.P. Herbert', *Encyclopaedia Britannica*, available at: https://www.britannica.com/biography/A-P-Herbert (last visited 5 November 2021).

60 Soli J. Sorabjee, 'Judges Must be Expensive', *Illustrated Weekly of India*, 22 August 1971, page 16.

61 *Illustrated Weekly of India*, 12 September 1971, page 6.

Chapter 6: 'This is Nothing to Panic About'

1 'Many Opponents of Mrs. Gandhi Arrested in India', *New York Times*, 26 June 1975, page 1.

2 Ibid.

3 'Security in Peril, Says P.M.', *Times of India*, 27 June 1975, page 1.

4 'Chimanbhai Patel Assumes Office', *Times of India*, 19 July 1973, page 1.

5 Granville Austin, *Working a Democratic Constitution: A History of the Indian Experience* (New Delhi: Oxford University Press, 2003), pages 298–299. Technically speaking, the country was still under an Emergency declared in 1971. Ibid., page 299.

6   See 'Student Stir to Go On in Ahmedabad', *Times of India*, 9 January 1974, page 1, 'Army Out in Baroda as Gujarat Riots Spread', *Times of India*, 11 January 1974, page 1; 'PM: No Scrapping of Gujarat Assembly', *Times of India*, 1 March 1974, page 1; 'Gujarat Assembly Dissolved', *Times of India*, 16 March 1974, page 1.

7   'Army Out in Baroda as Gujarat Riots Spread', *Times of India*, 11 January 1974, page 1.

8   Ibid.

9   Ibid.

10 'Student Stir to Go On in Ahmedabad', *Times of India*, 9 January 1974, page 1.

11 'Army Out in Baroda as Gujarat Riots Spread', *Times of India*, 11 January 1974, page 1; 'Police Open Fire Six Times in Gujarat', *Times of India*, 13 January 1974, page 1.

12 'Police Open Fire Six Times in Gujarat', *Times of India*, 13 January 1974, page 1.

13 'Army Out in Baroda as Gujarat Riots Spread', *Times of India*, 11 January 1974, page 1.

14 'Police Open Fire Six Times in Gujarat', *Times of India*, 13 January 1974, page 1.

15 'Army Out in Baroda as Gujarat Riots Spread', *Times of India*, 11 January 1974, page 1.

16 See 'Stir Now for Poll in Gujarat', *Times of India*, 12 February 1974, page 1; 'Gujarat Assembly Dissolved', *Times of India*, 16 March 1974, page 1.

17 'Students Being Exploited: PM', *Times of India*, 2 March 1974, page 5.

18 'Morarji Begins Fast', *Times of India*, 12 March 1974, page 1. He later undertook an indefinite fast again, in order to ensure that elections would be held in Gujarat. Granville Austin, *Working a Democratic Constitution: A History of the Indian Experience* (New Delhi: Oxford University Press, 2003), page 301.

19 'Students Being Exploited: PM', *Times of India*, 2 March 1974, page 5.

20 'Gujarat Assembly Dissolved', *Times of India*, 16 March 1974, page 1.

21 Ibid.

22 'Why Emergency?', a paper laid by the Ministry of Home Affairs, Government of India, before both houses of Parliament on 21 July 1975, page 5.

23 Khushwant Singh, 'Ten Years of Indira Gandhi', *Illustrated Weekly of India*, 25 January 1976, page 8.

24 He was the convenor of the National Coordination Committee for the Railwaymen's Struggle, an apex body of various trade unions. See 'Railmen's Arrest a Bid to Crush Struggle', *Times of India*, 3 May 1974, page 3.

25 See 'No Suburban Trains During Strike', *Times of India*, 29 April 1974, page 1.

26 See 'Why Emergency?', a paper laid by the Ministry of Home Affairs, Government of India, before both houses of Parliament on 21 July 1975, pages 14–15.

27 See 'Little Coal with Power Units', *Times of India*, 3 May 1974, page 3.

28 See 'Fernandes Ready for Talks Even in Jail', *Times of India*, 9 May 1974, page 1.

29 Ibid.; 'Railmen Call Off Strike', *Times of India*, 28 May 1974, page 1.

30 See 'Fernandes Ready for Talks Even in Jail', *Times of India*, 9 May 1974, page 1.

31 'Arrest of Rail Leaders Sparks City Bandh', *Times of India*, 3 May 1974, page 1; 'More than 1,000 held', *Times of India*, 5 May 1974, page 1. See further Granville Austin, *Working a Democratic Constitution: A History of the Indian Experience* (New Delhi: Oxford University Press, 2003), page 299.

32 Khushwant Singh, 'Total Revolution', *Illustrated Weekly of India*, 6 April 1975, page 6 (at page 10). See further 'Jayaprakash Narayan', *Encyclopaedia Britannica*, available at: https://www.britannica.com/biography/Jayaprakash-Narayan (last visited 6 November 2021).

33 '"Total revolution" call', *Times of India*, 14 July 1974, page 1; 'Bihar Agitation: New Phase', *Times of India*, 9 August 1974, page 4; 'Indira Rule Paradise for Capitalists: JP', *Times of India*, 28 January 1975, page 9; Khushwant Singh, 'Total Revolution', *Illustrated Weekly of India*, 6 April 1975, page 6 (at page 10).

34 'Bihar Agitation: New Phase', *Times of India*, 9 August 1974, page 4.

35 'Why Emergency?', a paper laid by the Ministry of Home Affairs, Government of India, before both houses of Parliament on 21 July 1975, pages 7–13.

36 'Indira Rule Paradise for Capitalists: JP', *Times of India*, 28 January 1975, page 9.

37 'Bihar Agitation: New Phase', *Times of India*, 9 August 1974, page 4.

38 Ibid.

39 'J.P. Finalises Plan for Bihar Stir', *Times of India*, 23 May 1975, page 1.

40 'Why Emergency?', a paper laid by the Ministry of Home Affairs, Government of India, before both houses of Parliament on 21 July 1975, pages 7–13.

41 Ibid.

42 Ibid.

43 Ibid., page 31.

44 Ibid, pages 26–27.

45 See Kenneth G. Lieberthal, 'Cultural Revolution', *Encyclopaedia Britannica*, available at: https://www.britannica.com/event/Cultural-Revolution (last visited 17 May 2021).

46 'Why Emergency?', a paper laid by the Ministry of Home Affairs, Government of India, before both houses of Parliament on 21 July 1975, pages 14–15, 18.

47 'L.N. Mishra among 23 Hurt in Bomb Blast', *Times of India*, 3 January 1975, page 1.

48 'L.N. Mishra Dies After Surgery', *Times of India*, 4 January 1975, page 1.

49 Justices J.M. Shelat, K.S. Hegde and A.N. Grover.

50 'Ray was Stunned by Grenades', *Times of India*, 22 March 1975, page 1.

51 Ibid.

52 'Chief Justice Escapes Bomb Attempt', *Times of India*, 21 March 1975, page 1.

53 Ibid.

54 'Charges and Rejoinders', *Times of India*, 19 March 1975, page 1.

55 Ibid.

56 See Justice Sudhir Narain, 'A Building Par Excellence', in, *Gavel and Pen* (Lucknow: Bennett, Coleman & Co. Ltd., 2016), page 430.

57 'Court Room Gets Face-lift for PM's Deposition', *Times of India*, 17 March 1975, page 9.

58 'PM Faces Gruelling 4-hr. Cross-examination in Court', *Times of India*, 19 March 1975, page 1.

59 'Court Room Gets Face-lift for PM's Deposition', *Times of India*, 17 March 1975, page 9.

60 'PM Faces Gruelling 4-hr. Cross-examination in Court', *Times of India*, 19 March 1975, page 1.

61 'High Court Verdict Unseats Indira', *Times of India*, 13 June 1975, page 1.

62 Ibid.

63 'Opposition to Press for PM's Resignation', *Times of India*, 13 June 1975, page 1; 'P.M.'s Decision is Shameful, says JP', *Times of India*, 14 June 1975, page 1; 'Anti-P.M. Dharna Continues', *Times of India*, 15 June 1975, page 1.

64 'Hearing on Monday', *Times of India*, 21 June 1975, page 1.

65 Kesavananda Bharati v. State of Kerala, (1973) 4 SCC 225.

66 Rustom Cavasjee Cooper v. Union of India, (1970) 1 SCC 248.

67 Madhav Rao Jivaji Rao Scindia v. Union of India, (1971) 1 SCC 85.

68 Granville Austin, *Working a Democratic Constitution: A History of the Indian Experience* (New Delhi: Oxford University Press, 2003), page 302.

69 See George H. Gadbois, Jr., *Judges of the Supreme Court of India: 1950–1989* (New Delhi: Oxford University Press, 2011), page 211.

70 Upendra Baxi, *Courage, Craft and Contention: The Indian Supreme Court in the Eighties* (Bombay: N.M. Tripathi Pvt. Ltd., 1985), page 27.

71 Ibid.

72 'Court Order on PM's Petition Today', *Times of India*, 24 June 1975, page 1.

73 Ibid.

74 'No Bar on Indira Continuing as PM', *Times of India*, 25 June 1975, page 1.

75 'No Bar on Indira Continuing as PM', *Times of India*, 25 June 1975, page 1.

76 'City Split on "Conditional PM"', *Times of India*, 25 June 1975, page 1.

77 Ibid.

78   Ibid.

79   'News Summary and Index', *New York Times*, 25 June 1975, page 15; Granville Austin, *Working a Democratic Constitution: A History of the Indian Experience* (New Delhi: Oxford University Press, 2003), page 304.

80   'No Comment: Indira', *Times of India*, 25 June 1975, page 1.

81   'Indira Calls on Ahmed', *Times of India*, 26 June 1975, page 1.

82   'Security in Peril, says PM', *Times of India*, 27 June 1975, page 1.

83   Granville Austin, *Working a Democratic Constitution: A History of the Indian Experience* (New Delhi: Oxford University Press, 2003), pages 306–307.

84   Ibid.

85   Granville Austin, *Working a Democratic Constitution: A History of the Indian Experience* (New Delhi: Oxford University Press, 2003), page 308.

86   *Shah Commission of Inquiry: Interim Report II* (26 April 1978), page 141.

87   Fali S. Nariman, *Before Memory Fades: An Autobiography* (New Delhi: Hay House Publishers (India) Pvt. Ltd., 2010), page 165.

88   Soli J. Sorabjee, 'Foxing the Censor During the Emergency', *Times of India*, 25 September 1989, page 13.

89   Ram Jethmalani, *Big Egos, Small Men* (New Delhi: Har Anand Publications Pvt. Ltd., 2000), page 6.

90   Soli J. Sorabjee, *The Emergency, Censorship and the Press in India, 1975–77* (New Delhi: Central News Agency Pvt. Ltd., 1977), page 11.

91   'Many Opponents of Mrs. Gandhi Arrested in India', *New York Times*, 26 June 1975, page 1.

92   Soli J. Sorabjee, *The Emergency, Censorship and the Press in India, 1975–77* (New Delhi: Central News Agency Pvt. Ltd., 1977), page 13.

93   Ibid.

94   Ibid., page 11.

95   Ibid., page 14.

96   Ibid., page 18.

97   Ibid., pages 17–18; Soli J. Sorabjee, 'Foxing the Censor during the Emergency', *Times of India*, 25 September 1989, page 13.

98   See 'Publication of High Court Judgment Allowed', *Times of India*, 25 November 1975, page 5.

99 Soli J. Sorabjee, *The Emergency, Censorship and the Press in India, 1975–77* (New Delhi: Central News Agency Pvt. Ltd., 1977), page 14.

100 Ibid., pages 15–16.

101 Ibid., page 16.

102 Ibid., page 15.

103 Ibid., page 15.

104 Ibid.

105 Ibid., pages 18–19.

106 Sabina Sehgal, 'For Justice and Jazz', *Times of India*, 3 October 1993, page 12.

107 Soli J. Sorabjee, *The Emergency, Censorship and the Press in India, 1975–77* (New Delhi: Central News Agency Pvt. Ltd., 1977), page 19.

108 This is based on 19 reported judgments in which Sorabjee's appearance was recorded, obtained by the author from the Manupatra and SCC Online databases.

109 See 'Crashed Caravelle Had Defects', *Times of India*, 20 November 1976, page 5; 'Pilot Required to Note Vibrations', *Times of India*, 24 November 1976, page 9.

110 Ramesh Ramlal Narang v. MG Mugwe, (1974) SCC Online Bom 112; Rajabally Hirji Meghani v. Union of India, (1974) SCC Online Bom 124.

111 Bharti Nayyar v. Union of India, MANU/DE/0129/1975; Murli Dhar Dalmia v. Union of India, MANU/DE/0127/1976; Additional District Magistrate, Jabalpur v. Shivakant Shukla, (1976) 2 SCC 521. He was one among several hundred lawyers who appeared for Ram Jethmalani in the Bombay High Court during the Emergency after a speech Jethmalani made in Kerala. Ram Jethmalani, *Big Egos, Small Men* (New Delhi: Har Anand Publications Pvt. Ltd., 2000), pages 50–51.

112 (1977) 1 SCC 677.

113 Interview with Avinash Rana dated 13 May 2021.

114 See Ram Jethmalani, *Big Egos, Small Men* (New Delhi: Har Anand Publications Pvt. Ltd., 2000), pages 50, 53.

115 See profile of M.R. Masani on the website of the Lok Sabha, available at: http://loksabhaph.nic.in/writereaddata/biodata_1_12/1252.htm (last visited 6 November 2021).

116 Binod Rao v. Minocher Rustom Masani, (1976) SCC Online Bom 100.

117 Ibid., paragraph 45.

118 Ibid., paragraphs 61, 66, 69.

119 Ibid., paragraph 98.

120 Ibid.

121 See profile of Justice J.L. Nain on the website of the Bombay High Court, available at: https://bombayhighcourt.nic.in/jshowpuisne. php?bhcpar=amdldGlkPTE2NSZwYWdlbm89OQ== (last visited 6 November 2021).

122 Binod Rao v. Minocher Rustom Masani, (1976) SCC Online Bom 100, paragraph 130.

123 Ibid., paragraph 131.

124 Ibid., paragraphs 115–116.

125 Ibid., paragraph 129.

126 Ibid.

127 Ibid., paragraphs 118–119.

128 Ibid., paragraphs 114, 124–125.

129 Chamber No. 9.

130 Soli J. Sorabjee, 'Foxing the Censor During the Emergency', *Times of India*, 25 September 1989, page 13.

131 Ibid.

132 Ibid.

133 Soli J. Sorabjee, *Law of Press Censorship in India* (Bombay: N.M. Tripathi Pvt. Ltd., 1976).

134 Soli J. Sorabjee, 'Foxing the Censor During the Emergency', *Times of India*, 25 September 1989, page 13.

135 Ibid.

136 In the introduction to the book, Sorabjee wrote that free speech was 'a reaffirmation of mankind's fundamental belief that thought remains a soliloquy unless men can communicate their ideas to one another, that it is [a] free and frank exchange of views between individuals and groups that ensures the progress of civilisation, the flowering of democracy, the creations of human culture.' 'The greater the freedom of opinion', he added, 'the greater is the flow of significant communication throughout

every area of life.' Soli J. Sorabjee, *Law of Press Censorship in India* (Bombay: N.M. Tripathi Pvt. Ltd., 1976), page 4. This entire paragraph, however, with some minor changes, seems to have been borrowed by Sorabjee, without attribution, from an American author, Corliss Lamont, in his book published in 1956. Corliss Lamont, *Freedom is as Freedom Does: Civil Liberties Today* (New York: Horizon Press, 1956), page 5, available at: https://archive.org/details/ldpd_8331676_000/page/n29/mode/2up?q=soliloquy (last visited 24 May 2021).

137 That is, by the division bench in appeal.

138 Soli Sorabjee, 'Preserve the Courts', *Illustrated Weekly of India*, 8 February 1976, page 26 (at page 27).

139 (1976) 2 SCC 521.

140 Ibid., paragraph 513.

141 'Executive Bound to Act As Per Law: Counsel', *Times of India*, 5 February 1976, page 13.

142 'Indian Court Upholds Political Jailings', *New York Times*, 29 April 1976, page 81.

143 Ibid.

144 Soli J. Sorabjee, *The Emergency, Censorship and the Press in India, 1975–77* (New Delhi: Central News Agency Pvt. Ltd., 1977), page 27.

145 Ibid., page 16 (footnote 2).

Chapter 7: 'Court to Keep Maneka's Passport'

1   See Soli J. Sorabjee, *The Emergency, Censorship and the Press in India, 1975–77* (New Delhi: Central News Agency Pvt. Ltd., 1977), page 62.

2   See State of Rajasthan v. Union of India, (1977) 3 SCC 592 (paragraph 100).

3   Soli J. Sorabjee, *The Emergency, Censorship and the Press in India, 1975–77* (New Delhi: Central News Agency Pvt. Ltd., 1977), page 62.

4   'Congress Faces Defeat', *Times of India*, 21 March 1977, page 1.

5   'Ram in 19-member Morarji Cabinet', *Times of India*, 26 March 1977, page 1.

6   'Morarji Takes Over as PM', *Times of India*, 25 March 1977, page 1.

7   'MPs Take Pledge at Raj Ghat', *Times of India*, 25 March 1977, page 9.

8   'Ram in 19-member Morarji Cabinet', *Times of India*, 26 March 1977, page 1. The headline in this article seems to contain an error, as the article itself only speaks of 18 cabinet members.

9   'Morarji Takes Over as PM', *Times of India*, 25 March 1977, page 1.

10 'Sorabjee Named Additional Solicitor-general', *Times of India*, 12 April 1977, page 4.

11 See 'S.V. Gupte Felicitated', *Times of India*, 21 March 1963, page 9.

12 See 'No Appeal for Detentions under Art. 21 Only', *Times of India*, 20 December 1975, page 13.

13 See 'Kacker for Poll Bar on Indira', *Times of India*, 9 September 1979, page 9.

14 See 'Sanjay's Say in Hotels, Too', *Times of India*, 11 May 1977, page 1.

15 Ibid.

16 Interview with Upendra Baxi dated 23 May 2021. Baxi attended many of those parties and met many judges of the Supreme Court there. He was introduced to Parsi vegetarian food, including dhansak, at some of those parties.

17 Bihar, Haryana, Himachal Pradesh, Madhya Pradesh, Orissa, Punjab, Rajasthan, Uttar Pradesh and West Bengal. See State of Rajasthan v. Union of India, (1977) 3 SCC 592 (paragraph 100). The text of the letter is at paragraph 27 of the judgment.

18 See 'Dissolution: Govt. Decision Put Off', *Times of India*, 26 April 1977, page 1.

19 'JP Wants Assemblies to be Dissolved', *Times of India*, 3 April 1977, page 1.

20 See State of Rajasthan v. Union of India, (1977) 3 SCC 592 (paragraph 28).

21 State of Rajasthan v. Union of India, (1977) 3 SCC 592 (paragraph 103).

22 Article 131(a), Constitution.

23 'Dissolution: Govt. Decision Put Off', *Times of India*, 26 April 1977, page 1.

24 See ibid.

25 Ibid.

26 Ibid.

27 State of Rajasthan v. Union of India, (1977) 3 SCC 592 (paragraphs 21–23).

28 See 'Parliament's Okay Needed for Dissolution: Counsel', *Times of India*, 30 April 1977, page 11.

29 Ibid.

30 'Court Rejects Plea against Dissolution', *Times of India*, 30 April 1977, page 1.

31 6 May 1977.

32 State of Rajasthan v. Union of India, (1977) 3 SCC 592: paragraphs 97 (MH Beg CJ), 107 (Chandrachud J), 142 (Bhagwati and Gupta JJ), with dissents at paragraphs 170 (Goswami J), 181 (Untwalia J), 195 and 198 (Fazal Ali J).

33 State of Rajasthan v. Union of India, (1977) 3 SCC 592: paragraphs 33, 41 and 64 (MH Beg CJ), 129 (Chandrachud J), 150 (Bhagwati J), 176 (Goswami J), 185 (Untwalia J), 210 and 216 (Fazal Ali J).

34 Ibid., paragraph 33 (Beg CJ).

35 Ibid., paragraph 150 (Bhagwati and Gupta JJ).

36 Justice Y.V. Chandrachud wrote that though this subject was considered to be well-settled, only one proposition was really 'well-settled' in this branch of constitutional law, i.e., that '[n]o question in this branch of law is well-settled.' Ibid., paragraph 134.

37 Ibid., paragraphs 35 (Beg CJ), 130 (Chandrachud J), 152 (Bhagwati and Gupta JJ), 176 (Goswami J), and 215 (Fazal Ali J). During the hearing, Justice Untwalia suggested that the government might have felt that there might be a revolution among the people if the Congress governments continued in the states after being defeated at the centre. 'Isn't Issue Political, Judges Ask De', *Times of India*, 27 April 1977, page 9.

38 State of Rajasthan v. Union of India, (1977) 3 SCC 592, paragraph 178.

39 Ibid., page 697. See further Abhinav Chandrachud, *Supreme Whispers: Conversations with Judges of the Supreme Court of India, 1980–1989* (Gurgaon: Penguin Random House, 2018), pages 11–13.

40 'Jatti Bows to Cabinet Advice: 9 Assemblies Dissolved', *Times of India*, 1 May 1977, page 1.

41 'Majority for Janata in Six States', *Times of India*, 16 June 1977, page 1; 'Kaipoori to Take Oath Tomorrow', *Times of India*, 23 June 1977, page 1.

42 See 'Shah Commission Starts Work', *Times of India*, 5 June 1977, page 9.

43 *Shah Commission of Inquiry: Interim Report II* (26 April 1978), page 141.

44 See 'Indira Indicted by Gupta Panel', *Times of India*, 1 June 1979, page 1.

45 See 'Inquiry Against Bansi Lal Begins', *Times of India*, 3 August 1977, page 1.

46 See 'Favour to Maruti: Bansi Found Guilty', *Times of India*, 12 May 1978, page 1.

47 See 'Nagarwala Case to be Reopened', *Times of India*, 21 April 1979, page 1; 'SBI Rules Violated in Nagarwala Affair', *Times of India*, 15 Jun 1978, page 4; 'Nagarwala Said Ex-PM Told Him to Collect Cash: Witness', *Times of India*, 23 July 1978, page 4. See further George H. Gadbois, Jr., *Judges of the Supreme Court of India: 1950–1989* (New Delhi: Oxford University Press, 2011), page 145. Reddy was not able to find an answer to the question in the Nagarwala probe.

48 See 'Inquiry against Bansi Lal Begins', *Times of India*, 3 August 1977, page 1; 'No Duplication in Bansi Probe Case', *Times of India*, 13 October 1977, page 7.

49 'Sanjay, Dhirendra Lose Pilot Licenses', *Times of India*, 3 June 1977, page 1.

50 Ibid.; 'Passport: Maneka's Plea against Order', *Times of India*, 20 July 1977, page 13.

51 'Mrs. Gandhi May Not Get Passport', *Times of India*, 2 September 1977, page 1; 'Passport for Indira on Court Permission', *Times of India*, 12 August 1978, page 15.

52 'Mrs. Sanjay Gandhi Claims Phones Tapped', *The Hartford Courant*, 30 June 1977, page 72.

53 'Passport: Maneka's Plea against Order', *Times of India*, 20 July 1977, page 13; 'Maneka's Passport Plea Admitted', *Times of India*, 21 July 1977, page 5.

54 Maneka Gandhi v. Union of India, (1978) 1 SCC 248: paragraph 5 (Bhagwati, Untwalia, Fazal Ali JJ), paragraph 48 (Chandrachud J), paragraphs 80, 82, 85 (Krishna Iyer J).

55 Ibid., paragraph 7 (Bhagwati, Untwalia, Fazal Ali JJ), paragraph 94 (Krishna Iyer J).

56 Ibid., paragraph 14 (Bhagwati, Untwalia, Fazal Ali JJ), paragraph 56 (Chandrachud J), paragraph 93 (Krishna Iyer J).

57 Ibid., paragraph 15 (Bhagwati, Untwalia, Fazal Ali JJ), paragraph 93 (Krishna Iyer J).

58 Ibid., paragraph 38 (Bhagwati, Untwalia, Fazal Ali JJ), paragraph 56 (Chandrachud J).

59 Ibid., page 403.

60 See 'Soli Sorabjee, Sinha Tender Resignation', *Times of India*, 15 January 1980, page 9.

61 See 'The Missing Ingredient', *Times of India*, 24 April 1977, page 8; 'Television', *Times of India*, 22 April 1977, page 3; Amita Malik, 'AIR's Reminiscences', *Times of India*, 5 March 1978, page 8; 'No Comeback for Indira: Shekhar', *Times of India*, 14 June 1978, page 9; Amita Malik, 'The International Scene', *Times of India*, 18 February 1979, page 8.

62 Amita Malik, 'Where are the Men', *Times of India*, 1 May 1977, page 8. I have changed the spelling of 'caviare' in the article to 'caviar'.

63 'Sounds of Childhood', *Times of India*, 11 December 1977, page 8.

64 Ibid.

65 Amita Malik, 'The Art of Biography', *Times of India*, 17 December 1978, page 8.

66 'PM's Conduct Should Not be Beyond Probe: Sorabjee', *Times of India*, 20 May 1977, page 7.

67 Soli J. Sorabjee, *The Emergency, Censorship and the Press in India, 1975–77* (New Delhi: Central News Agency Pvt. Ltd., 1977).

68 See 'Note on Contributors', in Soli J. Sorabjee et al., *The Governor: Sage or Saboteur* (New Delhi: Roli Books International, 1985).

69 347 U.S. 483 (1954).

70 National Association for the Advancement of Colored People.

71 'Brown Observance', *New York Amsterdam News*, 19 May 1979, page 52; 'On the Crucial Issue of Affirmative Action', *New York Amsterdam News*, 30 June 1979, page 20.

72 Gurbaksh Singh Sibbia v. State of Punjab, (1980) 2 SCC 565.

73 Ibid., paragraphs 9, 12–13, 17, 31.

74 (1980) 2 SCC 684.

75 Ibid., paragraph 209.

76 Sunil Batra v. Delhi Administration, (1978) 4 SCC 494; Sunil Batra (II) v. Delhi Administration, (1980) 3 SCC 488.

77 Sunil Batra v. Delhi Administration, (1978) 4 SCC 494 (paragraph 213).

78 Sunil Batra v. Delhi Administration, (1978) 4 SCC 494 (paragraphs 220, 223, 224, 228).

79 Ibid., paragraphs 236, 241.

80 Sunil Batra (II) v. Delhi Administration, (1980) 3 SCC 488 (paragraphs 32, 86).

81 (1978) 1 SCC 405 (paragraph 8).

82 That is, cases in which there was either a clearly discernible winner or loser.

83 See State of Karnataka v. Union of India, (1977) 4 SCC 608 (paragraph 218).

84 Ibid.

85 C.B. Muthamma v. Union of India, (1979) 4 SCC 260 (paragraph 8). See further Gurcharan Singh v. State (Delhi Administration), (1978) 1 SCC 118 (paragraph 32); State of Punjab v. Labour Court, Jullundur, (1980) 1 SCC 4 (paragraph 11).

86 Upendra Baxi, *Courage, Craft and Contention: The Indian Supreme Court in the Eighties* (Bombay: N.M. Tripathi Pvt. Ltd., 1985) page 27.

87 Sunil Batra v. Delhi Administration, (1978) 4 SCC 494 (paragraph 64). See further Sunil Batra (II) v. Delhi Administration, (1980) 3 SCC 488 (paragraph 1); Rajasthan State Road Transport Corporation v. Narain Shanker, MANU/SC/0323/1980 (paragraph 5).

88 (1979) 4 SCC 260.

89 Rahul Machaiah, 'C.B. Muthamma's Battle against a Gendered Foreign Service', *Live Wire*, 14 October 2020, available at: https://livewire.thewire. in/gender-and-sexuality/cb-muthammas-gendered-foreign-service/ (last visited 20 May 2021).

90 C.B. Muthamma v. Union of India, (1979) 4 SCC 260 (paragraph 8).

91 See 'CBI Unfolds "*Kissa Kursi Ka*"', *Times of India*, 15 July 1977, page 1.

92 State (Delhi Administration) v. Sanjay Gandhi, (1978) 2 SCC 411 (paragraph 2).

93 Ibid.

94 Ibid.

95 Ibid., paragraph 3.

96 'Sanjay and Shukla to Appear in Court', *Times of India*, 26 July 1977, page 9.

97 'Pandemonium in Court as Sanjay, Shukla Come', *Times of India*, 28 August 1977, page 1.

98 Ibid.

99 Ibid.

100 Ibid.

101 See 'Approver in *Kissa* Case Turns Hostile', *Times of India*, 22 February 1978, page 9; '"*Kissa*" Witness Turns Hostile', *Times of India*, 28 April 1978, page 4; 'Another Witness Turns Hostile in *Kissa* Case', *Times of India*, 29 April 1978, page 14.

102 'Sanjay Calls Prosecutor Scoundrel', *Times of India*, 13 April 1978, page 1. Jaisinghani allegedly drew attention to the fact that Sanjay was handling the court papers, and pointed out that he was accused of destroying a film.

103 'Special Leave Plea Filed: "Kissa" Case', *Times of India*, 21 April 1978, page 1.

104 'No Violation of Court Dignity: Chief Justice', *Times of India*, 26 April 1978, page 1.

105 State (Delhi Administration) v. Sanjay Gandhi, (1978) 2 SCC 411 (paragraph 13).

106 Ibid., paragraphs 19–20.

107 Ibid., paragraph 26.

108 'Sanjay in Tihar Jail', *Times of India*, 6 May 1978, page 1.

109 Ibid.

110 Ibid.

111 Ibid.

112 'Sanjay in Jail, Watches TV', *Times of India*, 9 May 1978, page 4.

113 'Maneka Harassed, Alleges Sanjay', *Times of India*, 25 May 1978, page 1.

114 '"*Kissa*" Witness Turns Hostile', *Times of India*, 11 May 1978, page 5; 'Two More Witnesses in Maruti Case Hostile', *Times of India*, 17 May 1978, page 5; 'Witness Turns Hostile in "*Kissa*" Case', *Times of India*, 27 July 1978, page 4.

115 'N.K. Singh's Son Dies in Hospital', *Times of India*, 16 May 1978, page 5.

116 '*Kissa* Case: Shukla, Sanjay Convicted', *Times of India*, 27 February 1979, page 1.

117 'Two years' R.I. for Shukla, Sanjay', *Times of India*, 28 February 1979, page 1.

118 Ibid.

119 Ibid.

120 Ibid.

121 'Charge on Judge's Elevation Denied', *Times of India*, 7 March 1979, page 9.

122 'Sanjay, Shukla File Appeals', *Times of India*, 21 March 1979, page 9.

123 'Shukla, Sanjay Plea Admitted', *Times of India*, 22 March 1979, page 5.

124 '"*Kissa*" Case', *Times of India*, 18 May 1979, page 15; '"*Kissa*" Case for Supreme Court', *Times of India*, 29 August 1979, page 1.

125 'CBI Plea against Sanjay's Bail: Hearing Next Week', *Times of India*, 10 November 1979, page 13.

126 'Chief Justice Alleges Threat', *Times of India*, 14 November 1979, page 1.

127 Ibid.

128 Ibid.

129 'No Cancellation of Sanjay's Bail', *Times of India*, 20 November 1979, page 1.

130 V.C. Shukla v. State (Delhi Administration), (1980) 2 SCC 665.

131 'Nahata to remake "Kissa Kursi Ka"', *Times of India*, 29 July 1977, page 1.

132 'Censor Board Recommends 15 Cuts in "Kissa Kursi Ka"', *Times of India*, 19 November 1977, page 15.

133 'Amrit Nahata to Quit Janata', *Times of India*, 7 May 1979, page 5.

Chapter 8: A Chief Justice on Trial

1   See '4,633 in Lok Sabha Election Fray', *Times of India*, 19 December 1979, page 9.

2   'President Invites Indira to Form Government', *Times of India*, 11 January 1980, page 1.

3   'Two-thirds Majority Got', *Times of India*, 10 January 1980, page 1.

4   'President Invites Indira to Form Government', *Times of India*, 11 January 1980, page 1.

5   Ibid.

6   Ibid.

7   Ibid.

8   Ibid.

9   Morarji Desai had resigned in July 1979. See Abhinav Chandrachud, *The Informal Constitution: Unwritten Criteria in Selecting Judges for the Supreme Court of India* (New Delhi: Oxford University Press, 2014), page 101.

10 'It is Indira's Personal Victory: Morarji', *Times of India*, 10 January 1980, page 3.

11 'Soli Sorabjee, Sinha Tender Resignation', *Times of India*, 15 January 1980, page 9.

12 The following data have been compiled by the author from all the reported judgments in which Sorabjee's name appeared between the date of his resignation as a Janata law officer and the date of his appointment as Attorney General in December 1989, in the SCC Online and Manupatra databases.

13 13 per cent of his reported cases were in the Delhi High Court.

14 See 'Shabana Azmi and Javed Akhtar: Torrid Suit', *India Today*, 30 April 1987, available at: https://www.indiatoday.in/magazine/eyecatchers/story/19870430-i-will-only-act-in-south-indian-movies-says-kamalahasan-798785-1987-04-30 (last visited 25 May 2021).

15 'Bench Upholds Secrecy of Source', *Times of India*, 13 November 1987, page 1. See further 'Disclosing Sources is "Unfair": Stardust Case', *Times of India*, 22 August 1987, page 3.

16 Ibid.; '"Stardust" Appeal Allowed', *Times of India*, 20 September 1987, page 5; 'Shabana Libel Case Judgment Begins', *Times of India*, 19 September 1987, page 3.

17 Together, around 15 per cent of his reported judgments were in the fields of labour law, service law and indirect tax.

18   Soli J. Sorabjee, 'Court's Contempt and the Press', *Times of India*, 1 June
     1980, page SM6; Soli J. Sorabjee, 'The Ball is in Your Court', *Times of
     India*, 13 September 1980, page SM6; Soli J. Sorabjee, 'No Gags on the
     Press', *Times of India*, 2 January 1983, page A4 (*Times of India* wrongly
     calls him 'Soli S. Sorabjee' in this article); Soli J. Sorabjee, 'Press: Watchdog
     or Consort?', *Times of India*, 20 November 1988, page A1.

19   Soli J. Sorabjee, 'Should Law Keep Pace with the Times?', *Times of India*,
     26 January 1985, page IV; Soli J. Sorabjee, 'Through the Peephole', *Times
     of India*, 15 June 1986, page A1.

20   Soli J. Sorabjee, 'The Supreme Court of India: Erosion of Judicial
     Collectivism', *Times of India*, 5 January 1987, page 8; Soli J. Sorabjee, 'In
     Nehru's Judgment', *Times of India*, 30 April 1989, page A1.

21   Soli J. Sorabjee, 'Heresies about the Constitution', *Times of India*, 6 May
     1987, page 8; Soli J. Sorabjee, 'A Sage Counsellor, a Friend', *Times of India*,
     17 May 1987, page I; Soli J. Sorabjee, 'Centre's Onslaught on Nagaland',
     Times of India, 10 August 1988, page 8.

22   Soli J. Sorabjee, 'The Governor—Sage or Spy?', *Times of India*, 10 July
     1988, page A1.

23   See e.g., Soli J. Sorabjee, 'The Rhythm of Poetry in All That Jazz', *Times
     of India*, 8 July 1989, page 13; Soli J. Sorabjee, 'When I was Scorched by
     the Lighter Side of Life', *Times of India*, 19 August 1989, page 15; Soli J.
     Sorabjee, 'My First Clash with the Secrecy Syndrome', *Times of India*, 5
     August 1989, page 11.

24   'Display Ad 24', *Times of India*, 5 November 1988, page A8. The poet he
     referred to was William Wordsworth.

25   Shah Babulal Khimji v. Jayaben D. Kania, (1981) 4 SCC 8.

26   Natraj Studios (P) Ltd. v. Navrang Studios, (1981) 1 SCC 523.

27   State of Maharashtra v. Ramdas Shrinivas Nayak, (1982) 2 SCC 463.

28   D.C. Wadhwa v. State of Bihar, (1987) 1 SCC 378. Sorabjee's appearance
     is shown in the Manupatra report at MANU/SC/0072/1986.

29   S.L. Kapoor v. Jagmohan, (1980) 4 SCC 379.

30   S.P. Mittal v. Union of India, (1983) 1 SCC 51.

31   R.K. Garg v. Union of India, (1981) 4 SCC 675.

32   S. Rangarajan v. P. Jagjivan Ram, (1989) 2 SCC 574.

33 See 'Judicial Independence', *Times of India*, 19 November 1980, page 8.

34 See the views of H.M. Seervai, in 'Eminent Jurists Uphold Freedom of Judiciary', *Times of India*, 21 November 1980, page 5; and the views of Ahilya Rangnekar in 'The Challenge of 1981', *Times of India*, 18 January 1981, page A4. See further 'Feeble Apologia', *Times of India*, 18 April 1981, page 8; 'Opposition Wants Chandrachud to Quit', *Times of India*, 23 July 1981, page 5.

35 See 'Minister Defends Judges' Transfer', *Times of India*, 3 February 1981, page 11; speech of the union law minister in Parliament, as reported in 'Note on Judges Defended', *Times of India*, 17 April 1981, page 1; 'Move on Judges to Fight Parochialism', *Times of India*, 16 July 1981, page 4.

36 'Allahabad Judge Resigns', *Times of India*, 26 July 1980, page 1. See further 'No Harassment of Judge', *Times of India*, 29 July 1980, page 1.

37 S.P. Gupta v. Union of India, (1981) Supp SCC 87 (paragraph 596). See further 'Chief Justices Transferred', *Times of India*, 21 January 1981, page 15.

38 'Ismail's Transfer is Challenged', *Times of India*, 23 January 1981, page 1.

39 'Status quo Ordered in Judges Case', *Times of India*, 4 February 1981, page 1.

40 The letter was sent to the Governor of Punjab and it was not sent to the Chief Ministers of the north-eastern states. See S.P. Gupta v. Union of India, (1981) Supp SCC 87, page 195.

41 Article 224, Constitution.

42 'Bar Council Assails Circular on Transfer', *Times of India*, 14 April 1981, page 4; 'Bar "Condemns" Law Minister's Note on Transfer', *Times of India*, 8 April 1981, page 14.

43 'High Court Work at a Standstill', *Times of India*, 16 April 1981, page 4.

44 'Walk-out by Opposition', *Times of India*, 15 April 1981, page 1.

45 'Transfers: Judges Urged Not to Sign Consent', *Times of India*, 22 April 1981, page 15.

46 S.P. Gupta v. Union of India, (1981) Supp SCC 87 (paragraph 2).

47 See speech of the union law minister in Parliament, as reported in 'Note on Judges Defended', *Times of India*, 17 April 1981, page 1.

48 '36 Judges Give Transfer Consent', *Times of India*, 14 July 1981, page 4.

49 'Official Letter to CMs Challenged', *Times of India*, 21 April 1981, page 1. An intra-court appeal against Justice Pendse's order was dismissed. S.P. Gupta v. Union of India, (1981) Supp SCC 87 (paragraph 2).

50 'Lawyers Flay Govt. on Judges Issue', *Times of India*, 8 June 1981, page 9.

51 'No Regrets, Says "Retired" Judge', *Times of India*, 9 June 1981, page 5.

52 'Delhi Judge Sees Malice in Denial of Extension', *Times of India*, 18 July 1981, page 9.

53 'Govt.'s Duty to Provide Judges: Sorabjee', *Times of India*, 22 August 1981, page 14.

54 'Sack of Additional Judges Illegal, Argues Sorabjee', *Times of India*, 27 August 1981, page 13.

55 S.P. Gupta v. Union of India, (1981) Supp SCC 87 (paragraph 1).

56 See 'Judgment is Reserved in Judges' Transfer Case', *Times of India*, 20 November 1981, page 9.

57 'Verdict in Judges' Case Today', *Times of India*, 30 December 1981, page 1.

58 Ibid; George H. Gadbois, Jr., *Judges of the Supreme Court of India, 1950–1989* (New Delhi: Oxford University Press, 2011), page 231.

59 Abhinav Chandrachud, *The Informal Constitution: Unwritten Criteria in Selecting Judges for the Supreme Court of India* (New Delhi: Oxford University Press, 2014), page 105.

60 S.P. Gupta v. Union of India, (1981) Supp SCC 87: paragraph 55 (Bhagwati J), paragraphs 397 and 425 (Fazal Ali J), paragraph 776 (Desai J), paragraph 1239 (Venkataramiah J).

61 Ibid.: paragraph 135 (Gupta J), paragraph 666 (Tulzapurkar J), paragraph 899 (Pathak J), paragraph 1222 (Venkataramiah). See further paragraph 786 (Desai J).

62 Ibid.: paragraph 681 (Tulzapurkar J), paragraph 1257 (Venkataramiah J), paragraph 139 (Gupta J), paragraphs 935–936 (Pathak J).

63 See Abhinav Chandrachud, *Supreme Whispers: Conversations with Judges of the Supreme Court of India, 1980–1989* (Gurgaon: Penguin Random House, 2018), pages 20–28.

64 According to Granville Austin, Bhagwati had personally demanded that Chandrachud file the affidavit. Granville Austin, *Working a Democratic*

Constitution: *A History of the Indian Experience* (New Delhi: Oxford University Press, 2003), page 529.

65 Seervai, who appeared in the case, wrote that the court had directed Chandrachud to file an affidavit, referring to paragraph 553 of the judgment of Justice Fazal Ali, who wrote in his judgment that the counter-affidavit was filed by Chandrachud 'as directed by us'. See H.M. Seervai, *Constitutional Law of India: A Critical Commentary* (New Delhi: Universal Law Publishing Co. Pvt. Ltd., 2014), 4th edition, vol. 3, page 2897. Though Chandrachud filed an affidavit, he did not appear before the court through any advocate.

66 S.P. Gupta v. Union of India, (1981) Supp SCC 87 (paragraph 114).

67 S.P. Gupta v. Union of India, (1981) Supp SCC 87 (paragraph 686).

68 'Sanjiva's Denial on C.J.'s Affidavit', *Times of India*, 20 November 1981, page 7.

69 S.P. Gupta v. Union of India, (1981) Supp SCC 87 (paragraph 686). See further paragraph 681.

70 S.P. Gupta v. Union of India, (1981) Supp SCC 87 (paragraph 686). See further paragraph 681.

71 Ibid.

72 The Times of India, in an editorial on 21 November 1981, wrote that it was 'not particularly difficult to find a possible explanation for President Sanjiva Reddy's decision to ask the solicitor-general' to make that statement, though it refused to spell out the explanation on the grounds that it would 'inevitably be circumstantial, inferential, speculative and therefore undesirable.' 'President & Chief Justice', *Times of India*, 21 November 1981, page 8.

73 S.P. Gupta v. Union of India, (1981) Supp SCC 87 (paragraph 686).

74 'Verdict in Judges Case Assailed', *Times of India*, 11 February 1982, page 19.

75 Kasturi Deshpande Naganathan, *An Analytical Study of India's Satellite Instructional Television Experiment* (doctoral dissertation, University of Oklahoma, 1985), page 45; William J. Brown, *Effects of 'Hum Log', A Television Soap Opera, on Pro-Social Beliefs in India* (doctoral dissertation, University of Southern California, 1988), page 7; B.D. Dhawan, 'School

Education Through Television', *Economic and Political Weekly*, 1973, pages 2111–2113, at page 2113 (footnote 3).

76 Naganathan, ibid., 46.

77 'Television', *Times of India*, 12 August 1974, page 3.

78 Ibid.

79 'Today's TV', *Times of India*, 18 March 1979, page 4.

80 Arvind Singhal and Everett M. Rogers, 'Television Soap Operas for Development in India', *International Communication Gazette*, April 1988, pages 109–126, at page 117.

81 Ibid.

82 'Television', *Times of India*, 24 July 1984, page 3.

83 See William J. Brown, *Effects of 'Hum Log', A Television Soap Opera, on Pro-Social Beliefs in India* (doctoral dissertation, University of Southern California, 1988), pages 18–19.

84 Ibid., page 17.

85 Ibid., page 18.

86 Ibid., page 19. Another estimate was 50.4 million. Seema Sirohi, 'India's Soap Opera Sent Social Message', *Times of India*, 10 January 1986, page E2.

87 Seema Sirohi, 'India's Soap Opera Sent Social Message', *Times of India*, 10 January 1986, page E2.

88 William J. Brown, *Effects of 'Hum Log', A Television Soap Opera, on Pro-Social Beliefs in India* (doctoral dissertation, University of Southern California, 1988), page 21.

89 'Television', *Times of India*, 1 February 1987, page 5.

90 See 'Television', *Times of India*, 6 May 1986, page 3; 'End of a Saga: Exit *Buniyaad*', *Times of India*, 29 May 1987, page 8.

91 Arvind Singhal and Everett M. Rogers, 'Television Soap Operas for Development in India', *International Communication Gazette*, April 1988, pages 109–126, at pages 109 and 117.

92 'The Godfather Game', *Times of India*, 23 August 1987, page A2.

93 Ramesh v. Union of India, (1988) 1 SCC 668 (paragraph 5).

94 'Akademi's award for Nirad', *Times of India*, 8 December 1975, page 1.

95 See Ramesh v. Union of India, (1988) 1 SCC 668 (paragraph 12).

96 'Will "Tamas" See the Light?', *Times of India*, 22 January 1988, page 1.

97 'Television', *Times of India*, 9 January 1988, page 5; 'Television', *Times of India*, 16 January 1988, page 5.

98 'Television', *Times of India*, 16 January 1988, page 5.

99 'BJP Agitation against "Tamas" from Jan. 23', *Times of India*, 21 January 1988, page 6.

100 Ibid.

101 'Stir Threat against "Tamas" Telecast', *Times of India*, 22 January 1988, page 3.

102 See '"Tamas" Defended Secularism: Nihalani', *Times of India*, 16 February 1988, page 3; 'BJP Calls for Ban on "Tamas"', *Times of India*, 26 January 1988, page 3.

103 '"Tamas" Defended Secularism: Nihalani', *Times of India*, 16 February 1988, page 3. See further Ramesh v. Union of India, (1988) 1 SCC 668 (paragraph 7).

104 See Ramesh v. Union of India, (1988) 1 SCC 668 (paragraph 6).

105 'Will "Tamas" See the Light?', *Times of India*, 22 January 1988, page 1.

106 'Pratap Order Minutes was Pinned to Plea', *Times of India*, 31 January 1988, page 5.

107 Ibid.

108 Justice Pratap's order was passed on a handwritten sheet of paper. The parties were then free to copy the contents of the order in their own handwriting and then to have the order typed themselves. Ibid. M.A. Rane, a senior advocate on the appellate side, opined that it was permissible in cases of urgency for the parties to have the order typed themselves and to file an appeal without appending the minutes of the order, but with an undertaking that they would annex the minutes upon obtaining them. See '"Tamas" case', *Times of India*, 30 January 1988, continued from page 1.

109 See profile of Chief Justice Sujata Vasant Manohar on the website of the Bombay High Court, available at: https://bombayhighcourt.nic.in/cjshow.php?bhcpar=amdldGlkPTI3JnBhZ2Vubz0y (last visited 25 May 2021).

110 'Bench Upholds Secrecy of Source', *Times of India*, 13 November 1987, page 1.

111 'Will "Tamas" See the Light?', *Times of India*, 22 January 1988, page 1; 'Judges See "Tamas", Decision Today', *Times of India*, 23 January 1988, page 9.

112 'Pratap Order Minutes was Pinned to Plea', *Times of India*, 31 January 1988, page 5.

113 See 'Blaze Minuet', *Times of India*, 29 January 1969, page 6.

114 'Judges See "Tamas", Decision Today', *Times of India*, 23 January 1988, page 9.

115 '"Tamas" Cleared by Judges', *Times of India*, 24 January 1988, page 1.

116 See Ramesh v. Union of India, (1988) 1 SCC 668 (paragraph 20).

117 'BJYM, Sena Plan to Challenge "Tamas" Ruling', *Times of India*, 25 January 1988, page 3.

118 'Anti-"Tamas" Rally Outside TV Centre', *Times of India*, 28 January 1988, page 3. See further, 'Photo Standalone 1', *Times of India*, 1 February 1988, page 3.

119 'BJYM, Sena Plan to Challenge "Tamas" Ruling', *Times of India*, 25 January 1988, page 3.

120 'BJP Calls for Ban on "Tamas"', *Times of India*, 26 January 1988, page 3.

121 'PM Urged Not to Ban "Tamas"', *Times of India*, 30 January 1988, page 9.

122 'Place "Tamas" Case Elsewhere: Judge', *Times of India*, 29 January 1988, page 5.

123 Ibid.

124 'Pratap Order Minutes was Pinned to Plea', *Times of India*, 31 January 1988, page 5.

125 'Place "Tamas" Case Elsewhere: Judge', *Times of India*, 29 January 1988, page 5.

126 'Urgency Led to Ruling: "Tamas" Case', *Times of India*, 30 January 1988, page 1.

127 See '"Tamas" Case', *Times of India*, 30 January 1988, continued from page 1.

128 'SC Quashes "Tamas" Ban Plea', *Times of India*, 2 February 1988, page 1.

129 Ibid.

130 See further Ramesh v. Union of India, (1988) 1 SCC 668 (paragraph 11).

131 'SC Quashes "Tamas" Ban Plea', *Times of India*, 2 February 1988, page 1.

132 'Firing in Andhra Over "Tamas"', *Times of India*, 5 February 1988, page 1.

133 Ibid.

134 '"Tamas" Most Popular Book at Exhibition', *Times of India*, 11 February 1988, page 18.

135 'Television', *Times of India*, 13 February 1988, page 5. See further '"Tamas" to be Made Feature Film', *Times of India*, 25 April 1988, page 3.

136 Ramesh v. Union of India, (1988) 1 SCC 668 (paragraph 13).

137 Ibid., paragraph 15.

138 Ibid., paragraphs 9, 19. It had not yet been made into a feature film. See '"Tamas" to be Made Feature Film', *Times of India*, 25 April 1988, page 3.

139 Ramesh v. Union of India, (1988) 1 SCC 668 (paragraph 20).

140 Ibid.

141 This was the first major free speech case that Sorabjee himself argued at the Supreme Court. Earlier, Sorabjee was led by Nani Palkhivala in Bennett Coleman & Co. Ltd. v. Union of India, (1972) 2 SCC 788 (his appearance is recorded in the Manupatra version at MANU/SC/0038/1972), a case in which Palkhivala and Sorabjee had succeeded. Another victory in a free speech case came to Sorabjee shortly after the *Tamas* case in S. Rangarajan v. P. Jagjivan Ram, (1989) 2 SCC 574.

Chapter 9: 'We are being Impeached Every Day'

1 Arun Subramaniam, 'The Catastrophe at Bhopal', *Business India*, December 17–30, 1984, available at: Abhilekh Patal (Identifier: PR_000004001966; File No. 17/2049/A/85-PMS, vol. 7), page 24.

2 Ibid. There remained doubts about what gas was exactly released into the air that night. See Digvijay Singh's letter to Rajiv Gandhi dated 29/8/1985, available at: Abhilekh Patal (Identifier: PR_000004001966; File No. 17/2049/A/85-PMS, vol. 7), page 12; 'Bhopal Gas Still a Mystery', *Times of India*, 26 September 1987, page 7.

3 Arun Subramaniam, 'The Catastrophe at Bhopal', *Business India*, December 17–30, 1984, available at: Abhilekh Patal (Identifier: PR_000004001966; File No. 17/2049/A/85-PMS, vol. 7), page 24.

4   See '375 Die in Bhopal Gas Leak', *Times of India*, 4 December 1984, page 1.

5   Union Carbide Corporation v. Union of India, (1991) 4 SCC 584 (paragraph 127).

6   Union Carbide Corporation v. Union of India, (1991) 4 SCC 584 (paragraph 26).

7   Ibid., paragraph 127.

8   Arun Subramaniam, 'The Catastrophe at Bhopal', *Business India*, December 17–30, 1984, available at: Abhilekh Patal (Identifier: PR_000004001966; File No. 17/2049/A/85-PMS, vol. 7), page 25.

9   Union Carbide Corporation v. Union of India, (1991) 4 SCC 584 (paragraph 33).

10 Letter from Deepchand Yadav to Prime Minister Rajiv Gandhi dated 13 February 1986, available at: Abhilekh Patal (Identifier: PR_000004001969; File No. 17/2049/A/85-PMS, vol. 2), page 11.

11 'Thousands Leaving Bhopal Despite Assurance', *Times of India*, 13 December 1984, page 1.

12 'Mishap—Plagued Unit', *Times of India*, 9 December 1984, page 9.

13 'Union Carbide Chiefs Arrested in Bhopal', *Times of India*, 8 December 1984, page 1.

14 'Anderson Leaves for U.S.', *Times of India*, 10 December 1984, page 1. He repeatedly avoided court summonses and died in the US on 29 September 2014. See 'A Bhopal Timeline', *University of Wisconsin Law School Digital Repository*, available at: https://repository.law.wisc.edu/s/uwlaw/page/a-bhopal-timeline (last visited 26 May 2021).

15 G.V. Krishnan, 'U.S. lawyers' Hunt for Bhopal Clients', *Times of India*, 10 January 1985, page 17. As Sorabjee wrote later on: 'The Transatlantic ambulance chasers moved with jet speed.' Soli J. Sorabjee, 'The Keenan Decision', *Times of India*, 2 June 1986, page 8. See further Charan Lal Sahu v. Union of India, (1990) 1 SCC 613 (paragraph 4).

16 See '$15b. Suit against Union Carbide', *Times of India*, 9 December 1984, page 1; '80 b. Suit against Union Carbide', *Times of India*, 30 December 1984, page 9; 'Yet Another Suit against Carbide', *Times of India*, 2 January 1985, page 7; 'Carbide Suits Consolidated', *Times of India*, 8 February 1985, page 15.

17 See 'Carbide Suits Consolidated', *Times of India*, 8 February 1985, page 15; 'Govt. Hires Law Firm: Bhopal', *Times of India*, 10 March 1985, page 1; Julia Brodsky, 'Honorable John F. Keenan '54 Receives Dean's Medal of Recognition', *Fordham Law News*, 12 June 2019, available at: https://news.law.fordham.edu/blog/2019/06/12/honorable-john-f-keenan-54-receives-deans-medal-of-recognition/ (last visited 27 May 2021).

18 Bhopal Gas Leak Disaster (Processing of Claims) Ordinance, 1985, available at: Abhilekh Patal (Identifier: PR_000004001975, File No. 17/2049/A/85-PMS, vol. 2), at page 80; 'Ordinance to Help Fight Gas Cases', *Times of India*, 21 February 1985, page 9.

19 'Indian Govt. Sues Carbide', *Times of India*, 10 April 1985, page 1.

20 Ibid.

21 'Pre-trial Begins in Carbide Case', *Times of India*, 17 April 1985, page 12.

22 Affidavit of Marc S. Galanter dated 5 December 1985, available at: https://repository.law.wisc.edu/s/uwlaw/media/301821 (last visited 26 May 2021), page 163.

23 Affidavit of N.A. Palkhivala dated 18 December 1985, page 226.

24 Ibid., page 229.

25 K. Parasaran's note dated 12 February 1985, available at: Abhilekh Patal (Identifier: PR_000004001975; File No. 17/2049/A/85-PMS, vol. 2), pages 37–38.

26 Secret/Internal note prepared by Arvind Pande, Joint Secretary, Prime Minister's Office, dated 15 January 1986, available at: Abhilekh Patal (Identifier: PR_000004001968; File No. 17/2049/A/85-PMS, vol. 1), page 1.

27 Ibid., page 1.

28 He also imposed three conditions on Union Carbide. The conditions were that Union Carbide Corporation would accept the jurisdiction of the court in India (and waive defences based on limitation), it would abide by the court's decision provided it satisfied the 'minimum requirements of due process', and it would subject itself to US discovery norms in India. The court of appeal later deleted the second and third conditions. Charan Lal Sahu v. Union of India, (1990) 1 SCC 613 (paragraphs 8, 10).

29   Soli J. Sorabjee, 'The Keenan Decision', *Times of India*, 2 June 1986, page 8.

30   Soli J. Sorabjee, 'Judiciary Can Rise to the Challenge', *Times of India*, 3 June 1986, page 8.

31   Union Carbide Corporation v. Union of India, (1991) 4 SCC 584 (paragraph 38).

32   Soli J. Sorabjee, 'Judiciary Can Rise to the Challenge', *Times of India*, 3 June 1986, page 8.

33   Ibid.

34   'Suit against Carbide Filed', *Times of India*, 6 September 1986, page 1.

35   K. Parasaran's note dated 12 February 1985, available at: Abhilekh Patal (Identifier: PR_000004001975; File No. 17/2049/A/85-PMS, vol. 2), pages 37–38.

36   Secret/internal note of the government dated 3 December 1986, available at: Abhilekh Patal (Identifier: PR_000004001974; File No. 17/2049/A/85-PMS, vol. 7), page 2.

37   'Carbide Told to Keep $3 b. Assets', *Times of India*, 1 December 1986, page 1; Secret/internal note of the government dated 3 December 1986, available at: Abhilekh Patal (Identifier: PR_000004001974; File No. 17/2049/A/85-PMS, vol. 7), page 2.

38   'Carbide Offers $3 b. Bond', *Times of India*, 28 November 1986, page 1.

39   'India, Carbide Close to Settlement', *Times of India*, 4 November 1987, page 17. See further '$ 650-m. Deal with Carbide Likely', *Times of India*, 17 November 1987, page 17.

40   Praful Bidwai, 'Justice for Bhopal Victims', *Times of India*, 11 November 1987, page 8. The sum would be a little higher for the families of those who had died due to the tragedy. See further 'Govt. Letting Carbide Off Easily', *Times of India*, 12 November 1987, page 7.

41   'Bhopal Gas Victims Win Rs. 350-crore IR', *Times of India*, 18 December 1987, page 1.

42   'Judge is Biased, says Carbide', *Times of India*, 7 May 1988, page 9.

43   Ibid.

44   Union Carbide Corporation v. Union of India, (1991) 4 SCC 584 (paragraph 41).

45 'SC Orders Rs 715-cr Compensation', *Times of India*, 15 February 1989, page 1.

46 Ibid.

47 Ibid.

48 'Carbide Accord Not a Come-Down: A-G', *Times of India*, 13 April 1989, page 9.

49 Union Carbide Corporation v. Union of India, (1991) 4 SCC 584 (paragraph 45).

50 'Mixed Reactions to Compensation', *Times of India*, 15 February 1989, page 7.

51 Upendra Baxi, 'The Bhopal Award', *Times of India*, 16 February 1989, page 12.

52 Sheila Tefft, 'Bhopal Settlement Challenged', *Washington Post*, 4 March 1989, page A15.

53 V.M. Tarkunde, 'Carbide Settlement Merits Welcome', *Times of India*, 23 February 1989, page 14.

54 Ibid. Chief Justice Misra made the same point in his concurring judgment in the Bhopal review case. Union Carbide Corporation v. Union of India, (1991) 4 SCC 584 (paragraph 17).

55 V.M. Tarkunde, 'Carbide Settlement Merits Welcome', *Times of India*, 23 February 1989, page 14.

56 Bhopal Gas Leak Disaster (Processing of Claims) Act, 1985. The law was upheld by the court in Charan Lal Sahu v. Union of India, (1990) 1 SCC 613.

57 'A New Bhopal Bench', *Times of India*, 4 March 1989, page 12.

58 Sheila Tefft, 'Bhopal Settlement Challenged', *Washington Post*, 4 March 1989, page A15.

59 Ibid.

60 'Bhopal Act Hearing Begins', *Times of India*, 9 March 1989, page 13. Chief Justice Misra referred to the media 'tirade' in paragraph 12 of his judgment. Union Carbide Corporation v. Union of India, (1991) 4 SCC 584.

61 Abhinav Chandrachud, *The Informal Constitution: Unwritten Criteria in Selecting Judges for the Supreme Court of India* (New Delhi: Oxford University Press, 2014), page 115.

62 Ibid.

63 'VP to be Sworn in PM Today', *Times of India*, 2 December 1989, page 1.

64 'Sorabjee Appointed Attorney General', *Times of India*, 9 December 1989, page 1.

65 'I'm Not a Govt. Agent: Sorabjee', *Times of India*, 10 December 1989, page 7.

66 Letter from Nani A. Palkhivala to Soli J. Sorabjee dated 11 December 1989.

67 'Lawyers Facing a Dilemma: Nariman', *Times of India*, 27 December 1989, page 5.

68 'Centre to Oppose Carbide Deal', *Times of India*, 13 January 1990, page 1.

69 Ibid.

70 Upendra Baxi, 'Govt. Move on Carbide Historic', *Times of India*, 14 January 1990, page 1.

71 'SC Order on Carbide Case Challenged', *Times of India*, 19 July 1990, page 6; 'Carbide Verdict Reserved', *Times of India*, 30 August 1990, page 11.

72 'Bhopal Deal Denial of Natural Justice', *Times of India*, 16 November 1990, page 10; Union Carbide Corporation v. Union of India, (1991) 4 SCC 584 (paragraph 8).

73 George H. Gadbois, Jr., *Judges of the Supreme Court of India, 1950–1989* (New Delhi: Oxford University Press, 2011), page 288.

74 'Bhopal Case to be Reheard', *Times of India*, 7 October 1990, page 1.

75 'Mandal Order Stayed', *Times of India*, 2 October 1990, page 1. See further 'SC to Decide Quota Hearing Schedule', *Times of India*, 30 November 1990, page 15.

76 'Photo Standalone 6', *Times of India*, 6 October 1990, page 9.

77 Section 320, Code of Criminal Procedure, 1973.

78 'SC Order on Carbide Case Challenged', *Times of India*, 19 July 1990, page 6.

79 Or, for that matter, an 'assistant public prosecutor'.

80 Section 321, Code of Criminal Procedure, 1973.

81 'A-G's Powers Queried in Carbide Case', *Times of India*, 24 November 1990, page 8.

82 Ibid.

83 'SC Order on Carbide Case Challenged', *Times of India*, 19 July 1990, page 6.

84 'A-G's Powers Queried in Carbide Case', *Times of India*, 24 November 1990, page 8.

85 'Carbide Plea Dangerous', *Times of India*, 28 November 1990, page 7.

86 'SC Can't Grant UCC Immunity', *Times of India*, 9 August 1990, page 11.

87 'Carbide Settlement Premature, Meagre', *Times of India*, 26 July 1990, page 10.

88 'Govt. Move Queried in Bhopal Case', *Times of India*, 28 July 1990, page 7. See further Union Carbide Corporation v. Union of India, (1991) 4 SCC 584 (paragraph 144).

89 'Petitioner Urges New Bhopal Settlement', *Times of India*, 15 November 1990, page 7; 'Govt. Move Queried in Bhopal Case', *Times of India*, 28 July 1990, page 7.

90 'Govt. Move Queried in Bhopal Case', *Times of India*, 28 July 1990, page 7.

91 'Petitioner Urges New Bhopal Settlement', *Times of India*, 15 November 1990, page 7.

92 'Carbide Plea Dangerous', *Times of India*, 28 November 1990, page 7.

93 See Union Carbide Corporation v. Union of India, (1991) 4 SCC 584 (paragraph 54).

94 Union Carbide Corporation v. Union of India, (1991) 4 SCC 584 (paragraph 83).

95 Section 320, Code of Criminal Procedure, 1973.

96 Section 321, Code of Criminal Procedure, 1973.

97 Section 482, Code of Criminal Procedure, 1973.

98 Union Carbide Corporation v. Union of India, (1991) 4 SCC 584 (paragraph 83).

99 Ibid., paragraphs 86, 92. See further paragraph 221 (Ahmadi J), paragraph 9 (Misra J).

100 Ibid., paragraph 90. See further paragraph 87.

101 Ibid., paragraph 91.

102 Ibid., paragraph 103.

103 Ibid., paragraphs 203–204. Justice Ahmadi dissented on this point, holding that this was only a recommendation. Ibid., paragraph 217.

104 Ibid., paragraphs 207–209.

105 Ibid., paragraph 202.

106 Ibid., paragraph 198.

107 Ibid., paragraphs 160, 166, 171, 172, 176.

108 Ibid., paragraph 63. The court held that: (i) Under Articles 136 and 142 of the Constitution, it could, even while hearing an appeal against an interim order, dispose of the final suit [paragraphs 58–61, 63]; (ii) The settlement was not void in the absence of a notice being given to the victims [paragraphs 69–70]; (iii) The sum of $470 million was not paid to stifle the prosecution [paragraphs 106–108] because: (a) the bargain was struck by the government, not a private party [paragraph 118], (b) dropping the criminal charges was the motive for the settlement, but not the consideration [paragraph 121], and (c) it was inconceivable that the government would coerce Union Carbide to pay a sum so as to stifle a prosecution [paragraph 122]; (iv) No 'fairness hearing' was necessary under Section 4 of the Bhopal Act, which had been upheld in Charan Lal Sahu's case [paragraphs 124, 131, 135, 140]; (v) In the event the settlement were to be set aside, Union Carbide would be entitled to a refund of $470 million, provided that it restored its undertaking not to alienate its assets worth $3 billion before the district court [paragraphs 144, 146, 148, 153–155].

109 As a law officer with the Janata government, he did even less customs and excise work—only 13 per cent of his reported judgments at that time were in excise/customs.

110 'Devi Lal—Astute Politician', Times of India, 3 December 1989, page 11.

111 K.M. Sharma v. Devi Lal, (1990) 1 SCC 438 (paragraph 3).

112 Ashoka Marketing Ltd. v. Punjab National Bank, (1990) 4 SCC 406.

113 Dorab Cawasji Warden v. Coomi Sorab Warden, (1990) 2 SCC 117.

114 Delhi Judicial Service Association v. State of Gujarat, (1991) 4 SCC 406.

115 Soli J. Sorabjee, untitled article, Times of India, 30 December 1990, page SM3.

116 Ibid.

117 Ibid.

118 Ibid.

119 Ibid.

120 'VP "Godfather of ULFA": Cong.', *Times of India*, 7 December 1990, page 17; 'Jaipal Denies Sorabjee's Remarks', *Times of India*, 8 December 1990, page 13.

121 Soli J. Sorabjee, untitled article, *Times of India*, 30 December 1990, page SM3.

122 Abhinav Chandrachud, *The Informal Constitution: Unwritten Criteria in Selecting Judges for the Supreme Court of India* (New Delhi: Oxford University Press, 2014), page 117 (footnote 193).

123 'The Build-up to the Fall Out', *Times of India*, 28 October 1990, page 13.

124 Ibid.

125 Soli J. Sorabjee, untitled article, *Times of India*, 30 December 1990, page SM3.

126 'V.P. Singh Loses Trust Vote, Quits', *Times of India*, 8 November 1990, page 1.

127 Soli J. Sorabjee, untitled article, *Times of India*, 30 December 1990, page SM3.

128 Abhinav Chandrachud, *The Informal Constitution: Unwritten Criteria in Selecting Judges for the Supreme Court of India* (New Delhi: Oxford University Press, 2014), page 117.

129 'Dandavate Quits Plan Panel Post', *Times of India*, 11 November 1990, page 1.

130 'Solicitor-general's Aides Quit', *Times of India*, 9 November 1990, page 14.

131 Soli J. Sorabjee, untitled article, *Times of India*, 30 December 1990, page SM3.

132 Ibid.

Chapter 10: 'Sack Bommai, Advises Governor'

1 Gian Kaur v. State of Punjab, (1996) 2 SCC 648.

2 Dr M. Ismail Faruqui v. Union of India, (1994) 6 SCC 360.

3   Tata Cellular v. Union of India, (1994) 6 SCC 651.

4   Kihoto Hollohan v. Zachillhu, (1992) Supp (2) SCC 651.

5   Secretary, Irrigation Department, Government of Orissa v. G.C. Roy, (1992) 1 SCC 508.

6   Vasant Pratap Pandit v. Anant Trimbak Sabnis, (1994) 3 SCC 481.

7   Debasish Gupta v. Soli Sorabjee, (1997) SCC Online Cal 347.

8   Interview with Nisha Bagchi dated 2 June 2021.

9   Roxna Swamy, 'The Slave-driver of "Paw Prints" Fame', *The Commonwealth Lawyer*, vol. 31, August 2021, page 8.

10   Interview with Siboney Sagar dated 9 June 2021.

11   Interview with Ujjwal Rana dated 4 June 2021.

12   He also did not like a large number of judgments to be cited in the pleadings and felt that those judgments might get reversed by the time the case is finally ready for arguments.

13   Interview with Nisha Bagchi dated 2 June 2021.

14   Sabina Sehgal, 'For Justice and Jazz', *Times of India*, 3 October 1993, page 12.

15   'Display Ad 42', *Times of India*, 5 May 1994, page 15.

16   'SC's Dismissal of Plea in "Saamna" Case Shocks Eminent Jurists', *Times of India*, 29 January 1995, page 5.

17   Joseph Bain D'Souza v. State of Maharashtra, (1994) SCC Online Bom 461.

18   'Citizens' Plea to Defeat BJP–Sena Alliance', *Times of India*, 11 February 1995, page 5.

19   'Kranti Ranga Forms Front with Janata', *Times of India*, 20 December 1982, page 9.

20   'Hegde's Return to Portals of Power', *Times of India*, 10 January 1983, page 5; 'Hegde's Dramatic Rise to Power', *Times of India*, 13 January 1983, page 19.

21   A.S. Abraham, 'Value Based Politics', *Times of India*, 15 February 1986, page 8.

22   H. Kusumakar, 'Bommai Starts on a Sticky Wicket', *Times of India*, 22 August 1988, page 8.

23   'Hegde Quits Over Arrack Case', *Times of India*, 12 February 1986, page 1.

24 'Hegde Likely to be Re-elected', *Times of India*, 15 February 1986, page 1; 'Hegde Back in Saddle', *Times of India*, 17 February 1986, page 1.

25 'Hegde Quits on Moral Grounds', *Times of India*, 11 August 1988, page 1.

26 See 'Bommai, a Seasoned Politician & Gandhian', *Times of India*, 11 January 1983, page 7.

27 'Bommai Succeeds Hegde as CM', *Times of India*, 13 August 1988, page 1; 'Gowda Given Back Old Portfolio', *Times of India*, 17 August 1988, page 9; 'Bommai, a Seasoned Politician & Gandhian', *Times of India*, 11 January 1983, page 7.

28 '4-party Merger by Aug. 15: V.P.', *Times of India*, 27 July 1988, page 1.

29 'V.P. Leads Janata Dal', *Times of India*, 12 October 1988, page 1.

30 Ibid.

31 'Now the Janata Dal', *Times of India*, 13 October 1988, page 8.

32 'Janata Dal Born in Karnataka', *Times of India*, 4 January 1989, page 1.

33 'Rebels Plan against Janata Dal', *Times of India*, 27 October 1988, page 9; 'Janata Dal a Fact: Hegde', *Times of India*, 30 December 1988, page 13.

34 'Gowda May Quit Cabinet', *Times of India*, 1 January 1989, page 1; E. Raghavan, 'What Made Gowda a Rebel', *Times of India*, 22 January 1989, page 13.

35 'Bommai Diplomacy Fails', *Times of India*, 15 December 1988, page 13.

36 See 'Karnataka Ministry Expanded', *Times of India*, 14 March 1989, page 9.

37 '13 Ministers Added to Bommai Team', *Times of India*, 16 April 1989, page 10.

38 Ibid.

39 'Bommai Faces Dissidence', *Times of India*, 19 April 1989, page 13.

40 Ibid. See further E. Raghavan, 'JD Men's Fatal Greed', *Times of India*, 23 April 1989, page 11.

41 'Sack Bommai, Advises Governor', *Times of India*, 21 April 1989, page 1.

42 Ibid.

43 Ibid.

44 See 'Governor Silent on Resignation', *Times of India*, 13 March 1989, page 1.

45 'Sack Bommai, advises Governor', *Times of India*, 21 April 1989, page 1.

46 'Krishna Iyer assails action', *Times of India*, 24 April 1989, page 7.

47 Twelve out of nineteen withdrew their letters. 'Coup in Karnataka', *Times of India*, 22 April 1989, page 12.

48 'Sack Bommai, Advises Governor', *Times of India*, 21 April 1989, page 1.

49 Ibid.

50 'Delhi Rule Imposed on Karnataka', *Times of India*, 22 April 1989, page 1.

51 Ibid.

52 'We Will Teach Cong. a Lesson: V.P.', *Times of India*, 23 April 1989, page 9.

53 'HC Admits Plea by Bommai', *Times of India*, 28 April 1989, page 12.

54 'Central Rule in Karnataka Invalid', *Times of India*, 8 July 1989, page 9.

55 'More Data Sought in Bommai Case', *Times of India*, 7 July 1989, page 8.

56 Ibid.

57 Ibid.

58 Ibid.

59 'Central Rule in Karnataka Invalid', *Times of India*, 8 July 1989, page 9.

60 S.R. Bommai v. Union of India, (1989) SCC Online Kar 253.

61 Ibid., paragraph 38(6).

62 'All-time Record by Karnataka Cong.', *Times of India*, 28 November 1989, page 22; 'Cong. Victory March in South', *Times of India*, 28 November 1989, page 1.

63 See S.R. Bommai v. Union of India, (1994) 3 SCC 1 (paragraphs 128–130).

64 Soli J. Sorabjee, 'Decision of the Supreme Court in S.R. Bommai v. Union of India: A Critique', (1994) 3 SCC (Jour) 1.

65 S.R. Bommai v. Union of India, (1994) 3 SCC 1: paragraph 35 (Ahmadi J), paragraph 47 (Verma and Dayal JJ), paragraph 374 (Jeevan Reddy and Agrawal JJ), paragraphs 2 and 8 (Pandian J—who agreed with the reasoning of Justice Jeevan Reddy and did not express any contrary opinion on this issue).

66 Ibid., paragraph 153(I) (Sawant and Kuldip Singh JJ), paragraph 2 (Pandian J), paragraph 435 (Jeevan Reddy and Agrawal JJ).

67 Ibid., paragraph 153(II) (Sawant and Kuldip Singh JJ), paragraph 2 (Pandian J), paragraph 435 (Jeevan Reddy and Agrawal JJ), paragraph 33 (Ahmadi J), paragraph 48 (Verma and Dayal JJ).

68 Ibid., paragraph 86 (Sawant and Kuldip Singh JJ), paragraph 48 (Verma and Dayal JJ), paragraph 33 (Ahmadi J). A court would be justified in directing the government to disclose the materials, subject to privilege: paragraph 380 (Jeevan Reddy and Agrawal JJ), paragraph 48 (Verma and Dayal JJ), paragraph 86 (Sawant and Kuldip Singh JJ). See further paragraphs 208–210 (Ramaswamy J).

69 Ibid., paragraphs 153(I) (Sawant and Kuldip Singh JJ), paragraph 2 (Pandian J), paragraph 435 (Jeevan Reddy and Agrawal JJ).

70 Ibid., paragraph 49 (Verma and Dayal JJ), paragraph 35 (Ahmadi J), paragraph 290 (Jeevan Reddy and Agrawal JJ), paragraphs 2 and 8 (Pandian J—who agreed with the reasoning of Justice Jeevan Reddy and did not express any contrary opinion on this issue).

71 Ibid., paragraph 153(VI) (Sawant and Kuldip Singh JJ), paragraph 2 (Pandian J), paragraph 435 (Jeevan Reddy and Agrawal JJ).

72 Ibid., paragraph 153(V) (Sawant and Kuldip Singh JJ), paragraph 2 (Pandian J), paragraph 435 (Jeevan Reddy and Agrawal JJ).

73 Ibid., paragraph 153(IV) (Sawant and Kuldip Singh JJ), paragraph 2 (Pandian J), paragraph 435 (Jeevan Reddy and Agrawal JJ).

74 Ibid., paragraph 153(VIII) (Sawant and Kuldip Singh JJ), paragraph 2 (Pandian J), paragraph 435 (Jeevan Reddy and Agrawal JJ). See further paragraph 186 (Ramaswamy J), paragraphs 29, 36 (Ahmadi J).

75 Ibid., paragraph 105 (Sawant and Kuldip Singh JJ), paragraph 31 (Ahmadi J), paragraphs 299–300 (Jeevan Reddy and Agrawal J—who held that the recommendations of the Sarkaria Commission on this point 'merit serious consideration'), paragraphs 2 and 8 (Pandian J—who agreed with the reasoning of Justice Jeevan Reddy, and did not express any contrary opinion on this issue).

76 See Soli J. Sorabjee, 'Decision of the Supreme Court in S.R. Bommai v. Union of India: A Critique', (1994) 3 SCC (Jour) 1.

77 S.R. Bommai v. Union of India, (1994) 3 SCC 1: paragraphs 2 and 8 (Pandian J—who agreed with the reasoning of Justice Jeevan Reddy

and did not express any contrary opinion on the floor-test in his separate judgment), paragraphs 82(III), 118–119 (Sawant and Kuldip Singh JJ), paragraphs 391–392 and 395 (Jeevan Reddy and Agrawal JJ). On this point, Justice Ramaswamy dissented (paragraph 263).

78 'A "Bandit Queen" Surrenders in India', *New York Times*, 13 February 1983, page A23.

79 Ibid.

80 Ibid.

81 Ibid.

82 'Dacoit Queen Phoolan Freed', *Times of India*, 20 February 1994, page 1.

83 'U.P. Withdraws Cases against Phoolan', *Times of India*, 24 January 1994, page 6.

84 See Phoolan Devi v. State of M.P., (1996) 11 SCC 19 (paragraph 1).

85 'Bandit Queen Goes to Cannes', *Times of India*, 15 May 1994, page 14.

86 'Phoolan Threatens Self-immolation Over Film', *Times of India*, 27 August 1994, page 11.

87 'Delhi HC ban on "Bandit Queen"', *Times of India*, 11 September 1994, page 30.

88 Ibid.

89 '"Bandit Queen" to Compete for Oscar', *Times of India*, 25 November 1994, page 1.

90 '"Bandit Queen" Barred from Oscar Panel', *Times of India*, 20 January 1995, page 1.

91 '"Bandit Queen" Knocked Out of Oscar Race', *Times of India*, 3 March 1995, page 3.

92 '"Bandit Queen" to Compete for Oscar', *Times of India*, 25 November 1994, page 1.

93 '"Bandit Queen" copies available in Delhi', *Times of India*, 25 January 1995, page 17.

94 'HC Ban on "Bandit Queen" Lifted', *Times of India*, 11 March 1995, page 1; '"Bandit Queen" Finds Itself in Hot Waters Once Again', *Times of India*, 15 February 1996, page 5.

95 '"Bandit Queen" to be Released Next Month', *Times of India*, 12 March 1995, page 10.

96 'I Don't Stand by this Film: Shekhar', *Times of India*, 29 December 1995, page A1; 'I Don't Want Bandit Queen Released Here: Shekhar Kapur', *Times of India*, 1 September 1995, page A1.

97 Bobby Art International v. Om Pal Singh Hoon, (1996) 4 SCC 1 (paragraph 11).

98 'Amitabh had Threatened Me, says Phoolan', *Times of India*, 18 February 1996, page 26.

99 'Ban Bandit Queen, Say Women's Groups', *Times of India*, 9 February 1996, page A1.

100 'Din Over Bandit Queen in Karnataka House', *Times of India*, 1 March 1996, page 9.

101 'CBFC Member Quits from Panel in Protest', *Times of India*, 15 February 1996, page 5; 'CBFC Failed to Curb Obscenity, Alleges Member', *Times of India*, 16 February 1996, page 6.

102 Namit Sharma, 'Soft-porn Fans Flip for Phoolan Devi', *Times of India*, 2 February 1996, page A1; '"Bandit Queen" draws crowds and protests', *Times of India*, 15 February 1996, page 1.

103 '"Bandit Queen" Finds Itself in Hot Waters Once Again', *Times of India*, 15 February 1996, page 5.

104 Moneisha Gandhi and Rekha Borgohain, 'Soft-porn Movies Draw Crowds', *Times of India*, 13 April 1996, page 5.

105 'HC Judge Views "Bandit Queen"', *Times of India*, 14 February 1996, page 10.

106 Om Pal Singh Hoon v. Union of India, (1996) SCC Online Del 235 (paragraph 39).

107 Ibid., paragraph 34.

108 Ibid., paragraph 35.

109 Ibid., paragraph 36.

110 Ibid., paragraph 36.

111 'Delhi High Court Continues to Dwell Over the Issues of "Bandit Queen"', *Times of India*, 13 March 1996, page 12.

112 'Ban on "Bandit Queen" to Continue', *Times of India*, 28 March 1996, page 12.

113 Ibid.

114 'HC Rejects Verbal Apology by Daily', *Times of India*, 20 March 1996, page 7.

115 See Sameera Khan, 'Let Bandit Queen Be', *Times of India*, 15 March 1996, page 16.

116 'An Apology', *Times of India*, 20 March 1996, page 10.

117 'Cases Stayed on "Bandit Queen" Distributor', *Times of India*, 4 April 1996, page 7.

118 Ibid.

119 Ibid.

120 Ibid.

121 Bobby Art International v. Om Pal Singh Hoon, (1996) 4 SCC 1 (paragraph 27).

122 Ibid.

123 Ibid.

124 Ibid.

125 Ibid.

126 Ibid.

127 Ibid., paragraph 29.

128 Ibid., paragraph 6.

129 Ibid., paragraph 32.

130 Ibid., paragraph 5.

131 Ibid., paragraph 4.

132 Ibid., paragraph 30.

133 Ibid., paragraph 31.

134 Ibid., paragraph 3.

135 'Ban on "Bandit Queen" Lifted', *Times of India*, 2 May 1996, page 7.

136 'Shekhar Kapur Wins Best Director Award for "Bandit Queen"', *Times of India*, 24 February 1997, page 7.

137 See 'The 71st Academy Awards, 1999', available at: https://www.oscars.org/oscars/ceremonies/1999 (last visited 29 May 2021). It won an Oscar for makeup.

138 'U.P. Gives BJP its Worst Drubbing of the Decade', *Times of India*, 8 October 1999, page 9.

139 'Phoolan Devi Shot Dead in Delhi', *Times of India*, 26 July 2001, page 1.

140 Soli J. Sorabjee, 'Phoolan Devi, Riaz Khokar and Chandraswami', *Times of India*, 6 May 1996, page 11.

141 Ibid.

142 Soli J. Sorabjee, 'Photo Finish, President's Rule & the Pope', *Times of India*, 26 March 1998, page 13.

143 Ibid.

144 Ibid.

Chapter 11: Coalition Dharma

1   'V.P. Singh Loses Trust Vote, Quits', *Times of India*, 8 November 1990, page 1. See further Abhinav Chandrachud, *The Informal Constitution: Unwritten Criteria in Selecting Judges for the Supreme Court of India* (New Delhi: Oxford University Press, 2014), page 117.

2   Chandrachud, ibid., pages 117–118.

3   Vinay Sitapati, *Half Lion: How P.V. Narasimha Rao Transformed India* (Gurgaon: Penguin Random House India, 2016), page 183.

4   Abhinav Chandrachud, *The Informal Constitution: Unwritten Criteria in Selecting Judges for the Supreme Court of India* (New Delhi: Oxford University Press, 2014), page 118.

5   'Vajpayee Gets Sharma's Nod, Will be Sworn in Today', *Times of India*, 16 May 1996, page 1; 'Vajpayee Sworn in as P.M.', *Times of India*, 17 May 1996, page 1.

6   See *Statistical Report on General Elections, 1996, to Eleventh Lok Sabha* (New Delhi: Election Commission of India, 1996?), vol. 1, available at: https://eci.gov.in/files/file/4123-general-election-1996-vol-i-ii/ (last visited 30 May 2021), page 91.

7   Soli J. Sorabjee, 'Vajpayee's Act was the One and Only Redeeming Factor', *Times of India*, 4 June 1996, page 11.

8   '13-day Govt. is the Shortest Ever', *Times of India*, 29 May 1996, page 1.

9   'Jethmalani at the Receiving End for Once', *Times of India*, 25 May 1996, page 12.

10 Soli J. Sorabjee, 'Vajpayee's Act was the One and Only Redeeming Factor', *Times of India*, 4 June 1996, page 11.

11 Ibid.

12 Soli J. Sorabjee, 'If only "Hindutva" would be replaced with "Bharatva"', *Times of India*, 20 May 1996, page 13.

13 'Sharma should invite BJP: Palkhivala', *Times of India*, 13 May 1996, page 3.

14 'Sharma hands over baton to Gowda as Vajpayee bows out', *Times of India*, 29 May 1996, page 1.

15 'Cong.-Front tussle to form govt. begins', *Times of India*, 23 May 1996, page 9; 'NF-LF will bring pressure on govt.', *Times of India*, 25 February 1996, page 32.

16 'Collective Guilt', *Times of India*, 22 May 1996, page 12; Smita Gupta, 'Third front on a comeback trail?', *Times of India*, 24 March 1996, page 7.

17 *Statistical Report on General Elections, 1996, to Eleventh Lok Sabha* (New Delhi: Election Commission of India, 1996?), vol. 1, available at: https://eci.gov.in/files/file/4123-general-election-1996-vol-i-ii/ (last visited 30 May 2021), page 91.

18 'Cong. warns United Front to fall in line', *Times of India*, 5 January 1997, page 1.

19 Ibid.

20 'CBI's probe against Kesri is politically motivated: Cong.', *Times of India*, 21 January 1997, page 1.

21 'Congress pulls rug from under UF, stakes claim to form govt.', *Times of India*, 31 March 1997, page 1.

22 'Kesri-Rao camp differences come to the fore', *Times of India*, 31 March 1997, page 1; 'Pawar's proximity to Gowda prompted Kesri's action', *Times of India*, 31 March 1997, page 1.

23 'Gujral Crops Up As a Consensus Candidate for PM', *Times of India*, 9 April 1997, page 9; 'After the Vote', *Times of India*, 23 April 1997, page 12.

24 See Chief Justice G. Rohini, 'Full Court Reference...', 15 May 2015, available at: https://delhihighcourt.nic.in/writereaddata/upload/Condolence/CondolenceFile_WQAWPCKU.PDF (last visited 30 May 2021).

25 Smita Gupta and Askari H. Zaidi, 'PM, Kesri Defuse Jain Report Row Over Dinner', *Times of India*, 14 November 1997, page 1; 'Solely Sonia', *Times of India*, 22 November 1997, page 14.

26 'Gujral Govt. Falls in UF—Congress Tug-of-war', *Times of India*, 29 November 1997, page 1.

27 'President Ends War of Attrition, Rings in Polls', *Times of India*, 5 December 1997, page 1.

28 *Statistical Report on General Elections, 1998 to the 12th Lok Sabha* (New Delhi: Election Commission of India, 1998?), available at: https://eci. gov.in/files/file/4124-general-election-1998-vol-i-ii/ (last visited 30 May 2021), vol. 1, page 90.

29 'Vajpayee Sails Home on TDP Support', *Times of India*, 29 March 1998, page 1.

30 'Soli Sorabjee Takes Over as the New Attorney-general', *Times of India*, 8 April 1998, page 1. Fali Nariman may have been Vajpayee's first choice for the position. See Fali Nariman, *Before Memory Fades: An Autobiography* (New Delhi: Hay House Publishers (India) Pvt. Ltd., 2016), pages 409–410.

31 'Legal Community Hails Sorabjee's Appointment', *Times of India*, 10 April 1998, page 9.

32 V.P. Singh, Chandra Shekhar, Narasimha Rao, Atal Bihari Vajpayee, H.D. Deve Gowda, I.K. Gujral, and Vajpayee again (not counted twice).

33 Article 76(1), Constitution.

34 Ashok Pandey v. Satish Chandra Mishra, MANU/UP/1116/2003. The qualifications for being a Supreme Court judge are set out in Article 124(3) of the Constitution.

35 Bhaskar Roy, 'BJP Bends Over Backwards to Please Allies', *Times of India*, 12 February 1999, page 1.

36 *Statistical Report on General Elections, 1998 to the 12th Lok Sabha* (New Delhi: Election Commission of India, 1998?), available at: https://eci. gov.in/files/file/4124-general-election-1998-vol-i-ii/ (last visited 30 May 2021), vol. 1, page 101.

37 J. Jayalalitha v. Union of India, (1999) 5 SCC 138 (paragraph 5).

38 Ibid.

39 'Jayalalitha is Prime Accused in Hotel Case', *Times of India*, 9 August 1996, page 8.

40 Ibid.

41 'Another Case Filed against Jayalalitha', *Times of India*, 19 September 1996, page 7.

42 'Jaya Will be Allowed Only Prison Diet', *Times of India*, 8 December 1996, page 9; V.R. Mani, 'Jayalalitha's Imprisonment May Evoke Sympathy', *Times of India*, 12 December 1996, page 8.

43 'Jaya Will be Allowed Only Prison Diet', *Times of India*, 8 December 1996, page 9.

44 'Jayalalitha Granted Bail, Released from Jail', *Times of India*, 4 January 1997, page 7.

45 J. Jayalalitha v. Union of India, (1999) 5 SCC 138, paragraph 20.

46 Ibid., paragraph 5.

47 'SC Ends the Year with Hectic Schedule', *Times of India*, 28 December 1998, page 9; 'PM is Tolerating Jaya to Remain in Power: DMK Chief', *Times of India*, 30 December 1998, page 1.

48 J. Jayalalitha v. Union of India, (1999) 5 SCC 138 (paragraph 2); 'Centre Transfers Jaya Cases to Regular Courts', *Times of India*, 8 February 1999, page 1.

49 'Centre Transfers Jaya Cases to Regular Courts', *Times of India*, 8 February 1999, page 1.

50 'BJP Says it Will Send Jayalalitha's Cases Back to Special Court', *Times of India*, 22 April 1999, page 7.

51 'TN Lawyers Burn Copies of Central Notification', *Times of India*, 13 February 1999, page 7.

52 'SC Admits TN's Plea in Jayalalitha Cases', *Times of India*, 23 February 1999, page 13.

53 'Centre Tells SC it Does Not Want to Block Jaya's Trial', *Times of India*, 18 March 1999, page 7.

54 S. Thirunavukkarasu v. J. Jayalalitha, MANU/TN/0870/1997.

55 'Jayalalitha Assures Support to Vajpayee Govt.', *Times of India*, 21 February 1999, page 10.

56 'Jaya Disappointed by Railway Budget', *Times of India*, 27 February 1999, page 7.

57 Sudha G. Tilak, 'Jaya Spurns Invite to Attend BJP Meet', *Times of India*, 3 March 1999, page 7; 'Jaya May Stay Out of BJP's Tiruchi Meet', *Times*

of India, 19 March 1999, page 7; 'Waiting for Jaya', *Times of India*, 24 March 1999, page 12.

58 'Jayalalitha says Vajpayee's Foreign Policy is Lopsided', *Times of India*, 31 March 1999, page 7.

59 'If I am Guilty of Leaks...', *Times of India*, 9 April 1999, page 3.

60 'All Eyes on Jayalalitha as BJP Gears up for Trial of Strength', *Times of India*, 5 April 1999, page 6.

61 'BJP Shuts Door of Compromise on Jayalalitha', *Times of India*, 9 April 1999, page 1.

62 'Centre Defends Setting up of Special Courts to Try Jaya Cases', *Times of India*, 14 April 1999, page 7.

63 Ibid.

64 'SC Reserves Order in Jaya's Case', *Times of India*, 16 April 1999, page 7.

65 'Govt. Inches Towards the Magic Figure of 272', *Times of India*, 17 April 1999, page 1.

66 'Political Thriller Sees Vajpayee Go Down 269–270', *Times of India*, 18 April 1999, page 1.

67 Soli Sorabjee, 'Corruption and Human Rights', *Times of India*, 25 April 1999, page 16.

68 Ibid.

69 Ibid.

70 Ibid.

71 'BJP, Allies Form New Front to Fight Polls', *Times of India*, 16 May 1999, page 1.

72 J. Jayalalitha v. Union of India, (1999) 5 SCC 138 (paragraph 20).

73 Ibid., paragraph 20.

74 Ibid., paragraph 25. The court also upheld section 3(1) of the Prevention of Corruption Act. Ibid., paragraphs 13–17.

75 *Statistical Report on General Elections, 1999 to the Thirteenth Lok Sabha* (New Delhi: Election Commission of India, 1999?), vol. 1, available at: https://eci.gov.in/files/file/4125-general-election-1999-vol-i-ii-iii/ (last visited 31 May 2021), page 90.

76 Ibid., page 91.

77 'PM Talks Tough...', *Times of India*, 11 October 1999, page 1.

78 'Jaitley gets I&B...', *Times of India*, 14 October 1999, page 1.

79 'Soli Sorabjee is Attorney General Again', *Times of India*, 2 November 1999, page 7.

80 J. Jayalalitha v. State, (2001) SCC Online Mad 875.

81 State of Karnataka v. J. Jayalalitha, (2017) 6 SCC 263 (paragraphs 573–574).

82 See 'Telecom Sector in India: A Decadal Profile', a paper by the Telecom Regulatory Authority of India, 2012, available at: https://www.trai.gov.in/sites/default/files/NCAER--Report08june12.pdf (last visited 31 May 2021), page 9.

83 Paragraph 1.2, *New Telecom Policy, 1999*, Department of Telecommunications, available at: https://dot.gov.in/new-telecom-policy-1999 (last visited 31 May 2021).

84 'Why Not Go in for Mobile Phone?', *Times of India*, 27 May 1986, page 7.

85 *A Twenty Year Odyssey, 1997–2017* (Telecom Regulatory Authority of India, 2017), available at: https://www.trai.gov.in/sites/default/files/A_TwentyYear_Odyssey_1997_2017.pdf (last visited 31 May 2021), pages 7, 9.

86 'Objects of Desire', *Times of India*, 23 August 1998, page A4.

87 'Objects of Desire', *Times of India*, 14 June 1998, page B5.

88 'Objects of Desire', *Times of India*, 2 May 1999, page A4.

89 'Telecom Cos. Firm on Revenue-sharing', *Times of India*, 26 November 1998, page 13.

90 Ibid.

91 Ibid.

92 'Telecom Hawks Get the Better of Doves', *Times of India*, 26 January 1999, page 19.

93 'Telecom Operators May Forfeit Guarantees as HC Rejects Plea', *Times of India*, 9 March 1999, page 19; 'DoT Encashes Bank Guarantees of Reliance, Modicom and Fascel', *Times of India*, 25 March 1999, page 17.

94 'DoT Seeks Attorney General's Views on Licence Fees', *Times of India*, 14 April 1999, page 23; *New Telecom Policy, 1999*, Department of Telecommunications, available at: https://dot.gov.in/new-telecom-policy-1999 (last visited 31 May 2021).

95 Ibid., paragraph 1.2.

96 Ibid., paragraphs 3.1.1, 3.1.2.

97 'Portfolio Change Not Due to Tough Stand: Jagmohan', *Times of India*, 10 June 1999, page 17.

98 Ibid.

99 *Report of the Joint Parliamentary Committee to Examine Matters Relating to Allocation and Pricing of Telecom Licenses and Spectrum* (New Delhi: Lok Sabha Secretariat, 2013), page 19.

100 Ibid., page 20.

101 Ibid.

102 Vinay Pandey, 'Telecom Migration Package Comes under Audit Fire', *Times of India*, 5 February 2000, page 13.

103 Ram Jethmalani, *Big Egos, Small Men* (New Delhi: Har Anand Publications Pvt. Ltd., 2000), page 68.

104 Ibid., pages 70–71.

105 *Report of the Joint Parliamentary Committee to Examine Matters Relating to Allocation and Pricing of Telecom Licenses and Spectrum* (New Delhi: Lok Sabha Secretariat, 2013), page 22, paragraph 3.9.

106 Ibid., page 22, paragraph 3.10.

107 Ibid., page 20, paragraph 3.4.

108 Ibid., page 21, paragraph 3.8.

109 Ibid., page 25, paragraph 3.12.

110 'High Court Adjourns Telecom Hearing', *Times of India*, 4 August 1999, page 7.

111 *Report of the Joint Parliamentary Committee to Examine Matters Relating to Allocation and Pricing of Telecom Licenses and Spectrum* (New Delhi: Lok Sabha Secretariat, 2013), page 28, paragraph 3.20.

112 Ibid., pages 33 and 154, paragraphs 3.41 and 10.12.

113 Ibid., page 31, paragraph 3.37.

114 'Shiv Sena Admits to Role in Bombay Riots', *Times of India*, 15 January 1993, page 1.

115 'Hearing in Riot Probe Concludes', *Times of India*, 4 July 1997, page 5.

116 'Srikrishna to Probe City Riots', *Times of India*, 26 January 1993, page 1.

117 'Hearing in Riot Probe Concludes', *Times of India*, 4 July 1997, page 5.

118 Ibid.

119 'Finally, Srikrishna Panel Wins against Odds', *Times of India*, 17 February 1998, page 7; 'Srikrishna Report Submitted to Govt.', *Times of India*, 17 February 1998, page 1.

120 'Make Srikrishna Report Public, Urge Cong., JD', *Times of India*, 20 February 1998, page 1.

121 'Govt. Rejects Srikrishna Panel Report', *Times of India*, 7 August 1998, page 1.

122 Ibid.

123 Ibid.

124 'SC's Dismissal of Plea in "Saamna" Case Shocks Eminent Jurists', *Times of India*, 29 January 1995, page 5; Joseph Bain D'Souza v. State of Maharashtra, (1994) SCC Online Bom 461.

125 'Govt. Rejects Srikrishna Panel Report', *Times of India*, 7 August 1998, page 1.

126 'Srikrishna Report', *Times of India*, 10 August 1998, page 12.

127 'SC Issues Notices to Centre, State on Srikrishna Report', *Times of India*, 9 October 1998, page 7.

128 'Govt. Accused of Going Back on Srikrishna Panel Report', *Times of India*, 15 September 2000, page 3.

129 'Srikrishna Report Will be Implemented, Affirms Bhujbal', *Times of India*, 25 October 1999, page 7; 'State to Implement Srikrishna Report', *Times of India*, 13 November 1999, page 1; 'State Fails to Keep its Word on Implementing Srikrishna Panel Report', *Times of India*, 8 February 2000, page 3.

130 'Police Gear Up to Maintain Peace in Mumbai', *Times of India*, 19 July 2000, page 1.

131 Ibid.

132 'Srikrishna Leela', *Times of India*, 22 July 2000, page 10.

133 Ram Jethmalani, *Big Egos, Small Men* (New Delhi: Har Anand Publications Pvt. Ltd., 2000), at page 108.

134 See Sections 467–473, Code of Criminal Procedure, 1973.

135 'Srikrishna Leela', *Times of India*, 22 July 2000, page 10.

136 Ram Jethmalani, *Big Egos, Small Men* (New Delhi: Har Anand Publications Pvt. Ltd., 2000), at page 108.

137 'Srikrishna Leela', *Times of India*, 22 July 2000, page 10. The minister was Mr. Ram Naik.

138 Rakesh Bhatnagar, 'SC Orders Centre to Spell Out Stand...', *Times of India*, 22 July 2000, page 1.

139 Ibid.

140 Ibid.

141 Ibid.

142 Ibid.

143 Ibid.

144 Ibid.

145 'Jethmalani is Defiant in Face of SC Criticism', *Times of India*, 22 July 2000, page 8.

146 Ibid.

147 Ibid.

148 Ibid.

149 Ram Jethmalani, *Big Egos, Small Men* (New Delhi: Har Anand Publications Pvt. Ltd., 2000), pages 7–8.

150 Ibid., page 8.

151 Ibid., page 50.

152 Ibid., pages 59–60.

153 Ibid., page 8.

154 Ibid., page 103.

155 Ibid., page 76.

156 Ibid., page 161.

157 Ibid., page 119.

158 'What is the Bofors Scam Case?', *Indian Express*, 3 February 2018, available at: https://indianexpress.com/article/india/what-is-the-bofors-scandal-case-why-is-it-being-opened-now-4823576/ (last visited 31 May 2021).

159 Ram Jethmalani, *Big Egos, Small Men* (New Delhi: Har Anand Publications Pvt. Ltd., 2000), page 117.

160 Ibid., page 120.

161 Ibid., page 151.

162 Ibid., page 123.

163 Ibid., pages 121–122.

164 Ibid., page 156.

165 Ibid.

166 'Court Throws Out Case Against Thackeray, State to Appeal', *Times of India*, 26 July 2000, page 1.

167 'Judge Decided Thackeray Case Before Chargesheet was Filed', *Times of India*, 9 August 2000, page 6; 'High Court Dismisses Case against Thackeray Sr', *Times of India*, 24 February 2007, page 2.

168 'SC: What Action Taken...?', *Times of India*, 12 February 2020, available at: https://timesofindia.indiatimes.com/city/mumbai/sc-what-action-taken-on-srikrishna-panel-report-on-mumbai-riots/articleshow/74092343.cms (last visited 31 May 2021).

169 'Vajpayee's Surgery Went Off Smoothly', *Times of India*, 11 October 2000, page 3; 'Soli Sorabjee is Also Operated Upon', *Times of India*, 11 October 2000, page 6.

170 Rekha Dixit, 'Sorabjee Says He Took His Mind Off...', *Times of India*, 15 October 2000, page 3.

171 Ibid.

172 'Sorabjee Resigns', *Times of India*, 26 May 2004, page 1.

173 Nick Robinson et al., 'Interpreting the Constitution: Supreme Court Constitution Benches since Independence', *Economic and Political Weekly*, 26 February 2011, available at: https://papers.ssrn.com/sol3/papers.cfm?abstract_id=1883272 (last visited 31 May 2021), page 28.

174 Re: Special Reference No. 1 of 1998, (1998) 7 SCC 739.

175 Murli S. Deora v. Union of India, MANU/SC/0703/2001.

176 Pradeep Kumar Biswas v. Indian Institute of Chemical Biology, (2002) 5 SCC 111.

177 State of Gujarat v. Hon'ble High Court of Gujarat, MANU/SC/0632/1998.

178 Javed Abidi v. Union of India, (1999) 1 SCC 467.

179 TMA Pai Foundation v. State of Karnataka, (2002) 8 SCC 481.

180 Ex. Capt. Harish Uppal v. Union of India, (2003) 2 SCC 45.

181 PUCL v. Union of India, MANU/SC/1036/2003.

182 Mardia Chemicals Ltd. v. Union of India, (2004) 4 SCC 311.

183 See profile of Justice Santosh Hegde, Supreme Court of India, available at: https://main.sci.gov.in/chief-justice-judges (last visited 1 June 2021).

184 Gayatri Ramanathan, 'Street Lawyer', *Times of India*, 24 June 2001, page B2.

185 Ram Jethmalani, *Big Egos, Small Men* (New Delhi: Har Anand Publications Pvt. Ltd., 2000), page 61.

186 Ibid.

187 Interview with Avinash Rana dated 13 May 2021.

188 Gayatri Ramanathan, 'Street Lawyer', *Times of India*, 24 June 2001, page B2.

189 Interview with Avinash Rana dated 13 May 2021.

190 'First Person', *Times of India*, 11 April 1999, page 17.

191 Sorabjee took an independent view, one which was different from that taken by the government. See Raju Ramachandran, 'Afterword', in, Mool Chand Sharma and Raju Ramachandran (eds.), *Constitutionalism, Human Rights and the Rule of Law* (Delhi: Universal Law Publishing Co. Pvt. Ltd., 2005) page 285.

192 Nirmal Mishra, 'Vacancies in Mumbai HC Negate Speedy Justice', *Times of India*, 14 September 2002, page A5.

193 Rakesh Bhatnagar, 'Sorabjee Told Apex Court Puja Could be Allowed', *Times of India*, 14 March 2002, page 7.

194 Ibid.

195 Rakesh Bhatnagar, 'Apex Court Rejects Centre's Prayer for Symbolic Puja', *Times of India*, 14 March 2002, page 1.

196 Rakesh Bhatnagar, 'Would You Allow Puja in Rashtrapati Bhavan?', *Times of India*, 14 March 2002, page 7.

197 Ibid.

198 Ibid.

199 Rajesh Ramachandran, 'NDA Partners Stick Together, Stand Firmly Behind Govt', *Times of India*, 14 March 2002, page 7.

200 Smita Gupta, 'No One Gave Me Instructions, Says Attorney General', *Times of India*, 14 March 2002, page 7; 'NDA Partners Stick Together, Stand Firmly Behind Govt', *Times of India*, 14 March 2002, page 7.

201 Smita Gupta, 'No One Gave Me Instructions, Says Attorney General', *Times of India*, 14 March 2002, page 7.

202 Soli Sorabjee, 'Nigeria, NATO & Norvo', *Times of India*, 11 April 1999, page 16; Soli J. Sorabjee, 'Nigeria, Pinochet and Goondaism', *Times of India*, 6 December 1998, page 18.

203 'Human Rights Said to Improve in Nigeria', *Times of India*, 2 December 1998, page A36.

204 'Soli Sorabjee is appointed U.N. envoy for E. Timor', *Times of India*, 8 May 1999, page 19; Soli J. Sorabjee, 'US Supreme Court, East Timor and Bans', *Times of India*, 22 July 2001, page 12.

205 Rama Lakshmi, 'Loosening the Grip of India's Caste System', *Times of India*, 3 July 2001, page A1.

206 Soli J. Sorabjee, 'Padma Vibhushan, Lutyens & the National Anthem', *Times of India*, 3 February 2002, page 10.

207 See 'Sorabjee Slams Barter Tactic for Prisoners', *Telegraph Online*, 25 August 2003, available at: https://www.telegraphindia.com/india/sorabjee-slams-barter-tactic-for-prisoners/cid/965680 (last visited 13 November 2021).

Chapter 12: The Sunset Years

1   'Sorabjee Resigns', *Times of India*, 26 May 2004, page 1.

2   Zee Telefilms Ltd. v. Union of India, (2005) 4 SCC 649.

3   Zoroastrian Cooperative Housing Society Ltd. v. District Registrar, Cooperative Societies (Urban), (2005) 5 SCC 632.

4   PA Inamdar v. State of Maharashtra, (2005) 6 SCC 537.

5   State of Gujarat v. Mirzapur Moti Kureshi, (2005) 8 SCC 534.

6   Rameshwar Prasad v. Union of India, (2006) 2 SCC 1.

7   BSES Ltd. v. Fenner India Ltd., (2006) 2 SCC 728.

8   IR Coelho v. State of TN, (2007) 2 SCC 1.

9   Manzar Sayeed Khan v. State of Maharashtra, (2007) 5 SCC 1.

10 Prabhudas Damodar Kotecha v. Manhabala Jeram Damodar, (2013) 15 SCC 358.

11 KS Puttuswamy v. Union of India, (2017) 10 SCC 1.

12 '"Bloody Indians" Jibe No Big Deal: Experts', *Times of India*, 19 November 2006, page 3.

13 'Jaipur Court's Arrest Warrant for Gere Shocks Legal Experts', *Times of India*, 27 April 2007, page 1.

14 'Panel on Police Planned', *Times of India*, 18 August 2006, page 1.

15 'Soli Wants Police Battle-ready', *Times of India*, 12 December 2008, page 1.

16 'Sorabjee Gives up Street Fight', *Times of India*, 19 February 2009, page 2.

17 'I Have No Take on Supreme Court's Verdict on Carbide', *Times of India*, 20 June 2010, page 20.

18 'Failing to admit Lalu, Karan Quits as IIC Life Trustee', *Times of India*, 13 October 2006, page 11; 'Elite Delhi Club Accepts Karan Resignation', *Times of India*, 6 April 2007, page 11.

19 'What I Want to be Remembered for...', *Times of India*, 26 December 2005, page 14.

Appendix: Excerpts from Soli Sorabjee's Favourite Poems and Quotes

1 Soli J. Sorabjee, 'The Rhythm of Poetry in All That Jazz', *Times of India*, 8 July 1989, page 13.

2 Soli Sorabjee, 'New Year Resolutions', *Indian Express*, 24 December 2006, page 7.

3 Soli Sorabjee, 'Hijacking & a Tryst with Millennium', *Times of India*, 2 January 2000, page 14; Soli J. Sorabjee, 'Elections, Press Council & 1998', *Times of India*, 1 January 1998, page 13; Soli Sorabjee, 'Favourite Poems', *Indian Express*, 12 October 2003, page 7; Soli Sorabjee, 'New Year Literary Musings', *Indian Express*, 1 January 2006, page 6.

4 Soli Sorabjee, 'New Year Literary Musings', *Indian Express*, 1 January 2006, page 6.

5 Ibid.

6 Soli Sorabjee, 'Craze for Statues', *Indian Express*, 3 August 2008, page 7.

7 Soli Sorabjee, 'New Year Literary Musings', *Indian Express*, 1 January 2006, page 6.

8 Ibid.

9 Ibid.

10 Soli Sorabjee, 'Ninety Cheers for Sam Bahadur', *Indian Express*, 2 April 2003, page 8.

11 Soli Sorabjee, 'Intuitive Recognition and Jazz', *Indian Express*, 11 June 2006, page 7. He wrongly attributed this line to Emerson. See https://libquotes.com/edith-sitwell/quote/lbm9v7f (last visited 3 June 2021).

12 Soli Sorabjee, 'Bold Initiative', *Indian Express*, 11 May 2003, page 7; Soli J. Sorabjee, 'Centre's Onslaught On Nagaland', *Times of India*, 10 August 1988, page 8 (in this article, Sorabjee did not give credit to Oscar Wilde); Soli J. Sorabjee, 'Elections, Press Council & 1998', *Times of India*, 1 January 1998, page 13.

13 Soli Sorabjee, 'Favourite Poems', *Indian Express*, 12 October 2003, page 7.

14 Soli Sorabjee, 'Memories of the First Independence Day', *Indian Express*, 16 August 2009, page 9.

15 Soli Sorabjee, 'Trifles', *Indian Express*, 18 December 2005, page 7.

16 Soli Sorabjee, 'Joint Statement, Different Interpretations', *Indian Express*, 19 July 2009, page 7; Soli J. Sorabjee, 'Monkey Business, Refractory Wives & Lewis Carroll', *Times of India*, 31 March 2002, page 10. See further https://www.bartleby.com/73/2019.html (last visited 3 June 2021).

17 Soli Sorabjee, 'Art and Spiritual Censorship', *Indian Express*, 19 July 2009, page 7.

18 Soli Sorabjee, 'Complicated Laws and Disembarkation Card', *Indian Express*, 21 December 2003, page 7.

19 Soli Sorabjee, 'Overpowering Sleep', *Indian Express*, 23 July 2006, page 7. See https://www.thereader.org.uk/featured-poem-from-the-rime-of-the-ancient-mariner-by-samuel-taylor-coleridge/ (last visited 13 November 2021).

20 Soli Sorabjee, 'Overpowering Sleep', *Indian Express*, 23 July 2006, page 7.

21 Soli Sorabjee, 'Press Freedom', *Indian Express*, 23 November 2003, page 7.

22 Soli Sorabjee, 'New Year Resolutions', *Indian Express*, 24 December 2006, page 7.

23 Ibid.; Soli J. Sorabjee, 'Lokpal Drama', *Indian Express*, 1 January 2012, available at: https://indianexpress.com/article/opinion/columns/lokpal-drama/ (last visited 13 November 2021).

24 Soli Sorabjee, 'New Year Resolutions', *Indian Express*, 24 December 2006, page 7.

25 Ibid.

26 Ibid.

27 Ibid.

28 Soli Sorabjee, 'Defining Jazz', *Indian Express*, 24 May 2009, page 7; Soli Sorabjee, 'Taking Suffering Seriously', *Times of India*, 10 December 1995, page 10; Soli Sorabjee, '"Honour" Killing?', *Indian Express*, 12 September 2010, available at: http://archive.indianexpress.com/news/-honour--killing-/680518/ (last visited 13 November 2021).

29 Soli Sorabjee, 'Perils of Kissing', *Indian Express*, 25 May 2003, page 11.

30 Soli Sorabjee, 'Hazards of Kissing', *Indian Express*, 25 September 2005, page 7.

31 Soli Sorabjee, 'Election Histrionics', *Indian Express*, 26 April 2009, page 7; Soli Sorabjee, 'Strange Competition', *Indian Express*, 23 May 2004, page 6.

32 Soli Sorabjee, 'Election Histrionics', *Indian Express*, 26 April 2009, page 7.

33 Soli Sorabjee, 'The Lighter Side of Recession', *Indian Express*, 26 April 2009, page 7.

34 Ibid.

35 Soli Sorabjee, 'Fashion Trends', *Indian Express*, 29 October 2006, page 7.

36 Soli Sorabjee, 'Infinite Variety of Judges', *Indian Express*, 26 March 2006, page 7.

37 Soli Sorabjee, 'Philosophers', *Indian Express*, 31 August 2003, page 7.

38 Soli Sorabjee, 'Poets and Judgments', *Indian Express*, 6 January 2008, page 7.

39 Ibid.

40 Soli Sorabjee, 'Unusual Award', *Indian Express*, 30 March 2008, page 7; Soli Sorabjee, 'Historic Judgment, Name and Old Favourites', *Times of India*, 24 December 2000, page 10.

41 Soli Sorabjee, 'Unusual Award', *Indian Express*, 30 March 2008, page 7.

42 Soli Sorabjee, 'Names Do Matter', *Indian Express*, 30 March 2008, page 7; Soli Sorabjee, 'Names Matter', *Indian Express*, 25 April 2004, page 7; Soli

J. Sorabjee, 'When Words Can Break Bones', *Times of India*, 5 May 1995, page 13.

43 Soli Sorabjee, 'A Dream Come True', *Indian Express*, 9 November 2008, page 7.

44 Soli Sorabjee, 'Playing Favourites', *Indian Express*, 9 November 2008, page 7.

45 Soli J. Sorabjee, 'Information, Defaulters & New Year Resolution', *Times of India*, 5 January 2003, page 6.

46 Soli J. Sorabjee, 'Right to Shelter, Jazz & Unparliamentary Words', *Times of India*, 17 March 2002, page 10; Soli J. Sorabjee, 'Tea Parties, Zubin and Mahato', *Times of India*, 18 April 1997, page 11.

47 Soli J. Sorabjee, 'War & Children', *Times of India*, 26 May 2002, page 14; Soli Sorabjee, 'Varying Eccentricities', *Indian Express*, 29 August 2004, page 6.

48 A Latin line by the poet Horace, https://www.poetryfoundation.org/poems/46560/dulce-et-decorum-est (last visited 3 June 2021).

49 Soli J. Sorabjee, 'War & Children', *Times of India*, 26 May 2002, page 14.

50 Ibid.

51 Soli J. Sorabjee, 'Human Rights, Sri Lanka & Joe Henderson', *Times of India*, 5 August 2001, page 10.

52 Soli Sorabjee, 'Privacy, Clinton, Racism & Laloo', *Times of India*, 2 April 2000, page 14.

53 Soli Sorabjee, 'Charter Rights, Correct Language & Soni Raag', *Times of India*, 15 October 2000, page 14.

54 Soli Sorabjee, 'Rajkumar, US Courts & Fijian Judiciary', *Times of India*, 26 November 2000, page 10.

55 Soli Sorabjee, 'Historic Judgment, Name and Old Favourites', *Times of India*, 24 December 2000, page 10.

56 Soli Sorabjee, 'Litigation Lottery, Amnesty and Tolerance', *Times of India*, 3 January 1999, page 18.

57 Soli J. Sorabjee, 'Elections, Press Council & 1998', *Times of India*, 1 January 1998, page 13. See further https://www.poetryfoundation.org/poems/44299/elegy-written-in-a-country-churchyard (last visited 3 June 2021).

58 Ibid. See further 'WH Auden's Unsparing Poem on the Partition of India', *Scroll.in*, 15 August 2014, available at: https://scroll.in/article/674238/wh-audens-unsparing-poem-on-the-partition-of-india (last visited 13 November 2021).

59 Soli J. Sorabjee, 'Intolerance, Auden and Names', *Times of India*, 7 May 1998, page 11.

60 Soli J. Sorabjee, 'Genocide, Polygamy and Naughty Tricks', *Times of India*, 13 September 1998, page 16.

61 Soli J. Sorabjee, 'Impeachment, Secession and Kautilya', *Times of India*, 27 September 1998, page 18.

62 Soli J. Sorabjee, 'Split, Sharif & Saramago', *Times of India*, 11 October 1998, page 18.

63 Soli J. Sorabjee, 'The Rhythm of Poetry in All That Jazz', *Times of India*, 8 July 1989, page 13. See further https://www.poetryfoundation.org/poems/44481/on-first-looking-into-chapmans-homer (last visited 13 November 2021).

64 Ibid.

65 Soli Sorabjee, 'Musical Instruments', *Indian Express*, 9 October 2005, page 7.

66 Soli J. Sorabjee, 'My First Clash with the Secrecy Syndrome', *Times of India*, 5 August 1989, page 11.

67 Soli J. Sorabjee, 'The Rhythm of Poetry in All That Jazz', *Times of India*, 8 July 1989, page 13. See further https://www.poetryfoundation.org/poems/52773/dirge-without-music (last visited 13 November 2021).

68 Soli J. Sorabjee, 'The Rhythm of Poetry in All That Jazz', *Times of India*, 8 July 1989, page 13.

Index